TH

FINAL

HOUR

By Michael H. Brown
Co-Author of "Josyp Terelya—WITNESS"

Queenship

The publisher recognizes and accepts that the final authority regarding the apparitions in the Catholic Church rests with the Holy See of Rome, to whose judgment we willingly submit.

—*The Publisher*

This edition contains the complete text of the original edition published by Faith Publishing Company.

Copyright © 1992 Michael H. Brown

Library of Congress Number # 92-071997

Published by:
Queenship Publishing
P.O. Box 220
Goleta, CA 93116
(800) 647-9882 • (805) 692-0043 • Fax: (805) 967-5843

Printed in the United States of America

ISBN: 1-57918-133-3

"Children, it is the final hour; just as you heard that the antichrist was coming, so now many such antichrists have appeared. This makes us certain that it is the final hour." —*1 John* 2:18

Table of Contents

Lourdes, France as it is today.

Dedication

For Bill and Fran Reck,
whom Mary has chosen.

Publisher's Foreword

The twentieth century has provided the greatest advancement this planet has ever seen. It is the climax of the industrial revolution. Technology has provided mass production of computers, televisions, communication systems, machinery. Satellites roam the galaxy. Air travel is commonplace. The sciences claim to be the new god. Medicine has reached astonishing levels of success. Education has reached new highs. The world's population has exploded. Our standard of living is unparalleled. But is it all success? Or good?

This century has also produced the greatest amount of destruction and devastation the world has ever known. Two world wars have directly or indirectly claimed hundreds of millions of lives. Lesser wars have been constant. Godless communism ravaged two-thirds of the earth. While one-fourth of the world's population lives in relative comfort with bountiful food supplies, the other three-fourths live in total poverty, facing the daily regime of starvation. Crime, violence, persecution exist everywhere. The family unit has been largely dissolved. Blatant immorality and perversity run roughshod over respected and traditional values. God was declared dead and educational and medical advancements have resulted in egoism, greed, and the destruction of human life by the hundreds of millions through the use of abortion. From Masonry to the occult, diabolical venues become evident. The environment is threatened; racial and ethnic dissension abounds.

Is this the century of "good versus evil?" Is this the advent of the end times as foretold in the Scriptures? There is strong evidence to suggest that it is. Regardless of your particular religious beliefs (or none at all), it is no longer possible to deny the fact that the world sits precariously posed on the brink of self destruction.

In this book, *The Final Hour,* Michael H. Brown provides some startling and eye-opening data concerning these opposite and opposed hallmarks of this century. He spent many months covering the world to investigate the supernatural events that have been reported in this century, most in the past twenty-five years. More importantly, he has systematically linked these events not only with the evil of this century, but with the biblical prophecies given to us through the Bible.

Michael Brown, 40, brought to this project a great amount of expertise and past experience. It was he, as an investigative journalist, who exposed the infamous Love Canal toxic waste crisis. His previous books include *Laying Waste: The Poisoning of America, The Search for Eve,* and *The Toxic Cloud.* He also co-authored, with Josyp Terelya, the book *Witness.* Once a contributing editor to *Science Digest,* his work has appeared in periodicals such as *Reader's Digest, New York Magazine, The Atlantic Monthly, Discover,* and *The New York Times.* Having had a conversion experience in 1983, he has since visited 25 sites of alleged Marian apparitions around the world. He lives in Upstate New York.

In *The Final Hour,* Michael speaks to all peoples without regard to any religious preference. Though most of the events listed herein are documented through the Catholic Church, it is to all the people of the world that Michael speaks. It is simply the recognition that we are all under the domain of He Who created us and brought us life. Further, it is in recognition that we are all the object of the evil forces that attempt to destroy. It is the battle of good versus evil. At stake is your soul.

Faith Publishing Company

CHAPTER 1

This Present Hour

The reports come from deep in the former Soviet Union, where towering apparitions of Jesus and Mary seemed to announce the fall of Communism; from the damp, wind-swept peat of Ireland, where visions are given of the Crucifixion; from war-torn Yugoslavia, where the Virgin has appeared since 1981; and from a mountainside in Venezuela where the sun pulses and spins and throws off colors of great splendor.

During the past century, and especially the last ten years, we on earth have been experiencing a major supernatural episode. Reports of unusual events, spiritual events, are coming from every habitable continent. In Europe and Asia, in Nicaragua and the Middle East, in Africa and America, are accounts of an apparitional woman calling herself the Blessed Virgin Mary who appears to visionaries and gives them inspiration, instructions, and messages, including warnings about the future of the world.

She comes to children. She comes to adults. She speaks to peasants and aristocrats, Christians and non-Christians, believers and atheists. She appears in the glory of Heaven, beautiful beyond comparison and arrayed with angels, but often shedding tears of disappointment. She comes as a bright light in an era of spiritual darkness, a young mother calling her children away from danger and exposing the unseen

perils. Our era is evil, she tells us, our world has lost its
sense of God and spirituality, it has sold out to actual forces
of darkness, and as a result a time of cataclysmic events
threatens us all.

Just as the angel Gabriel once came to instruct her, so
does she now come to inform us. Just as Elijah and Moses
were seen on the mount (*Matt.* 17:7), so is Mary of Nazareth
now sighted on mountaintops.

Whether you're a believer or disbeliever, Catholic or
Protestant, Gentile or Jew, you are about to encounter a series
of unearthly events—call them *alleged* events—unlike any
reported in 2,000 years.

A good argument can be made that there haven't been
such extraordinary phenomena since Christ Himself appeared
after death to His apostles.

That may sound like an exceedingly large claim but the
reports of supernatural events, especially the apparitions
of a saintly woman whom Catholics call Our Lady or the
Queen of Heaven, are remarkably consistent. In Czechoslovakia and Japan, Ecuador and Mexico, in Italy and Arizona, are accounts of inexplicable and indeed nearly
inconceivable sights: like incidents in the Old and New
Testaments, fiery lights, tongues of flame, and strange
luminous clouds.

Witnesses feel the rush of wind and claim to experience
visits from a heavenly woman.

I'm not talking about dreams, phantoms, or vague ghostly
images. Nor am I speaking about anything New Age or
occult. I'm speaking of spectacular and often three-
dimensional apparitions, apparitions that move and breathe
like a living person.

Often there is a babe—the Christ Child—in her matronly
arms.

She comes to tell us about our present and dangerous hour.

We'll see how the cycle of Mary's appearances began in
the 19th century and almost always involve a lesson on the
evil of the times, a beseeching to pray so that God's anger
is allayed, and warnings that great and dreadful events are
a possibility if there is not mass conversion. We'll see how,
through the last hundred years, there have been hints of

the "end times" as mankind fell deeper into what I can only call anti-spiritualism. We let socialists and atheists set the social agenda, we offended God by a rash of occultic activities (from 19th-century seances to the current New Age Movement), and we succumbed to the deceptions of psychology, which dismissed the influence of the supernatural on our thought processes and instead explained away spiritual problems in mere mechanical—and non-spiritual—terms.

Our modern trends were also affected by secret societies, and while this book is not about secret societies, we'll glimpse a few such cults.

These general trends opened the door to the forces of evil and Mary has appeared constantly during the past century in an effort to point us back in the right direction, stepping up her activity greatly since 1981 and leaving us with an assortment of hints about the future and insight into great spiritual conflicts that most people do not see. Although I will not belabor the occultic or secular history of the times, I will present certain of the occultic seeds of destruction, and the growing indications, in certain of the more interesting apparitions, that bibilical prophecies are being fulfilled, and that the spirit of anti-christ has arisen through the century, punctuated by appearances of Mary as the constant waver of a red flag. We have moved from hours of occultism and modernism through hours of persecution and war to an hour that may lead up to the actual Anti-Christ himself, and to the hour of great tribulation that Christ spoke about.

I ask my Protestant and Jewish friends to bear with me and weigh the evidence. In the end you may be surprised. I was. While I'm now back to being a practicing Catholic, I went through my own years of turmoil and skepticism.

I understand the objections, and I write in the spirit of reconciliation between all countries and all faiths. Know this for now: Mary's mission is to point to Christ. By the merits of her earthly faith and suffering she has gained a special place in paradise. She is to be honored, not worshipped. She was full of grace while on earth and is full of grace as a key messenger of Heaven. It seems only logical that Christ would give her a special role, and I'm confident an open-minded reader will see her in a new light. She isn't here to replace Christ, but to serve as His forerunner, as she was His forerunner two millennia ago. She is not prayed *to* but prayed *with*. *"Holy Mary, mother of God, pray for us sinners. . ."* It's a prayer, the Hail Mary, that might be 1,600 years old and the majority of its words are drawn from the New Testament. She's a heavenly prayer-warrior. She helps us in our needs by petitioning her Son. Her fruits are peace and conversion, and with her aid, many are born again.

"Behold," Jesus said from the cross, *"your mother."*

As Martin Luther once said, "Without doubt Mary is the Mother of God. . .and in this one word is contained every honor which can be given to her."

She's not a godhead. She's not part of the Trinity. She's the handmaid of the Lord, and as such she's an instrument of the Holy Spirit.

In the 1980s David du Plessis, father of modern Pentecostalism, visited Medjugorje, Yugoslavia, the major apparitional site, and decided what he'd experienced was "something extraordinary." It was a revival the likes of which he had given up seeing in his lifetime, and he spotted no "bad fruit." The apparitions, concluded the great charismatic leader, were "of God."

While miracles associated with Mary go back to the first century (at Zaragoza, Spain, where she manifested herself to Saint James), at no other time in history has she appeared as much as she does now and at no other time has she spoken with such ardor. It's been an incredible episode with roots at places like Fatima and Lourdes. As one renowned Marian scholar, Rev. Michael O'Carroll of Ireland, puts it, "We can't find anything equivalent. There's nothing comparable in history. We must be in for some trying times. It's going to be something pretty awesome. Never has she been so apocalyptic. It's a unique manifestation and communication. I have no doubt about that at all."

There are those who propose we're approaching the great and terrible day of the Lord, or end times. There are those who relate what she says to biblical prophecies, especially those in *Daniel* and the Book of Revelation (or "Apocalypse").

We'll take a look at the entire century and what has been called the "Age of Mary" in the context of these apparitions.

We'll study many of the supposed secrets and warnings.

In the end we'll try to discern if a major shift in the world is about to take place, possibly in the next few years, before the end of our millennium.

For now suffice it to say that the Blessed Virgin seems to be capping off a century-long campaign to open our spiritual eyes—a campaign that seems to be reaching a crescendo.

It's said that the Virgin is appearing as never before because our planet has become so materialistic and lustful. She says there is an invisible confrontation raging around us and evil has infiltrated all aspects of modern reality. She said this at Fatima in 1917 and we ignored her.

Her words have been especially insistent during the past decade as we humans continue to wallow in corrupt societies and thus to risk Divine punishment.

According to dozens of visionaries, Heaven is trying to tell us something as the millennium dwindles down to an as yet uncertain conclusion.

"Children," Mary says at Medjugorje, *"darkness reigns over the whole world* (7/30/87)—*this unfaithful world walking in darkness* (6/5/86). *Satan exists! He seeks only to destroy!* (2/14/82). *Satan is working hard in the world* (1/14/85). *You can not imagine what is going to happen nor what the Eternal Father will send to earth* (6/24/83). *You must warn the bishop and the pope with respect to the urgency and the great importance of the message for all of mankind* (1983). *A great struggle is about to unfold, a struggle between my Son and Satan* (8/2/81). *Light and darkness are fighting each other. Many live in darkness. Show them the light* (3/13/85). *The present hour is the hour of Satan. The hour has come when the demon is authorized to act with all his force and power."*

Visionaries claim that for a century now the world has been under the extended influence of Satan. This vast and nefarious supernormal force has managed in an unprecedented way to take God out of our lives and to sow spiritual blindness, making us live only for the physical or demonic world. His greatest gimmick is to convince us he doesn't exist and he has quietly succeeded in doing so with many of our most influential intellectuals. He's the great spoiler. He's behind addiction, murder, war, atheism, pornography, promiscuity, blasphemy, mind control, witchcraft, totalitarianism, egoism, greed, terrorism, obsession, abortion, perversion, oppression, and sloth. He has caused a spirit of pride, vulgarity, and rebellion to dominate our popular culture, and he is as present in profane rock lyrics (or for that matter crooked stock deals) as he is in the eyes of Charles Manson.

He's in our laboratories, our hospitals, our universities. He is equally at home in a courthouse or a crackhouse. He sits in the control room at the networks and has a seat in the halls of Congress.

While this whole concept may seem superstitious or paranoid to some of you, I'm confident the following pages will aptly demonstrate the existence of such a diabolical entity and how he has led mankind onto a stray path from which we must hurriedly change course or risk terrific harm.

Currently, the Evil One is doing as much as he can as soon as he can and is full of rage because cast amongst us he knows his time is short.

He is the force of anti-christ, an energy visualized as a fallen angel of great beauty and rank, now with glowering eyes and scaly skin, horned of head, a serpent or dragon, the personification of evil known as Satan or Lucifer.

According to one modern visionary, Mirjana Dragicevic of Medjugorje, this filthy entity has been granted enhanced powers in our specific era, and in this book we'll see his actual footprints, in the form of occult manifestations from Marx to Hitler. "The Virgin told me God and the devil had a conversation, and the devil said that people believe in God only when life is good for them," says Mirjana. "When things turn bad, they cease to believe in God. Then people blame God, or act as if He does not exist. God therefore allowed the devil one century in which to exercise an extended power over the world, *and the devil chose the twen-*

tieth century (my italics). This century, she told me, is under the power of the devil."

You'll be encountering a number of hair-raising incidents. I have no choice but to tell the bad with the good, and I will not shrink from mention of the devil, for Our Lady herself speaks frequently and directly about him. In the Book of Genesis God told the serpent (*Gen.* 3:15) He would one day put enmity *"between you and the woman,"* and I believe the "woman" is the Virgin Mary. We'll see how Mary's most recent campaign began in the 1800s, just before our era, as Heaven tried to warn of the coming evils. With mankind reaching new moral lows, the apparitions have become more numerous than ever before. New reports arrive not each decade or year but every month. Something seems to be in the wind. Something seems to be coming to a head. Something seems ready to reveal itself. Those who speak with her say Mary has come to guide us back to her Son as we approach pivotal times and as war breaks out between the forces of Christ and anti-christ—that she has come as Heaven begins to more openly contend with the forces of Hell.

Again I address my Protestant friends: I know your concern that Catholics focus too much on Mary, and I greatly appreciate your concern that her apparitions might be a trick by the devil. Indeed, I'll report on cases indicating that such deceptions have occurred.

But I hasten to add that I'm equally convinced in the heavenly origin of many of the paranormal events, and my point is that this book is for all believers, written in the spirit of fellowship and reconciliation. It's for Franciscans but it's also for Anglicans and Orthodox, Baptists and Evangelicals, Jesuits but also Muslims. Yes, it focuses on phenomena associated with the Virgin Mary, and as such has a great Catholic flavor, but it is a *Christian* book since the end result is hopefully a better acquaintanceship with Jesus, and it's a Jewish book in that it's about a Jewish woman, and it's a Muslim book because it talks about the same God.

It might even be a book for some agnostics and atheists, since they may find certain evidence here that they haven't encountered elsewhere.

Not since the Pentecost has there been such an outpouring of supernatural verbiage. Not since Christ Himself appeared in glorified form have apparitions been such an instrument of conversion. Thousands and tens of thousands, even millions, profess to have recently undergone profound experiences and to have felt a transcendental peace and to have seen signs in the sky like the wonders predicted by the prophet Joel.

Often, as at Fatima and Medjugorje, the messages are accompanied by external phenomena—shooting stars, the sun miracle, strange cloud formations. In other cases the sites exhibit phenomena distinctly their own, such as weeping icons or healing wells. It is these phenomena, taken together, that compose the most impressive supernatural manifestations in twenty centuries.

If but a small majority of the recent accounts are true we are in a period that may indeed be the times spoken about in the Book of Revelation—times that will witness painful purification followed by glorious transformation. We'll look at what changes or cataclysms may be in store, and we'll also survey the influence of Lucifer. It's the premise of this book that we're nearing the end of a dark era and that these phenomena—the *legitimate* phenomena—are breaking through the night and heralding the epic confrontation between forces of good and evil, a confrontation that will determine the planet's destiny, a confrontation that the Blessed Virgin, as her Son's emissary, promises to win.

"These are my times," Mary has supposedly told an Italian priest, Stefano Gobbi. *"You are now living the events that I predicted to you. You are in the period in which the struggle between Me, the Woman Clothed With the Sun, and my adversary, the Red Dragon, is moving toward its conclusion, and for this reason I am appearing in a new and more extraordinary way. The struggle has now entered into its conclusive phase.* (As the century ends), *you are entering into the most difficult and decisive period. . ."*

It's hard to believe that a truly informed and detached observer, taking time to review all the reports, could deny that we're encountering a huge paranormal episode. It's widely remarked that there have been more than 300

noteworthy visions of the Virgin during the current century
and more in the past ten years than in all the 1800s. But
in reality no one has a reliable reckoning, and if individual
apparitions are taken into consideration—apparitions that
occur only once to a single individual and never gather public notice—the figure is much higher than 300, perhaps in
the thousands.

Many tens of thousands of others see lesser but nonetheless spectacular manifestations, like the spinning sun.

"One of the signs of our times," comments a Vatican official, Joseph Cardinal Ratzinger, "is that the announcements
of 'Marian apparitions' are multiplying all over the world."

I must immediately issue a warning, a warning that should
be considered with every single apparition or supernatural
incident. There is so much alleged phenomena that it's
impossible for the Church, let alone an individual, to render sound conclusions on the supernatural authenticity or
goodness of each case. Along with the occurrences that seem
of a heavenly origin are also reports, especially of locutions
(the hearing of an inner voice), that may be products of
the subconscious. Please keep this in mind throughout the
book. Assume the word "alleged" with each claim that has
not been approved by the Church. You're about to encounter some very strong and striking cases, but there will also
be phenomena that are too private and subtle to authenticate.

Assuming a case *is* true we must always be aware of that
other distinct possibility: that certain of the supernatural
events are being orchestrated *not* by Heaven but by sinister
forces that seek to dilute the bona fide phenomena and lead
us on a wild goose chase. In other words, the battle is so
treacherous that Satan is not beyond masquerading as the
Virgin to confuse and discourage us.

Every single event, no matter how good it seems at first,
must be weighed and discerned by means of extensive prayer.
And we also should remember that there are always cases
of collective suggestion and hysteria.

It's already clear, from cases you'll read, that wherever
Our Lady appears the devil also turns up. In some cases
Satan or his demons actually materialize as full-bodied apparitions, attempting to disrupt the events. In other cases
they're an invisible but influential force.

I'm not using the word "evil" in the secular sense. When I say evil I mean *evil*. We will presume that entities called "demons" actually exist, and we will take a new look at history with that presumption in mind. In short: I'll assume demons do exist, and that they are invisibly affecting us in ways we usually don't realize. Heavenly forces are squaring off against those led by an actual entity named Satan. We're in the middle of a war, an invisible war of great moment, a war that's been in the offing for a hundred years and is now being waged at every level on every continent and may soon reach a shattering conclusion.

Spurred in part by the supernatural occurrences, forces of goodness are regrouping and striking back at the pervasive evil. After decades of fearful silence the believers are finally entering the fray, and those of goodness and light—Catholics, Protestants, and Jews, all who believe in and love God—have the opportunity to win if they heed the authentic warnings.

If they don't, we'll succumb to turmoil and the growing spirit of anti-christ.

While victory awaits us, so does the beast who is rising from the sea. Skeptics, scoffers, and other zealots of agnosticism are warned that I'll make few attempts to appease their suspicions and no apologies for a shamelessly mystical viewpoint. This book is about *miracles,* and while it hasn't been fashionable during most of our era to profess the supernormal, the vast majority of Americans (94 percent) believe in some form of God. They are the ones with whom I chiefly concern myself.

While I'm a journalist by training—trained to be "objective" and "skeptical"—I write not as a secular reporter (which has come to mean an agnostic or atheist), but as a decidedly Judeo-Christian writer. I believe we no longer have the luxury of compromise with the forces of evil. This is not so much a work of journalistic or collegiate scholarship as a leap into an invisible dimension.

Right now earth remains in an era of great spiritual darkness. The world is black as anthracite, lit only by the flares of an otherwise invisible war. Take a look at Chapter 12 of *Revelation: "Now a great sign appeared in Heaven, a woman clothed with the sun, with the moon under her feet, and on her head a garland of twelve stars. . . And another sign appeared in Heaven: behold, a great fiery red dragon having seven heads and ten horns, and seven diadems on his heads. . . And war broke out in Heaven. . . "*

If we're in the middle of that battle then we may indeed be living in what bibical scholars refer to as the apocalyptic or last times. I'm always wary of such melodrama, but let's say we *are* in the latter times. If so we're not speaking about the end of the *world* but the end of an *era*—a period that will record radical change in the way we live, think, and believe, along with certain social, political, economic, and perhaps even geophysical upheavals.

Our world is about to change. The evil is about to be broken. But before it is, there may be great confusion and catastrophe.

In my opinion the incidents are an indication that we're entering a spiritually decisive period, and that Mary, the one who brought Christ into the world two millennia ago, has returned to bring Him back—ending the high reign of Lucifer.

CHAPTER 2

Woe to Earth

Our story starts in 1830, just after the French Revolution, as the world was about to begin the current era of godlessness, occultism, and "rationalism." On July 18, at about 11:30 p.m. in a novitiate (or seminary) known as Sisters of Charity at 140 Rue du Bac in Paris, a nun named Catherine Labouré woke with a start.

She heard a voice call her and drew the bed curtain.

There was an angelic "child" of about four or five years old, dressed in radiant white. "Come to the chapel," this apparitional figure said. "The Blessed Virgin is waiting for you."

For years Catherine Labouré had prayed to her guardian angel to bring Our Lady, and now there was the angel in response. She hurriedly dressed and followed the child. Lights came on by themselves as they stepped through the corridor. "When we reached the chapel the door opened as soon as the child touched it with the tip of his finger," she recounted.

The cherub led her to the sanctuary and they waited for what seemed like hours. "Toward midnight the child said, 'Here is the Blessed Virgin,'" said Catherine. "I heard a noise like the rustle of a silk dress. A very beautiful lady sat down in Father Director's chair. The child repeated in a strong voice, 'Here is the Blessed Virgin!' Then I flung myself at her feet on the steps of the altar and put my hands on her knees.

"There a moment passed, the sweetest of my life. I could not say what I felt. The Blessed Virgin told me how I must conduct myself with my director, and added several things that I must not tell. As to what I should do in time of trouble, she pointed with her left hand to the foot of the altar, and told me to come there and to open my heart, assuring me that I would receive all the consolation I needed."

Several months later, on November 27, Catherine encountered Our Lady for a second time, again in the chapel, near a picture of St. Joseph. The apparition was of average height and clothed in white, with a veil that flowed over the head and fell to the floor. Above the altar, a pyramid painted to represent God's all-knowing wisdom looked down on them.

Our Lady's feet rested on a white globe and there was also a green serpent with yellow spots that she was stepping on. In her hands was a golden ball that represented the world. Great streams of light issued from her hands, and she also showed Catherine an image of two hearts, the Sacred Heart wrapped in piercing thorns and her own heart punctured by a sword. The sword represented her suffering with Jesus.

After instructing Catherine to strike a medal of this pose (which became known as the medal of the Immaculate Conception or "Miraculous Medal"), Mary disappeared like an extinguished candle.

While the Virgin Mary has been appearing ever since Zaragoza in the first century, the 19th-century apparition at Rue du Bac introduced a new phase in the history of her apparitions. For our purposes it was a defining moment, important because it announced the onset of the great battle and forewarned that a dark era lay in the immediate future. It was the apparition leading up to the recent ones. Our Lady began to dispense secrets. And, with the globe, she revealed herself in worldwide dispute with the forces of dark. *"The times are evil,"* she told Catherine. *"Misfortunes will fall upon France. The throne will be overturned. The entire world will be overcome by evils of all kinds."*

Henceforth Mary's appearances would gain in frequency and meaning. Henceforth she would deliver secrets to the world. Henceforth she would reveal herself in direct and unmistakable conflict with the serpent.

What mankind didn't know but the Virgin did was that, henceforth, evil would be extolled as a modern "good"— in the form of many liberalisms—and God would be subjugated. Little seeds of the occult, spores from certain secret societies like the Masons, would eventually germinate into a large forest, altering the landscape of politics and human thought.

I have no intention of getting too deeply into politics but suffice it to say that Our Lady's appearance to Catherine Labouré was at a critical juncture in history. In France and across Europe intellectuals and politicians, intoxicated by a rebellious spirit, were starting to replace belief in the supernatural with belief solely in the material, three-dimensional world—only in what they could see, hear, taste, or feel. We call this "naturalism" and "materialism." It's a movement that almost immediately sought to remove religion from any position of authority and replace it with strictly secular or non-religious systems of authority.

We also call it "humanism" because everything suddenly revolved around humans. Mankind stood alone at the center of a mechanical and soulless universe.

And with that, the great cosmic struggle had begun. In one corner was Satan, inspiring mankind with the same pride and rebelliousness that had gotten him thrown out of Heaven. There was Satan, removing the concept of God from human thought. There was Satan, blinding the intellectuals to anything that wasn't of the "logical" and material world or dragging them into the occult and demon worship. But there was also Christ, represented by His mother. He was sending the person He had trusted most on earth, the person whose personal recollections had been responsible for much of the New Testament, as His personal emissary. For the time being, perhaps in wait for the Second Coming, the Holy Spirit was using Mary to help fend off and expose

Satan. If the first Eve had failed us, there was now a new covenant and in many ways a new "Eve." Satan had been given enhanced power, but so had Mary.

Sixteen years after Rue du Bac the Blessed Virgin returned to troubled France, this time on the other side of the country, high at the rounded summit of Mount Planteau in the towering Alps. She had more messages, secrets, and especially warnings.

The summit of Mount Planteau was so quiet the sound of a bird's wings startled visitors. The only other noise was the occasional and far-off rumor of a cow heavy with milk, and far below were mountain villages. In the closest hamlet, LaSalette, smoke unfurled from cobblestone chimneys.

By October the summit would be coated with snow and sleet, but it was September 19, 1846, and on the stone-strewn meadows two peasant children named Mélanie Mathieu (14) and Maximin Giraud (11) were watching cows near the summit when, to their incredulity, they spotted a large circle of light. It was in a ravine.

"I dropped the stick I was holding," recalled Mélanie. "Something inconceivably fantastic passed through me in that moment, and I felt myself being drawn. I felt a great respect, full of love, and my heart beat faster. I kept my eyes firmly fixed on this light, which was static, and as if it had opened up, I caught sight of another, much more brilliant light which was moving, and in this light I saw a most beautiful lady sitting with her head in her hands."

The Lady seemed to be crying. Slowly the apparitional woman rose, revealing a dress bursting with unnatural light, her slippers edged with flowers—roses—and her head topped with a glorious crown. She also wore a yellow pinafore that in Mélanie's words was "more brilliant than several suns put together." It wasn't of tangible material but of ethereal glory, scintillating and ravishingly beautiful.

There were tears on the woman's cheeks, crystalline tears, and every part of her was radiant. There were two lights next to her, bathing the children in their luminescence, and she said, *"Come, my children, and fear not. I am here to proclaim important news to you. . . If my people do not wish to submit themselves, I am forced to let go of the hand of my Son. It is so heavy and weighs me down so much I can no longer keep hold of it. I have suffered all the time for the rest of you! If I do not wish my Son to abandon you, I must take it upon myself to pray for this continually.*

"All the civil governments will have one and the same plan, which will be to abolish and do away with every religious principal, to make way for materialism, atheism, occultism and vice of all kinds.

"The chiefs, the leaders of the people of God, have neglected prayer and penance, and the devil has bedimmed their intelligence. They have become wandering stars which the old devil will drag with his tail to make them perish. God will allow the old serpent to cause divisions among those who reign in every society and in every family. Physical and moral agonies will be suffered. God will abandon mankind to itself and will send punishments which will follow one after the other for more than 35 years. The society of men is on the eve of the most terrible scourges and of gravest events. Mankind must expect to be ruled with an iron rod and to drink from the chalice of the wrath of God."

The Virgin also issued warnings about working on the Sabbath and about using Christ's name in vain. She said there were no longer souls worthy of making sacrifices for the world. Priests, she said, were angering God with their impiety in the celebration of the holy mysteries and their obsession with money, honors, and pleasures.

The same was true, she warned, for political leaders. Vengeance was at the door. Napoleon III, she correctly predicted, would soon fall on his own sword.

For months and years after the LaSalette apparition Mélanie and Maximin found themselves embroiled in controversy. The reason was not the apparition itself, which the Church approved in 1851, but the secrets, which were revealed only later. Bishops and cardinals fought over their authenticity and curious laymen tried to pry them from the two beleaguered children. When Mélanie and Maximin did release them, it was to the pope, Pius IX, who, it is said, reflected great emotion when he read what Mélanie had written. "There are scourges that menace France, but Germany, Italy, all Europe is culpable and merits chastisements," the pope said afterward.

The nuncio to Paris, Cardinal Fornari, proclaimed that for Heaven to send such warnings the evils had to be very great and the future ominous. "I am terrified," he said, "of these prodigies."

We'll look at more of the LaSalette secrets as we go on. The important point is that like Rue du Bac, the Virgin of LaSalette predicted great evil descending upon mankind in the near future. Self-indulgence, greediness, and a loveless, worldy spirit were entering mankind's collective heart. The spirit of rebellion, occultism, and humanism was continuing to pervade Europe. Three-fourths of France, said Mary, would lose the faith.

Most important was Maximin's claim that according to the Virgin a monster would rise and disrupt peace in the world at the end of the 19th century or the beginning of the twentieth. Keep this beast in mind. We'll see it soon. Keep in mind that it comes full force around the beginning our era.

Mary's dire observations coincided all too well with other mystical warnings. For many years visionaries and stigmatists had been saying that the pit of perdition was creaking open and furies from Hell were being loosed upon earth. As far back as the 1790s, and undoubtedly before then, there were prophecies to the effect that godlessness, greed, violence, and immorality would reign toward the year 2000—during our era, the end of the millennium.

Little by little, it was said, forces of evil, gaining power during the 1800s and then reaching full stride in the next century, would infiltrate government, business, the educational system, and organs of communication.

It was an incubation period. The stage was being set for a full-scale assault. Major leaders would extinguish belief in God, promote paganism, or even dabble with black magic. When that happened, said these mystics, the Church would be persecuted, believers would be martyred, and the influence of evil in all aspects of life would greatly accelerate.

In the midst of Satan's extended influence, however, mankind, they said, would be witness to supernatural signs and a purifying chastisement—great events that would break Satan's power.

Pope Pius IX himself predicted that after the Church suffered horrible ordeals—after a century-long trial during which demonic forces rushed the Church's very gates—there would be "a great sign which will fill the world with awe."

We'll discuss that "great sign" a little later. For now what's important is to understand that Pope Pius and the Virgin were most concerned with the social and intellectual upheavals wracking Europe. Secular humanists were trying to take marriage out of the domain of the Church, arguing that it was a purely legalistic matter; and they insisted on separating not just Church and state but *God* and state. In so doing they were re-establishing paganism and paving the way for what was known then as "Red Radicalism," which sought the destruction of all ranks of society, the abolition of private property, and establishment of common ownership for all goods.

In other words, the foundation was being built for Communism.

"In the year 1864, Lucifer, together with a large number of demons, will be unloosed from Hell," Mary told Mélanie. *"They will put an end to faith little by little... Evil books will be abundant on earth and the spirits of darkness will spread everywhere a universal slackening in all that concerns the service of God. They will have great power over Nature; there will be churches built to serve these spirits. People will be transported from one place to another by these evil spirits..."*

Devils would disguise themselves as spirits of the dead, Mary warned, or would come as false ministers preaching that there is no Hell or Heaven. The Church would suffer a frightful and implicitly long-lasting crisis. *"May the Pope guard against the performers of miracles. For the time has come when the most astonishing wonders will take place on the earth and in the air."* She was referring to the occult, UFOs, and psychic phenomena. The coming decades, she said, would witness performers of miracles who were in reality controlled by *"the demon of magic."*

Darkness. A time of darkness was emphasized at LaSalette. In bibilical terms "a time" can mean a century or more. Thus, LaSalette contained prophecies not just for the 19th century but for our own era. Indeed, there are reasons to believe the prophecies of LaSalette are more relevant now than then. In words that distinctly resembled Revelation, Mary said, *"God will strike in an unprecendented way. Woe to the inhabitants of the earth! God will exhaust His wrath upon them and no one will be able to escape so many afflictions together."*

She glanced in the direction of Rome, then faded into the light and vanished.

CHAPTER 3

The Door of Hell

Over the next few chapters I'll give little snippets to show how the demonic forces entered the world and affected our culture, politics, and thus the course of modern history through occultism. I don't like to dwell on the occult, but we must see evil as an actual force—and we must understand how it has perverted the world, forcing Mary to make urgent visits as we head to the brink of chastisements.

For example, just two years after LaSalette, during the winter of 1848, in nearly immediate fulfillment of the warnings, a mysterious and dangerous movement was born in Hydesville, New York. It was the "religion" of Spiritualism, whereby mediums communicate with the "dead." It was a forerunner of the New Age and "channeling" movements. It was also the door of Hell creaking open. Mary had warned that devils, seeking entrance into the world, would disguise themselves as deceased humans, and here they were.

It started when a family (named Fox) heard strange rappings, footsteps, and loud bangs from the pantry and cellar stairs of their modest home in Upstate New York. Soon two of the Fox children, Margaretta and Catherine, began communicating with the "ghost" by using a rapping code. In no time they were famous mediums, holding seances across the state and then around the nation. Hundreds and then thousands followed their example, tipping tables and listening to raps in the rising wood. Even President Lincoln attended a table-tilting session. In England a psychic named Daniel Douglas Home held seances for writers, scientists, and royalty. Home, it was claimed, could levitate not only tables but his own body, floating from one window to another in seeming fulfillment of a second LaSalette prediction, that people *"will be transported from one place to another by evil spirits."*

I don't know how much is true but many witnesses said spirit voices were heard around Home and eerie, moaning winds erupted near him.

"Then a fifth angel sounded: And I saw a star fallen from heaven to the earth," says Revelation 9:1-3. *"And to him was given the key to the bottomless pit. And he opened the bottomless pit, and smoke arose out of the pit like the smoke of a great furnace. And the sun and the air were darkened because of the smoke of the pit. Then out of the smoke locusts came upon the earth. And to them was given power, as the scorpions of the earth have power."*

In the midst of the demonic infestation, in the wave of popularized occultism, Mary came again to France, appearing to a young girl named Bernadette Soubirous, who had taken to wearing the Miraculous Medal. The first of 18 apparitions occurred at a shallow cave (or "grotto") near the River Gave in Lourdes on February 11, 1858. The Blessed Virgin announced her arrival with the sounds of a storm and Bernadette noticed a rosebush moving strangely. Then she saw a gold-colored cloud drift out of the grotto, followed by the apparition of a young woman above the wind-swept bush. Mary was 16 or 17, dressed in white with a blue sash or girdle. During her apparitions she identified herself as the *"Immaculate Conception."* This was important because it was the first affirmation of a declaration that Mary was conceived without original sin.

"Penitence!" she stressed. *"Pray for sinners."*

She even asked Bernadette to climb the slope on her knees and kiss the earth as a sign of reverence and sacrifice.

And she imparted a secret that Bernadette never revealed. Sacrifice was the key. People had to live pure lives—free of the occult and demons. People had to look toward their place in eternity.

"I do not promise to make you happy in this world," said the Lady, *"but in the next."*

In what became a custom of her apparitions, Mary prayed with Bernadette, indicating the rosary as a protection against Satan. "Without thinking of what I was doing, I took my rosary in my hands and went on my knees," recounted the young visionary. "The Lady made a sign of approval with her head and herself took into her hands a rosary which hung on her right arm. When I attempted to begin the rosary and tried to lift my hand to my forehead, my arm remained paralyzed, and it was only after the Lady had signed herself that I could do the same. The Lady had me pray by myself; she passed the beads of her rosary between her fingers but she said nothing; only at the end of each decade did she say the *'Gloria'* with me. When the recitation of the Rosary was finished, the Lady returned to the interior of the rock and the golden cloud disappeared with her."

At a certain moment during the apparitions Bernadette suddenly heard loud shouts, "like the clamor of a bawling crowd," coming from the area near the river, with one especially furious voice roaring at Bernadette: "Get out! Get out!" It was an attack by demonic spirits who tried to scare her from the grotto. The Virgin Mary merely glanced in their direction and with a simple and yet sovereign look reduced the invisible mob to silence.

Although only a few messages were given at Lourdes, Mary accomplished many things with the famous apparition. She established a presence with storm-like force, barging into a social climate that was increasingly dominated by occultism; she made herself known as the "Immaculate Conception;" she brought forth a miraculous spring of healing waters; and she showed in a very living way that she was in conflict with the devil.

She also tried to give an increasingly rationalistic and occultic world a taste of the *right* kind of the supernatural.

But Satan was always around and he gained footholds through both Spiritualism and atheism. The devil was working with earnest on the minds of the 19th-century philosophers. He drew them into seeing life as a purely physical event, and he replaced belief in the Creator with belief in Darwinism. The German philosopher Nietzsche soon rose to blaspheme God. He declared that a new "creator" was needed, and pronounced the goal of human existence to be that of evolution into a god-like "superman." It became fashionable for intellectuals to mock concepts of the real Creator as outdated and simple-minded ideologies.

This was all in Satan's strategy: negate God through either atheism or occultism—whatever means possible.

CHAPTER 4

Voice from the Abyss

Not long after LaSalette and Lourdes, on October 13, 1884, Pope Leo XIII, a fragile and sagacious man, experienced a horrifying vision. He was consulting with his cardinals after Mass in the private Vatican chapel when suddenly he paused at the foot of the altar and lapsed into what looked like a coma.

According to popular legend the pope's face turned pallid, leading to fears he was near death, and he was catatonic—disconcertingly motionless—for several tense minutes.

By some accounts a physician rushed to his side and had trouble finding a pulse.

After a short interval, however, Pope Leo rallied, his eyes flashing open, his slender face fixed in a dazed look. "Oh," he gasped, "what a horrible picture I was permitted to see!"

The pope later confided that during the strange episode he saw demons and heard the atrocious, guttural voice of Satan boasting to God that he could destroy the Church and drag the world to Hell if he were given sufficient time and power.

According to the Pontiff, Satan asked God for between 75 and 100 years of enhanced worldly influence and it was granted.

Leo was further given to understand that if the devil didn't accomplish his purpose in the allotted time, he would suffer a crushing and humiliating defeat.

Whatever its additional content, the vision was obviously a nerve-wracking one. Afterwards Pope Leo repaired to his office and urgently composed the famous prayer to the archangel Michael.

> *"St. Michael the Archangel, defend us against the enemy, be our safeguard against the wickedness and snares of the devil. May God rebuke him, we humbly pray, and do thou, O Prince of the Heavenly Host, by the power of God, cast into Hell Satan and the other evil spirits who prowl about the world for the ruin of souls."*

We can only imagine the devils Pope Leo saw. We can only speculate that they were the stuff of a nightmare—distorted, beastlike faces with the bodies of locusts and scorpions.

Did Leo see them crawling into bedrooms, there to inspire lust and adultery? Did he see them hiding in the courtyards of government? Did he see them manipulating the pens of philosophers and slinking beneath the lumbering oak doors of a noble cathedral, to corrupt the local clergy?

We know this much. Leo had read the secrets of LaSalette and was well aware of the massive infiltration of atheism, occultism, and other forms of evil into society. He was especially aware of secret cults such as the Masons that sought to destroy Christ's Church. In fact, just six months before his vision, Leo had written an encyclical entitled *Humanum Genus* that exposed the Masons for what they were: a device of the devil. While they seemed on the surface like nothing more than a social club (in America many prominent men, including presidents, belonged), the Masons were out to quash Catholicism, railing against the Church and in their robes and arcane rituals practicing what was in effect a new form of witchcraft. Born in the Middle Ages, Freemasonry had started as an early trade union but quickly evolved into an organization that personified materialism, occultism, and humanism. Its loyalty was to the physical world, putting *reason* in the place of *revelation*. When Masons did feign religious rituals, the rituals were inspired by ancient Egyptian paganism, European witchcraft, and alchemy. "The fundamental doctrine of the Naturalists, which they sufficiently make known by their very name, is that human nature and human reason ought in all things to be mistress and guide," Leo wrote. He saw Freemasonry as the coalescing of humanistic and materialistic factions for a full-scale assault on Christianity.

No wonder Mary appeared so much in France. The country's best astronomers, mathematicians, and politicians were openly preaching humanism and joining Masonic lodges. At Lourdes a parish church had even been confiscated by the local government and turned at one point into a "temple of reason."

"No longer making a secret of their purposes," fretted Leo, "they are now boldly rising up against God Himself."

And France was hardly alone. In Germany neo-pagan cults that had different rituals but the same Masonic philosophy were rising quickly. These organizations would soon influence national politics, resurrecting ancient mystical symbolism and inspiring ideas of Germanic or "Aryan" superiority. Highly influential in this spiritual underground was an enigmatic, white-bearded occultist named Guido von List, who wore long flowing robes and was immensely popular in Austria. List performed sex rites to raise the "spirits," and one morning in 1875 the magician went to a hill overlooking Vienna, chanted his special incantations, and buried nine wine bottles in the shape of an old occult symbol called the swastika.

I use List simply as an example of the occultic origins of rising political movements. I could use others. The Masonic lodges Pope Leo was so concerned about had been infiltrated, for example, by a supremely secretive organization called the "Illuminati" who since 1776 had been fomenting disruptions and changes in society. The Illuminati were spawned by a group that included banker Meyer Rothschild. They sought to form one world government that they would then exercise tremendous control over. First, though, they had to break down existing institutions and governments, and it was the Illuminati who, with other Masonic elements, helped give birth to the calamitous French Revolution. More to the point, in 1829, a year before the apparition at Rue du Bac, the Illuminati met in New York and formed a committee that later financed Karl Marx. Still later, the Bolshevik Revolution in Russia was financed by a group of international money-lenders that included Jacob Schiff, who gave Lenin millions to bring socialism to Russia. Both Lenin and his sidekick, Trotsky, had connections to the Masons.

While to the casual observer the world may have looked very calm during much of Leo's pontificate (an era of peace even seemed to be unfolding), the devil, preparing for his full assault, was manifesting in ever more complex and insidious ways. Mostly he sought to puff up man's pride and make him feel independent of God, an easy task in this seductive era of wondrous new technology. "Logic" was the new ideal, and finding Heaven on earth—through use of the brain and brain alone—became man's chief preoccupation.

There were splendid inventions everywhere, discoveries made possible by human powers of deductive reasoning. In 1884, the year of Leo's vision, inventors developed the linotype (which revolutioned the newspaper business) and isolated the diptheria bacillus. Miracles were no longer the sole province of Heaven. This was the heyday of materialism. There were trolleys and coated photographic paper and the first gasoline-driven motor and John D. Rockefeller to provide the petroleum. I'm certainly not out to condemn ingenuity. Who'd want to go back to the days before automobiles and air conditioning? But man became *intoxicated* with his new mechanical realm and began to look to machines for solace instead of seeking God's guidance, comfort, and peace.

We began to worship at the altar of technology, and electricity replaced the Holy Spirit. Who needed God for illumination? Let there be light, and someone simply turned on a switch.

With science as the new religion, there was no room for "childish" and medieval notions of demonology. Suddenly, instead of seeing demons as the cause of many men-

tal, spiritual, and emotional disorders (as most religions
have long believed), doctors began placing all such problems in the context of a new "science" called psychology.
No doubt many mental disturbances are caused by chemi-
cal imbalances, childhood traumas, and other behavioral
factors. But evil spirits also exert an influence. There are
cases of demonic possession that are no longer recognized
as such, diagnosed instead, now, as "psychosis,"
"schizophrenia," or "dual personality." As I stressed, the
devil's best device is to camouflage his existence.

It was the era of Freud, who set about establishing psy-
chotherapy as a new denomination of scientism. Although
the very female patient who inspired Freud's initial theory
was in reality a case of demonic oppression (she complained about an evil spirit inside her!), the famous psy-
choanalyst scoffed at such notions and was contemptuous
of religion. As far as he was concerned, she was delusional.
Any miracles or "demonic" attacks were explained away
as products of the subconscious, a childish reversion to
"primitive" days when people believed in such "nonsense" as devils and angels. Freud sought to replace the
idea of "good" and "evil" with his bizarre and to this day
unproven psychosexual theories.

It was all a grand deception, and while Freud was too
blind to see it, unaware that he was being used, that's what
it was: a supernatural scheme to hide the increasing presence of evil spirits. If Satan couldn't get people to worship
at his seances and occult altars, if he couldn't get them to
follow the Fox sisters or D. D. Home, the next best thing
was to blind them to all forms of the supernatural so his
demons could operate freely. There was a supernatural
conspiracy going on—a plan devised at unearthly levels—
and the spirit of satanism had risen into the world, spreading its clever deceptions. If you think it's outlandish to
believe that forces of evil conspire to affect and engineer
world events, consider the case of Karl Marx. Nowhere was
the connection to sinister forces clearer than with the very
founding father of socialism. He himself wrote of Hell and
the devil as if the devil were his friend. In public he may
have espoused atheism, calling religion the "opiate of the

people," but in private he obviously believed in supernatural realities and seems to have made a pact with Satan. Wrote Marx in a poem called "The Player:"

> The hellish vapors rise and fill the brain,
> Till I go mad and my heart is utterly
>   changed.
> See this sword?
> The prince of darkness
> Sold it to me.
> For me he beats the time and gives the signs.
> Ever more boldly I play the dance of death.

Marx also wrote a drama entitled *Oulanem,* which includes this dialogue:

> Yet I have power within my youthful arms
> To clench and crush you with tempestuous
>   force,
> While for us both the abyss yawns in
>   darkness.
> You will sink down and I shall follow
>   laughing,
> Whispering in your ears, "Descend, come
>   with me, friend."

As Marx himself admits in his writings, the real goal of Marxism was not to form a new social order but to drag as many souls as possible to the depths of Hell. The goal was to negate God and take up the sword of Satan. The goal was to replace Christianity with either naturalism or occultism. In *Oulanem* it was vowed that "soon I shall embrace eternity to my breast, and soon I shall howl gigantic curses on mankind." The netherworld, he said in *The Pale Maiden,* was his own destination:

> This heaven I've forfeited,
> I know it full well.
> My soul, once true to God,
> Is chosen for hell.

CHAPTER 5

The Hour of Power

A spirit of anti-christ, the beast Maximin mentioned at LaSalette, was stirring in the depths. By 1890 attacks on the Church were coming from everywhere. France's liberal government had seized Church property and broken diplomatic relations with the Holy See. It prohibited religious instruction without strict government control while a rationalistic movement known as "modernism" infiltrated the Church itself, demystifying the Bible and making the sacraments seem like nothing more than outdated rituals.

"As the holy Faith of God is forgotten, every individual will wish to be his own guide and be superior to his fellow men," Our Lady of LaSalette foresaw. *"Civil and ecclesiastical authority will be abolished. All order and all justice will be trampled underfoot. Nothing will be seen but murder, hatred, jealousy, falsehood, and the discord without love for the mother country or the family. . . The Church will suffer a terrible crisis."*

In 1879 she had also appeared at Knock, Ireland, in a "living picture" with St. Joseph, but the event had little impact and was all but ignored by the press. It was the hour of secular, anti-Christian influence. Newspapers eliminated religious articles from the front page and, following Freud's lead, relegated Scripture to the category of superstition. As the twentieth century neared, technology

30

exploded all around. New chemicals were invented and the development of celluloid paved the way to Hollywood. The first beauty contest was held in Belgium, glorifying the body above all human attributes, and Oscar Wilde promoted the previously condemned practice of homosexuality.

Political, sexual, and cultural trends washed away religious values.

Tolstoy had it right in a new book called *The Power of Darkness.*

That's what was happening on the surface. But many such societal trends had their origin below ground, in demonism, Masonry, and the occult. What seemed like mere societal trends were in actuality subtle manifestations of evil. And as our era began, the occult was spreading rapidly. In their secret lodges, the Masons were spawning sub-cults such as the Rosicrucians, movements that borrowed from Spiritualism or ancient sorcery and gave birth to a satanic cult called the Hermetic Order of the Golden Dawn. Among the Golden Dawn's membership was the magician Aleister Crowley, whose own mother referred to him as "The Beast" and who became the most infamous occultist of the dawning era. A user of drugs and practitioner of sexual magic, Crowley's emphasis was on man's "true inner self."

"Be strong, O man! Lust, enjoy all things of sense and rapture: fear not that any God shall deny thee for this," Crowley used to preach.

As he also said, "Do what thou wilt shall be the whole of the law."

Addressing Heaven at a satanic ceremony, Crowley, who rose to power precisely at the onset of our century, the year 1900, railed against Christ Himself: "Thine hour is come; as I blot thee out from this earth, so surely shall the eclipse pass; and Light, Life, Love and Liberty be once more the law of Earth. Give thou place to me, O Jesus; thine aeon is passed; the Age of Horus (an Egyptian demigod) is arisen by the Magick of the Master, the Great Beast."

Crowley's cult was only one of the esoteric organizations that were suddenly sprouting across Europe. These secret but influential cults were both anti-Semitic and anti-Catholic—opposed, certainly, to conventional Christianity. Their home base was Germany, and mesmerized by the idea of evolution, they, like Nietzsche, believed the Germanic people would evolve into a race of superhumans. As I've said, they resurrected pagan emblems like *the swastika,* a sign that had been used since prehistoric times as a sun symbol.

The swastika soon found its way onto the banner of another cult called the New Templars, and this was significant because the New Templars were a forerunner of the Nazi movement. The order acquired its first temple in 1907 and like the Masons its members wore ceremonial robes, practiced pagan rituals, and possessed an interest in astrology, phrenology (palm reading), and the Cabala. In 1909, at a brief meeting in Vienna, Dr. Jörg Lanz von Liebenfels, founder of the Templars, met with a 20-year-old man named Adolf Hitler who was likewise developing a keen interest in the black arts.

In addition to the Templars, Hitler was interested in occult practices like Theosophy, a demonic religion that combined Eastern mysticism, especially belief in reincarnation, with spiritualistic-type seances. It was popular in both Europe and America, where it also caught the attention of Margaret Sanger, the woman who founded Planned Parenthood and championed the most dangerous trend of the coming era, the "right" to abortion. I don't plan to delve deeply into Sanger's personal life, but she was a famous adulteress who treated her first husband with remarkable cruelty and neglected her children. Sexual promiscuity was her real cause and as one writer, Mabel Dodge, described her, "it was as if she had been more or less arbitrarily chosen *by the powers that be* (author's emphasis) to voice a new gospel of not only sex knowledge in regard to contraceptions, but sex knowledge about copulation and its intrinsic importance. She was the first person I ever knew who was openly an ardent propagandist for the joys of the flesh."

Her own husband complained that Sanger's movement was "not noble but an excuse for a Saturnalia of sex." A "Saturnalia" is a pagan sex festival.

We see then how paganism, a form of demon worship, was infecting not only politics and philosophy but personal morality. Sanger was a Rosicrucian and editor of a newspaper called *Woman Rebel,* the motto of which was "No Gods, No masters." She urged women to "look the whole world in the face with a go-to-hell" attitude.

But Sanger's true cause was less political than it was mystical. Unknowingly controlled by what Crowley called the "secret chiefs," she was trying, in essence, to involve an entire society in an occult ritual of Saturnalia. A massive sex rite! If Spiritualism was the demon of magic, this was the demon of lust. The sexual revolution was on its way, and its fruit, abortion, was tantamount to another ritual of witchcraft: blood sacrifice. For centuries witches have promoted just what Sanger was promoting: free, extramarital sex and the sacrifice of innocents. Now this too was being done on a massive scale! The occult spirit engendered by Spiritualism and nurtured by the secret cults was now integrating itself in society's mainstream under the disguise of liberated sex and feminism. Sanger was the Marx of sexuality. She described herself (in *My Fight For Birth Control*) as part of a "secret society" of "agnostics and atheists" who were waiting for the "coming revolution."

It was already here, a revolution orchestrated not by humans but by satanic forces.

CHAPTER 6

Beyond Cosmic Laws

It was a clever deception and like those propagated by the other cultural revolutionaries, the cause Sanger espoused was considered human "progress." Only the most astute observers, such as Pope Pius X, recognized the undercurrent of evil. He called doctrines of modernism the "synthesis of all heresies" and "felt a sort of terror, considering the disastrous conditions of humanity at the present hour."

The onslaught of wickedness even made him wonder if we were entering an apocalyptic century, "the beginning of the sorrows which must take place before the end of the world."

Pius knew about LaSalette, where Mary warned that God was going to abandon mankind to itself and *"send punishments which will follow one after the other for more than 35 years."*

War! The secrets of LaSalette had to do with unprecedented wars. Italy would have a war to fight, she predicted, and so would France, Spain, and England. *"A general war will follow which will be appalling. For a time, God will cease to remember France and Italy because the Gospel of Jesus Christ has been forgotten. The wicked will make use of their evil ways. Men will kill each other, massacre each other even in their homes... Paris will burn and Marseilles will be engulfed.''* Appearing to 22 peasant farmers on May 12, 1914 at a chapel in Hrushiw, Ukraine, where various supernatural phenomena had been reported for ages, Mary predicted eighty years of hardship. It was a site where there was a miraculous well, like at Lourdes, and during this apparition Mary said the people would witness three world wars. A month and a half later, on June 28, Archduke Francis Ferdinand, heir to the Austro-Hungarian empire, was assassinated in the Bosnia-Hercegovina region of Yugoslavia. It was the event that triggered World War I, which cost ten million lives; and in the midst of those hostilities the Blessed Virgin Mary made another appearance, her famous apparitions at Fatima, Portugal.

The Fatima episode began the year after Hrushiw, a time of persecution for the Portuguese faithful. As in France, the Republic had seized Church property and exiled hundreds of priests, including the Cardinal Patriarch of Lisbon. Masonic and other secular factions campaigned fervidly against local churches. As one scholar noted, "Not since the French Revolution had a European government made such determined efforts to stamp out religious institutions."

Signs of evil influence were cropping up everywhere. In Russia Czar Nicholas II and his wife Alexandra were under the spell of a Siberian occultist and "healer" known as Rasputin. Rasputin had been introduced to the monarchy by two princesses from Montenegro who were leaders in the East European Spiritualistic movement. He was a vile, foul-smelling man with long coal-black hair, long large fingers, and unforgettable blue-gray eyes. His was a shocking visage, but his hypnotic personality and his reputation as a healer endeared him to Russia's ruling elite. He weakened the czar and exerted unusual power over palace decision-making. When four men, including Prince Felix Yusupov, sought to save Russia by killing Rasputin, it was a scene out of a horror movie. Neither cyanide-laced wine nor a gunshot close to the heart could immediately kill him. As Yusupov told it, "All of a sudden his expression changed into one of fiendish hatred...I felt that, confronted with those satanic eyes, I was beginning to lose my self-control. A strange feeling of numbness took possession of me. My head reeled." At one point, wounded, Rasputin nonetheless found the supernormal strength to climb a set of stairs and roar at his killers.

Rasputin finally succumbed, but Russia and the world were in turmoil. The war was killing men at a rate never before known to the planet. Everything seemed to be in violent flux. On May 5, 1917, Pope Benedict XV made this strident plea to Heaven: "To Mary, then, who is the Mother of Mercy and omnipotent by Grace, let loving and devout appeal go up from every corner of the earth—from noble temples and tiniest temples, from royal palaces and mansions of the rich as from the poorest hut—from every place wherein a faithful soul finds shelter—from blood-drenched plains and seas. Let it bear to her the anguished cry of mothers and wives, the wailing of innocent little ones, the sighs of every generous heart: that her most tender and benign solicitude may be moved and the peace we ask for be obtained for our agitated world."

In the midst of that chaos, and with Portugal ready to join World War I, an angel had appeared to a broad-faced seven-year-old shepherdess named Lucia dos Santos about 90 miles north of Lisbon, in the hilly, impoverished farm region of Fatima. This was in 1915, just before the assassination of Rasputin. "We were just about to start praying the Rosary when I saw, poised in the air above the trees that stretched down to the valley which lay at our feet, what appeared to be a cloud in human form," Lucia recalled. It looked like a statue made of snow or a person wrapped in a sheet. A year later the angel appeared again, this time while she and two younger cousins, Francisco and Jacinta Marto, were tossing rocks into the valley. "As it drew closer, we were able to distinguish its features," said Lucia. "It was a young man, about 14 or 15 years old, whiter than snow, transparent as crystal when the sun shines through it, and of great beauty. As he drew nearer, we could distinguish his features more and more clearly. We were surprised, absorbed, and struck dumb with amazement. On reaching us, he said: *Do not be afraid. I am the Angel of Peace. Pray with me.*'"

So forceful was the presence of God that it "almost anni-hilated us. It seemed to deprive us even of the use of our bodily senses for a considerable length of time." The angel came twice more and granted the children special prayers and blessings.

"Pray," said the angel. *"Pray a great deal. The hearts of Jesus and Mary have merciful designs on you. Offer prayers and sacrifices continually to the Most High. Make everything you do a sacrifice."*

He explained that God was greatly insulted by the epi-demic of evil spreading across the physical and spiritual horizon. *"With all your power offer a sacrifice as an act of reparation for the sinners by whom He is offended, and of supplication for the conversion of sinners,"* the angel told them, adding that they should often repeat the words, *"My God, I believe, I adore, I hope, and I love You! I beg pardon of You for those who do not believe, do not adore, do not hope and do not love You!"*

At his last apparition the celestial messenger held a chalice in his left hand. Suspended above was a Host that dripped blood into the cup. He gave them another prayer for the conversion of sinners, then placed the Host on Lucia's tongue. *"Take and drink the Body and Blood of Jesus Christ, horribly outraged by ungrateful men! Make reparation for their crimes and console your God."*

Francisco and Jacinta were given to drink from the chal-ice before the angel prostrated himself, prayed to the Holy Trinity, and as Lucia said, "disappeared into the immense distance of the firmament."

Starting on May 13, 1917, eight days after Pope Benedict's plea, at nearly the exact spot where the angel appeared, Lucia, now 10, Francisco, 9, and Jacinta, 7, were visited by another apparition, but this time of the Virgin Mary. "It was a lady dressed all in white," recalled Lucia, "more brilliant than the sun, shedding rays of light clearer and stronger than a crystal glass filled with the most sparkling water and pierced by the burning rays of the sun."

The Virgin appeared to be only 16 years old, with a gar-ment of the finest white and a star near the hem of her flow-ing robe. She held white rosary beads, her hands delicate, her expression one of wistful solemnity—not sad, not happy, but serious. *"I am from Heaven,"* she explained to the awestruck Fatima children.

"And what is it you want of me?" asked Lucia.

"I come to ask you to come here for six months in succession, on the thirteenth day at the same hour. Then I will tell you who I am and what I want." The ethereal woman asked for recitation of the Rosary every day to end the war and bring peace.

She promised to take them to Heaven and asked, *"Are you willing to offer yourselves to God to bear all the sufferings He wills to send you, as an act of reparation for the sins by which He is offended, and of supplication for the conversion of sinners?"*

"Yes, we are willing," was their reply.

"Then, you are going to have much to suffer, but the grace of God will be your comfort."

The Blessed Virgin appeared on the 13th of each of the following five months, preceded by three flashes of light, accompanied at least once by a luminous globe, and leaving to the sound of thunder. At first local clerics feared the children were fabricating the story, or that they were encountering a deception by the devil. A white cloud was seen to descend on a small holm oak tree during the apparitions and a fragrant, unnatural odor issued from its branches.

As at Rue du Bac, streams of light issued from the Virgin's hands, encompassing the transfigured youngsters. Mary emphasized recitation of the Rosary as a means to end the war and showed them a heart pierced by thorns. *"Jesus wishes to make use of you to have me acknowledged and loved,"* she told Lucia. *"He wishes to establish in the world the devotion to my Immaculate Heart. . . My Immaculate Heart will be your refuge and the way that will lead you to God."*

The children were given visions of both Jesus and Mary, and following each decade of the Rosary, the Blessed Mother asked them to say the following prayer: *"Oh my Jesus, forgive us, save us from the fire of Hell, lead all souls to Heaven, especially those who are most in need."*

During one of her apparitions Mary opened her hands,

directed rays of light into the earth, and showed them the inferno of Hell. "Plunged in this fire were demons and souls in human form, like transparent burning embers, all blackened or burnished bronze, floating about in the conflagration, now raised into the air by the flames that issued from within themselves together with great clouds of smoke, now falling back on every side like sparks in a huge fire, without weight or equilibrium, and amid shrieks and groans of pain and despair, which horrified us and made us tremble with fear," said Lucia. "The demons could be distinguished by their terrifying and repellent likeness to frightful and unknown animals, all black and transparent. This vision lasted but an instant. How can we ever be grateful enough to our kind heavenly Mother, who had already prepared us by promising, in the first apparition, to take us to Heaven. Otherwise, I think we would have died of fear and terror."

That was the destiny for "poor sinners," and to save them, said Mary, God wished to establish devotion to her Immaculate Heart. *"If what I say is done, many souls will be saved and there will be peace. The war is going to end; but if people do not cease offending God, a worse one will break out during the pontificate of Pius XI. When you see a night illumined by an unknown light, know that this is the great sign given you by God that He is about to punish the world for its crimes, by means of war, famine, and persecution of the Church and of the Holy Father."*

It was a prophecy strikingly similar to that of the 1914 apparition of Hrushiw, Ukraine. The Blessed Virgin went on to request the consecration of Russia to her Immaculate Heart and Communion of reparation on the first Saturday of every month. *"If my requests are heeded, Russia will be converted, and there will be peace; if not, she will spread her errors throughout the world, causing wars and persecutions of the Church. The good will be martyred, the Holy Father will have much to suffer; various nations will be annihilated. In the end, my Immaculate Heart will triumph. The Holy Father will consecrate Russia to me, and she will be converted, and a period of peace will be granted to the world."*

These messages, and the vision of Hell, were kept secret for years, revealed only when Lucia felt the time was appropriate. There was also another message known as the Third Secret but it was never publicly released. It's said that during communication of the Third Secret Lucia took a deep breath, turned pale, and let out a shriek.

"Why do you look so sad?" people asked when the apparition was over.

"It's a secret," insisted Lucia. "It's a secret."

"Good or bad?"

"Good for some, for others, bad."

Despite threats from the local administrator, who belonged to a Masonic lodge in Leiria, pilgrims from across Portugal gathered at Fatima for the final apparition on October 13, 1917. They arrived the previous night in a storm of almost supernatural proportions.

"What a night!" wrote historian William Thomas Walsh. "It was as if the devil, somewhere in the ice and snow that could never slake the burning of his pain, had resolved to destroy with one blow all that remained of the Europe which had so long been his battleground against the Thing he hated most. Somewhere in the dark misery of Siberia, he was permitted, Heaven knows why, to disturb the equilibrium of the air, setting in motion a cold and cutting blast that shrieked across the continent to the western sea. It may have passed howling over a cabin in Finland where a little lynx-eyed man who called himself Lenin had been waiting to enter St. Petersburg (he had lately sown the seeds of revolution there), and to begin, in a very few weeks, the transformation and destruction of all the world which owed what was best and noblest in it to the teachings of Christ."

The rain slanted against the rustic countryside, turning roads to halting mud, but that didn't stop the people and neither did rumors that the Masonic authorities planned to explode a bomb at the moment of Mary's apparition. The determined pilgrims—farmers and fishermen, factory workers, peasant women in bare feet, children riding atop burros—continued to arrive until between 50,000 and 70,000 had gathered at a spot known as Cova da Iria. Early in the afternoon, when Lucia and her two cousins went into ecstasy, the clouds suddenly parted and Lucia saw Our Lady dressed in white with Saint Joseph beside her holding the Infant Jesus. Then Lucia saw a sorrowful Mary and an adult Jesus who looked with pity on the crowd and raised His hand to bless the pilgrims. At the end of her ecstasy Lucia saw Mary as *Our Lady of Mount Carmel,* dressed in dark brown.

While this was happening a disc of some sort moved in front of the sun and for ten minutes the sun danced like the firewheels in Ezekiel. Spinning and throwing off stupendous rays of crimson, causing reflections of green, red, orange, blue, and violet on the faces below, it gyrated at least three times, shuddered, and began to plunge downward in a zig-zag fashion, as if to destroy all the earth.

"We're going to die!" people screamed. "It's the end of the world!"

Then the sun returned to its normal position and to the crowd's amazement their clothes, dampened by hours of rain, were instantly dry.

As Avelino de Almeida reported in the newspaper *O Seculo,* "Before the astonished eyes of the people, whose attitude carries us back to biblical times and who, full of terror, heads uncovered, gaze into the blue of the sky, the sun has trembled, and the sun has made some brusque movements, unprecedented and outside of all cosmic laws..."

Was the fantastic display connected with the secrets? Did it portend a great catastrophe at some point in the future? Something from the sky?

Many years later versions of the Third Secret would leak out, and while their reliability is in dispute, one segment quoted the Virgin as saying, *"What I have already made known at LaSalette through the children Mélanie and Maximin, I repeat today before you. Mankind has not developed as God expected. Mankind has been sacrilegious and has trampled underfoot the gifts which were given it."*

A great punishment was going to come to all mankind, the Virgin supposedly said, *"not as yet today, nor even tomorrow, but in the second half of the twentieth century."*

Jacinta   Lucia   Francisco

The seers of Fatima, 1917.
The messages included the end of World War I and
actually foretold the start of World War II
and the rise of Communism.

CHAPTER 7

Kings of the Anti-Christ

As the Virgin predicted, World War I soon was brought to a halt. But mankind laid the foundation for another, monstrous struggle. A number of anti-christs were already walking the earth—not the Anti-Christ, but as LaSalette said, his forerunners. They were following in the footsteps of Marx. Chief among them were Lenin, Hitler, and Stalin.

In the case of Lenin, we need only know the significance of his name, the hardness of his appearance, and his awful fruits to realize that, like Marx, he was a miniature anti-christ. Lenin returned to Petrograd just three days after the last apparition at Fatima, disguised in a large gray wig and spectacles. He was in essence an agent of the bankers and Masons who wanted to tear down the existing societies of the world, and his code name with the Illuminati was supposedly "Spartacus." He once told an old friend, "We are...the real revolutionaries..! Yes, we are going to destroy everything, and on the ruins we will build our temple."

The founder of Soviet Communism was a cold, severe man with a pointed face and malign dark slitty eyes. His first name, Vladimir, a Slavonic name, meant "lord" or "ruler of the earth," which is precisely the phrase Mary used at LaSalette in warning that there would be *"kings of the Anti-Christ"* who would cause famines, annihilate

43

worship to God, and seek to replace Him as *"the only rulers of the world."* As if to mimic Christ, his mother's name was Maria and her mother's name was Ann (like the mother of Mary).

Mimicking Jesus is a trait of an anti-christ and indeed, one day soon every government building in the Soviet Union would have a little table altar with Lenin's picture next to those of Engels and Marx. As a child Lenin displayed an alarming lack of ordinary humanity, screaming at playmates and finding comfort only in the aria of the opera *Faust* (which is about a man selling his soul to the devil for knowledge and power); and in fifth grade he tore off a cross he was wearing, spat on it, and threw it to the ground or in the garbage.

That's the true spirit of anti-christ, and so is manslaughter. During Lenin's takeover and the Red Terror of 1918-1920, at least two million oppositionists were killed (including more than a thousand bishops and priests) and millions more during the civil war and subsequent uprising. "While no one knows the exact numbers, their scale can be grasped through the estimate that between 1914 and 1920 some twenty million perished—of whom 'only' 1.7 million were Russian war dead," note former intelligence agents Peter Deriabin and T. H. Bagley. "Numbers unknown, but surely in the millions, died in the famine of 1921-1922 which was mainly due to the policies of the new regime."

When Lenin died in 1924, a horrible howl was heard from his room, as if the demons he'd served so well had come to take him.

The spirit of rebellion, which the Bible (*1 Sam.* 15:23) compares to witchcraft, was also sweeping Germany. There its disguise was as the National Socialistic or "Nazi" movement, the political organization inspired by racist cults like the Templars. Though it masqueraded as a political revolt, Nazism was really a new and demonic religion based not only on the teachings of New Templars, but also Freemasons, Theosophists, Darwin, Rosicrucians, and a cult called the Thule Society—whose guru was the white-haired magician I mentioned in Chapter Four, Guido von

List, who buried the nine wine bottles in the pattern of a swastika.

These organizations were in spiritual brotherhood with Aleister "The Beast" Crowley, who must have been pleased with the Nazis' choice of the swastika for its banner. Dating back to the Bronze Age, this occult symbol was associated with the terrible goddess Kali and also represented the hammer of the Nordic god Thor. Such pagan idols are often major demons or "principalities" in disguise, and Hitler's favorite was the god of destruction, *Wotan.* As one of his own poems said:

> I often go on bitter nights
> to Wotan's oak in the quiet glade
> With dark powers to weave a union—
> The runic letters the moon makes with its
> magic spell
> And all who are full of impudence during the
> day
> Are made small by the magic formula!

Although secular biographies stay away from his occult disposition, Hitler was steeped in black magic. When he became a politician his advisers included Erik Jan Hanussen, who was a seer and astrologer, and Karl Haushofer, who taught him Theosophy from Madame Blavatsky's *The Secret Doctrine.* Hitler was an occultist by his own description and like many who practice black magic, there were strong indications that he was possessed by demons and had been since boyhood. During his confirmation ceremony at a cathedral in Linz, Hitler turned sulky and surly, repulsed by the holy ritual. He was also prone to satanic trances. He would turn pale, take on a sinister countenance, and launch into impassioned speeches with a hoarse, raucous voice.

"It was as if another being spoke out of his body, and moved him as much as it did me," remembered one of his few friends, August Kubizek. "It was not all a case of a speaker carried away by his own words. I rather felt as though he himself listened with astonishment and emotion to what burst forth from him with elementary force..."

A similar trance occurred while Hitler was recovering

from war injuries in the Prussian Military Reserve Hospital at Pasewalk. There he heard voices that told him he was Germany's messiah.

His most frightening moods were witnessed at a museum known as the Hofburg as he stood before a relic called the "spear of Longinus," a long, black, tapered spearhead that the centurion Longinus (also known as Cassius) supposedly used to pierce the side of Christ as He died on the cross. Hitler revered the artifact and in its presence he fell into what can only be described as demonic ecstasy. Standing in front of the velvet dais, his face would flush and his brooding eyes would shine with what one observer described as "an alien emanation." He swayed on his feet and "his whole physiognomy and stance (apparently) transformed as if some mighty Spirit now inhabited his very soul."

Hitler knew there was some kind of great evil attached to the relic. He says as much in describing one visit to this beloved relic, a visit that seems to have included the apparition of a demon at the museum: "The air became stifling so that I could barely breathe. The noisy scene of the Treasure House seemed to melt away before my eyes. I stood alone and trembling before the hovering form of the Superman—a Spirit sublime and fearful, a countenance intrepid and cruel. In holy awe, I offered my soul as a vessel of his will."

World War I gave the world massive destruction, death, and endless bread lines.

CHAPTER 8

An Hour of Famine

All the preceding is by way of showing that trends which defined our century often had evil roots. In the United States it was less obvious, taking the form of revolutions in entertainment and finances. Greed! It was the Roaring Twenties. It was the age of torrid romances, short skirts, and baseball scandals. And it fulfilled another LaSalette prophecy, that *"people will think of nothing but amusements"* and *"the wicked will give themselves over to all kinds of sin."*

In Pontevedra, Portugal, the Fatima visionary Lucia dos Santos, now a novice, watched the world from the safety of a cloister and waited for the sign that God's punishments were on the way. *"If people do not cease offending God,"* Our Lady of Fatima had told her, *"a worse (war) will break out during the pontificate of Pius XI. When you see a night illumined by an unknown light, know that this is the great sign given you by God that He is about to punish the world for its crimes, by means of war, famine, and persecution of the Church..."*

The Fatima visionary, training to be a nun in the order of Saint Dorothy (later a Carmelite), was the sole survivor of Mary's extraordinary visits to Cova da Iria. An epidemic of flu had claimed Francisco and his sister Jacinta in 1919 and 1920, leaving Lucia as sole possessor of the Third Secret.

Peering from the convent and knowing what lay in the future must have been unnerving. An earthquake had recently devastated Tokyo and Yokohama, but the secrets Lucia possessed were oriented more toward Russia and Europe. Stalin had taken over the Soviet Union, enforcing Lenin's philosophies with a brutality previously unknown in Eastern Europe, and Hitler was coming out with his own "bible," the book *Mein Kampf.* Pieces to the puzzle were falling into place and now in 1925, alone in her room, Lucia received another apparition of the Virgin on December 10. Mary was again accompanied by the Christ Child and this time the Child spoke. He told Lucia to have compassion on His mother's heart, which was pierced by the thorns of ingratitude.

The following February Lucia had another remarkable experience. "I went to throw out a panful of rubbish beyond the vegetable garden, in the same place where, some months earlier, I had met a child. I had asked him if he knew the Hail Mary, and he said he did, whereupon I requested him to say it so that I could hear him."

That February day, throwing the trash, she spotted the child again. This time Lucia, referring to a different prayer she'd taught him, a prayer invoking the Infant, said to the boy, "Did you ask our heavenly Mother for the Child Jesus?"

Whereupon the child turned to her with his own question. "And have you spread through the world what our heavenly Mother requested of you?"

He was referring to the First Saturday devotion, and with that, recounts Lucia, the youngster was transformed into a resplendent Jesus!

More than three years later, during holy hour on June 13, 1929, the Fatima visionary was at a convent chapel in Tuy when she had a vision of the Trinity as well as Mary as the Virgin of Fatima. Mary was holding the Immaculate Heart in her left hand and told Lucia that *"the moment has come in which God asks the Holy Father in union with all the bishops of the world to make the consecration of Russia to my Immaculate Heart, promising to save it by this means."*

Lucia conveyed the message to her spiritual director, Father Jose Bernardo Goncalves, and the priest turned it over to the bishop of Leiria, who wanted time to think about it. There are indications that Goncalves then tried to get Lucia's message to Pope Pius XI, but there is no evidence that the pope ever received Lucia's message.

Eventually the message would find its way to the proper authorities in Rome, but Russia was not consecrated and events in the Soviet Union aimed toward disaster.

"If my requests are heeded, Russia will be converted, and there will be peace," said Mary in 1917. *"If not, she will spread her errors throughout the world, causing wars and persecutions of the Church. The good will be martyred, the Holy Father will have much to suffer; various nations will be annihilated. In the end, my Immaculate Heart will triumph. The Holy Father will consecrate Russia to me, and she will be converted, and a period of peace will be granted to the world."*

There had already been government-caused food shortages in Ukraine (the large southern republic where the Virgin appeared in 1914, issuing warnings about the next eighty years), and there was an ongoing execution of landowners and intellectuals (from 1928 to 1930 nearly two million Ukrainians were deported or incarcerated and another 400,000 were destroyed *in situ*—hanged or shot). "Wild rumors circulated: the women were to become communal property, the children would all be sent away to China, the old people would be burned in a special machine to stop them eating, the Anti-Christ was coming, the end of the world was nigh," note writers Gwyneth Highes and Simon Welfare.

But that was only prelude to what happened in 1932 and 1933, when Stalin, seeking to quash Ukrainian nationalism and terrorize private farmers, hauled all that republic's wheat to Russia and created a severe, almost incomprehensible famine. In 1933 alone at least 4.6 million and perhaps as many as ten million Ukrainians perished.

"Practically every village has a mass grave from the artificial famine of 1933," Dr. James Mace, director of the

Commission on the Ukraine Famine, told me. "There was tremendous demographic damage—epic figures."

According to another scholar, Lubomyr Hajda of Harvard, it qualified as a case of actual genocide. The number of dead from this period alone nearly equalled and in fact *may* have equalled the number of people killed a few years later during the Nazi Holocaust. Says Hajda: "In terms of absolute data the Ukrainian numbers are probably higher than any other mass atrocity we're familiar with. It's not proportionately as high as what happened to the Jews—whose entire European population was nearly exterminated—and we don't have a good reckoning from China, but the Ukrainian experience has certainly been one of the most horrific of this century."

Their crops stolen by the Muscovites and their herds slaughtered for Russian consumption, Ukrainians were forced to eat nettles, tree bark, leaves, milkweed, worms, rodents, and crows. Entire villages were devoid of life—the cats and dogs devoured when the crows and rats were gone, followed by numerous incidents of cannibalism. In cities where children were abandoned by parents who couldn't provide so much as a morsel of black bread, trucks came each night and picked up corpses that littered every major thoroughfare. The bodies were piled like cordwood and there was actually a black market in human meat. Remembers one survivor, "We arrived at a nameless village. There was not a soul to be seen. Our purpose was to weed the beets. It was spring and the beets were still growing. I asked the leader why there was such a stench coming from a neighboring village. The name of the village was Katerynivka. There were some peasants gathering wild garlic to make dinner, he answered. Later on, I grew thirsty and they wouldn't give us water, so I went toward the village without permission. There I saw a truly horrible picture. Everywhere bodies were sitting and lying and they were decomposing."

Adds a witness now living in Detroit: "The mortality increased each day. People died of hunger in their houses, the fields, in the yards, streets, railroad stations, on the roofs of train cars. Bodies were collected everywhere and taken to a large hole where they were covered with lime.

One spring day I heard the cries of a child. Going up to the yard where the cries were coming from, I saw a young mother sitting on a bank of earth against the house. There was an infant on her breast which was frantically trying to suck its mother's breasts, which were as dry as empty bags. It seemed at first that she was asleep, but when I touched her shoulder, she fell like a blade of grass. She was dead. Her child rolled off her, hit its head against the ground, and also died.''

So enfamished were the peasants that mothers butchered their children and children consumed their parents. The genocide, says Congressman Daniel Mica, ''prepared the way for the paradigmatic act of genocide in all of human history—Hitler's destruction of the European Jews.''

As the Ukrainian scholar Robert Conquest puts it, ''The Soviet assault on the peasantry and on the Ukrainian nation was one of the largest and most devastating events in modern history, yet these events have not to this day been fully registered in the Western consciousness. There is a general knowledge that some sort of catastrophe struck or may have struck, but little more. I believe the famine deaths to have been about seven million—five million in the Ukraine, one million in the Kuban and North Caucasus, one million in the Don and Lower Volga. Three million had already died in the *dekulakization* and about one million of the four million Kazakhs had perished. To this 11 million we must add three million for the peasants (poor and middle peasants, *bedniaky* and *seredniaky*) in labor camps, leaving us with a reasonable estimate for the anti-peasant and anti-Ukraine operation of 14.5 million—more than died in all countries in World War I.''

Could anyone deny that Satan was gaining momentum? Could anyone not see the way he savored blood sacrifice? Could anyone not smell the stench of anti-christ?

The West had plunged into economic depression and Hitler continued to make headway in Germany. What Crowley called the ''new age'' had indeed arrived, and its flag bore the twisted cross. ''Hitler is one of our pupils,'' boasted Adolf Lanz of the New Templars. ''You will one day experience that he, and through him we, will be victorious and develop a movement that makes the world tremble.''

Just as she appeared before Lenin's rise, so did the Mother of God appear immediately before Hitler's ascension into power. These apparitions were in two Belgian towns named Banneaux and Beauraing. On November 29, 1932, while walking near a shrine dedicated to Lourdes in front of a railroad embankment in Beauraing, five children spotted a woman in white moving above a bridge. She was luminous and her feet were hidden by a little cloud. It was the first of 33 apparitions. As elsewhere her appearances followed a clap of thunder or involved what looked like a ball of fire amid the branches of a hawthorn—like the burning bush witnessed by Moses.

Mary pleaded with the people to *"pray, pray very much,"* issued several secrets that have never been disseminated, promised to convert sinners, and showed herself with a golden heart. This heart has been interpreted as a link with Fatima, where the Immaculate Heart was also such an important feature. The largest crowd arrived on December 8, the Feast of the Immaculate Conception, and while the children saw her that day, the majority of people witnessed no extraordinary phenomena—certainly not the great miracle they'd hoped for. But so impressive were the children's experiences that a well-known Communist editor was converted and the local bishop approved the apparition.

Twelve days after the last visit in Beauraing, the Blessed Virgin appeared fifty miles to the north in Banneaux, calling herself the "Virgin of the Poor" during this the era of the Great Depression. *"Pray much,"* she repeated. *"Believe in me and I will believe in you."* She came to encourage us not so much because of financial poverty as the poverty of sin that was lashing across the world. As usual she was young, beautiful, and had a most endearing and humble smile. There was an oval of light around her and her gown was dazzling white, chastely closed at the collar and falling in the simple dignity of broad pleats. She wore a sash of unforgettable sky blue and her veil, white as the gown, had a transparent nature about it. Nearby was a stream that became known as a source of healing. *"This spring,"* she said, *"is reserved for all nations."*

I mention these two apparitions because they seemed like a final warning. On January 30, 1933, just two weeks after she first appeared in Banneaux, Hitler won the chancellery in neighboring Germany.

In the true tradition of anti-christ, Hitler required German schoolchildren to recite prayers that put him on a par with Jesus. One was a plagiarism of the Lord's Prayer:

> Adolf Hitler, you are a great leader. Thy name makes the enemy tremble. Thy Reich comes, thy will alone is law upon the Earth. Let us hear daily thy voice and order us by thy leadership, for we will obey to the end even with our lives. We praise thee! Heil Hitler!

The Russian Revolution of 1917 brought:

Lenin, Stalin, and the evil of Communism.

CHAPTER 9

Burnt Offerings

On January 26, 1938, *The New York Times* printed a story with the headline, "Aurora Borealis Startles Europe; People Flee in Fear, Call Firemen."

Under it was the following subhead: "Britons Thought Windsor Castle Ablaze—Scots See Ill Omen—Snow-Clad Alps Glow."

In London awestruck residents had watched two magnificent arcs of light rising in the east and west, "from which radiated pulsating beams like searchlights in dark red, greenish blue, and purple."

It was the most brilliant display of the "northern lights" in at least fifty years, and "one of the novel features of tonight's show," said *The Times*, "was the vivid red glow."

Astronomers claimed it was caused by sunspot activity. From an airplane it looked like a "shimmering curtain of fire," so much so that in London they thought Windsor Castle was aflame. The phenomenon was seen as far east as Vienna. In southern Germany it struck special fear into the hearts of Catholics who knew that this day was the feast of St. Paul, who was blinded by a light from Heaven.

In Portugal, peasants ran through villages fearing the end of the world. Short-wave radio transmissions were disrupted, and in Grenoble, near LaSalette, huge blood-red

56

beams of light further convinced scientists that it was an aurora borealis of "exceptional magnitude."

From her lonely window at the convent in Tuy, Spain, Lucia marveled at the meteorological spectacle and remembered the words spoken to her 21 years before. *"When you see a night illumined by an unknown light, know that this is the great sign given you by God that He is about to punish the world for its crimes, by means of war, famine, and persecutions of the Church . . ."*
In a letter to the bishop, Lucia referred to the "aurora borealis" with an almost bemused tone. "God manifested that sign, which astronomers chose to call an aurora borealis," she wrote. "I don't know for certain, but I think if they investigated the matter, they would discover that, in the form in which it appeared, it could not possibly have been an aurora borealis. Be that as it may, God made use of this to make me understand His justice was about to strike the guilty nations."
A similar display of the northern lights preceded an apparition at Pontmain, France, but this was far more spectacular and far more foreboding. It also seemed pertinent to Pope Pius IX's prediction that a great sign would be followed by horrible persecutions. A week after the aurora borealis, on February 4, 1938, Hitler promoted himself to military chief and a month after that marched his Nazis into Austria and annexed that nation, declaring victory in Vienna, where List had planted those wine bottles. Upon arrival, Hitler and his sinister entourage dashed to the Hofburg museum and confiscated the relic that so infatuated him as a young man, the "spear of Longinus."
It was his most glorious moment and in many ways the beginning of World War II. There were more apparitions indicating ominous times, apparitions of Mary weeping and appearing as Our Lady of Sorrows. They occurred from Illinois to Brazil.

In Poland, which was also about to be invaded by the Nazis (another benchmark that some consider the official start of the war), a nun named Sister Mary Faustina was receiving what became known as the Divine Mercy devotions. She was given visions of Christ with the red and pale

rays from His heart—representing blood and water—and
He told her, in no uncertain terms, that His patience with
Russia was running out. *"I cannot suffer that country any
longer. Do not tie My hands, My daughter."* That was in
1936. Two years later, He warned Sister Faustina that He
would *"allow convents and churches to be destroyed"*
because convents and churches—apparently around the
world—had been filled with self-love and egoism. *"If you
did not tie My hands, I would send down many punishments upon earth,"* He said in 1938 to Sister Faustina, who
prayed fervently for the world. *"My daughter, your look
disarms My anger. Although your lips are silent, you call
out to Me so mightily that all Heaven is moved. I cannot
escape from your requests, because you pursue Me, not
from afar but within your own heart."*

On October 1, 1937, the Lord Jesus told Sister Faustina
that the prayers and sacrifices of small, hidden souls were
drops of consolation in a sea of bitterness. *"Daughter,"* He
said, *"I need sacrifice lovingly accomplished, because that
alone has meaning for Me. Enormous indeed are the debts
of the world which are due to Me; pure souls can pay them
by their sacrifice, exercising mercy in spirit."*

The world was not as powerful as it seemed, He said;
its strength is strictly limited. *"Know, My daughter, that
if your soul is filled with the fire of My pure Love, then
all difficulties dissipate like fog before the sun's rays and
dare not touch the soul. All adversaries are afraid to start
a quarrel with such a soul, because they sense that it is
stronger than the whole world . . ."*

But a cycle of the Lord's Mercy was about to run out.
In the very belly of the beast, Heede, Germany, four children saw the angels of justice, and Mary indicated the coming of a "minor judgment."

If this was a "minor judgment," we can imagine what
may be in our own future. It was a war unlike any previous
wars. At least five times as many people died than during
World War I and rare was the country that went unscathed:
supply routes reached to the southern tip of Africa and
Australia and submarines fought it out across the length
and breadth of the Atlantic.

But most of the activity was in Europe, where, as stated

at LaSalette, mankind was drinking from the chalice of the wrath of God. *"France, Italy, Spain, and England will be at war,"* Mary had predicted during the 1846 apparition. *"Blood will flow in the streets...For a time, God will cease to remember France and Italy because the Gospel of Jesus Christ has been forgotten."*

Indeed, Spain went through a civil war during this period, Italy joined Germany in attacking France, and smoke billowed around Saint Paul's Cathedral in London. *"Paris will burn, and Marseilles will be engulfed."*

While that city was never reduced to a cinder, it escaped such a fate only through circumstances that journalists have described as "miraculous." In August of 1944 Hitler slammed his fist on a table and shouted at his chief of staff, "Is Paris burning? Jod! I demand to know! Yes or no? Is Paris burning now?"

The battles raged from Norway to Egypt, then east into Russia and out to the Philippines. It was the war of U-boats and the *blitzkrieg*. It also involved the black arts. Both Rudolf Hess and Heinrich Himmler, two staunch leaders of Hitler's elite guard, the SS, were immersed in the occult. Hess had been a member of the Thule Society and Himmler claimed he was the reincarnation of King Heinrich I of Saxony, and that at night the "king" appeared to him and gave him orders. Himmler advocated public execution of the pope and both he and Hess were instrumental in the Holocaust. It was an atrocity that rivaled the Ukrainian genocide in sheer numbers (5.9 million Jews, or two-thirds the European Jewish population, were gassed and put in the ovens). This too had occult connotations. The use of poison was an ancient tactic of German sorcery, and the very word "Holocaust" comes from *holokaustein,* which is defined in witchcraft as "a burnt offering."

Another 44 million died in the war itself. Houses of worship were destroyed with demonic fervor. At a venerated shrine called Hoshiw, on the river Swicha in the Soviet Union, a miraculous icon of the Virgin Mary, an icon known to radiate supernatural light, disappeared without a trace and a 3,000-pound bell was melted into bullets for the invading Nazis. During the German occupation of Italy

Nazi guards wandered the Vatican's very grounds and watched the pope's windows with a high-powered telescope. Small bombs had even been dropped on Vatican City because the pope had given sanctuary to 15,000 Jews.

Alas, on October 13, 1944, the anniversary of Fatima, allied bombers pounded Neuremberg and turned most of the evil headquarters into a pile of rubble. American troops searching through the ruins came across the spear of Longinus, or *Heilige Lance,* the following spring. The precise time they took possession of it was 2:10 p.m. on April 30, 1945—within two hours of Hitler's suicide on this the afternoon of satanism's main annual festival, "Walpurgis Night."

That was the end of World War II in Europe, but hardly the end of Satan's offensive. He was about to focus still more attention on Russia, moving his headquarters there. Indeed, after the conquest of Berlin, invading Soviets carried away another prized Nazi relic known as the Pergamos altar of Zeus. This was interesting because in *Revelation* 2:13 Jesus Christ, addressing the angel of a city in Asia Minor of the same name, implies that Pergamos was "where Satan dwells." According to Romanian scholar Richard Wurmbrand, the satanic altar was hauled out of the Island Museum and taken to Moscow.

CHAPTER 10

An Hour of Persecution

Taking humanism to its ultimate, Stalin and his henchmen sought in one brutal stroke to crush belief in God. Throughout the Soviet Union red banners with hammer and sickle flapped with the same insistence as the swastika. And religious persecution reached greater heights than even in Germany.

"Priests and religious orders will be hunted down," said LaSalette, *"and made to die a cruel death."*

While diluted forms of religion were allowed to linger for years, the Communists carried forth a savage campaign to disembowel Christianity, particularly those churches with allegiance to Rome. Before World War I there were nearly 5,000 Orthodox churches, 25,000 mosques, and thousands of synagogues, Protestant churches, and Buddhist temples; by the 1980s, when Gorbachev arrived, there were fewer than 4,000 structures belonging to all sects combined, virtually none of these Catholic, for, in most parts of the union, that Church was outright illegal. In 1934 the golden domes of St. Michael's Cathedral in Kiev were destroyed and other churches were boarded, bulldozed, turned into grain depositories, or converted into museums of atheism. Precious icons were smashed and belltowers yanked to the ground.

Although the Russian Orthodox Church received better

treatment than the Catholics, it too was devastated, losing four-fifths of its monastic institutions in Ukraine. A Lutheran pastor named Teodor Varchuk disappeared, and a Reformed pastor named Teodosii Dovhaliuk met a martyr's death in the concentration camp on the frigid Solovetsky islands. There was a ban on teaching Hebrew and the vast majority of Judaic religious communities were disassembled, with only eight synagogues and one active rabbi left in the intensely religious Ukraine.

The godless Soviets were especially intent on quashing the Ukrainian Catholic (or "Eastern Rite") Church, which was based in that part of the Carpathians where the Mother of God had visited the tiny chapel of Hrushiw. On April 11, 1945, Cardinal Josyf Slipyj, head of the Eastern Rite, was arrested with all his bishops and within a year more than eight hundred priests would follow him into imprisonment. The following year Moscow forced Church leaders into a "synod" at which time the Eastern Rite was abolished and forcibly merged with the Russian Orthodox Church, which was Soviet-controlled. The chapel of Hrushiw, with its healing well and gorgeous iconography, was boarded and abandoned.

From here on, until Gorbachev came to power, it would be suicidal to practice the Catholic or Baptist faiths in Ukraine. Nuns were killed or sent to Siberia; priests were castrated or nailed in crucifixion; one bishop, Theodore G. Romzha, was poisoned in the hospital.

Priests were arrested for hearing confessions and monks faced three-year sentences if they were caught giving religious instruction. The average prison term was ten years and in the gulag they were forced to stand semi-nude in the frigid air and (in the Romanian prisons) eat excrement shaped as the Holy Eucharist, which Satan despised more than anything else.

By 1950 4,119 Catholic churches in the Ukraine alone were demolished or given to the Orthodox. Those priests who were still free lived an underground life as they snuck from village to village conducting Mass in forests, barns, or shaded homes. Including the great Ukrainian famine of 1933, the purges and terror between 1935 and 1939, the more than 15 million estimated to have died in camps, and the internal repressions during World War II, more than fifty million Soviet people—comparable to the population of France—may have died at the hands of the Communists.

By the most conservative estimates Stalin killed twenty million humans, a figure that doesn't include the ten or 12 million more who died on the battlefields.

It was true. Satan was exercising extended power. He'd been given the century and his demons were clawing for power—blood and power—in an earthly netherworld. I don't intend to run down all the major historical events up to our time, only to cite a few that represent its astonishing level of evil. We have now seen how materialism and secular humanism—the philosophies that permit the material world and only the material world—led to Lenin, Hitler, and Stalin, who together may have killed a hundred million. It wasn't survival of the fittest but survival of the most evil. Add to Soviet numbers the hundreds of thousands (and perhaps as many as fifty million) killed in Red China under Mao Tse-tung—along with the Communist-inspired wars and atrocities from Cambodia to Ethiopia—and we see a century during which there were as many terroristic and state killings—perhaps 150 or even 200 million—as there were people existing on the entire planet during the time of Jesus. Rationalism turned into Communism and that turned into the absence of God, which turned into Hell on earth. Marx could be heard from the grave: *Soon I shall embrace eternity to my breast, and soon I shall howl gigantic curses on mankind.*

It was what *Revelation* calls the Red Dragon. It was an era of human reptiles. I have seen no information offering direct evidence that Mao was demonically possessed, but there are little peripheral coincidences which do indicate diabolical synchronicity. Let's start with the fact that Mao was born in 1893, the "year of the snake;" that's pretty tenuous stuff, but now let's move on to his literature, for Mao, like all good revolutionaries, expressed himself in poetry. "To fight with Heaven," said one of his earliest poems, "is infinite pleasure!" Again, the essence of antichrist. He was a man of such erratic emotions that at times he had to be carried out of meetings, his eyes flitting in rage, spittle frothing around his mouth. His lust for power led the Red Army into a 20-year civil war with the God-fearing Nationalists led by Chiang Kai-shek. In the captures of Chengteh and Yenan alone there were 700,000 casualties. Mao's banner? A red dragon.

In Rome Pope Pius XII could only view these developments with incredulity and nausea. The Church had seen persecution throughout recent decades—by the Fascists in Italy, the Masons and civil warriors in Spain, by a similarly anti-Catholic regime in Mexico—but that was nothing compared to what happened in the wake of Hitler, Stalin, and now Mao. The oppression was spreading to East European countries like Hungary, and by the end of the decade 4,314 places of worship would be abandoned in Yugoslavia, with 186 priests executed and 519 in exile.

In China Protestantism would soon be declared a "foreign devil" and beginning in 1950 a systematic persecution of priests began, banishing all bishops from that country.

Instead of uniting to fight a common enemy, Christians continued to bicker and splinter, infected by their own epidemic of rebelliousness. Never before had there been so many sects. The schisms that began with the split of Orthodox a thousand years before, and with the subsequent formation of Protestantism in the 16th century, had widened to the point where no one could keep track of all the denominations. Pride, pride, and more pride. Everyone wanted their own church, and they flew in different directions like tektites from a comet. In response to the growing divisiveness both Pius XI and Pius XII issued official pleas for love and understanding among Christians. Those who believed in Jesus needed to unite against the insidious, expanding enemy.

But the devil continued to sow rebellion and magnify their differences, inspiring them to take biblical passages out of context and make differences of interpretation appear larger than they were. He focused special venom on Mary, degrading her importance and by doing so building a wall between Catholics and many Protestants.

Divide and conquer. It was Satan's golden rule. It was his war strategy. He set Catholics and Protestants against each other not only over the issue of Mary but by instilling a truly poisonous spirit of criticality on both sides. The bickering almost cost Pius XII his life, for in 1947 Bruno Cornacchiola, a former Catholic who'd come under the spell of both Communists and anti-Catholic "christians," plotted to stab the Pontiff and save the world from the "evils" of the papacy, the "idolatry" of communion with saints, and the "fraudulent" idea that Mary was the Mother of God.

An emotional man given to beating his wife, Bruno had been convinced by a German that the pope was the great beast of the Apocalypse and that the Catholic Church was behind everything that was bad in the world. "This false prophet had already succeeded in putting poison into my heart, the seed of hatred against the Holy Eucharist, against Our Lady, against all Sacraments," Bruno later said, recalling how he set about gathering all holy pictures in his house and incinerating them, including souvenirs from his First Holy Communion. He tore down a picture of Our Lady of the Rosary of Pompeii, threw it on the floor, stomped on it, and like Lenin hurled the holy object into the trash. On the wall near the bed was a crucifix, which Bruno, not one to leave anything behind, broke in two.

"Death to Priests," he wrote on the sides of trolley cars. "Death to the Pope!" he engraved on his dagger.

But the plan to kill Pius XII came to a screeching halt on April 12, 1947. On that day Bruno took his children to a field north of Rome called Three Fountains (or *Tre Fontane*), where St. Paul was beheaded. It was the octave of Easter, a day commonly called "the day of Our Lady," and Bruno was preparing an anti-Catholic speech as his children played ball. There was a grotto at Three Fountains—a cave used as a lover's lane—and Bruno plopped nearby, taking out a Bible and notebook to organize his talk, planned for the next day in Red Cross Square. The speech was specifically directed against Our Lady: Mary, he began to write, was not a virgin, was not immaculate, and was not assumed into Heaven. He was just finding his cadence when suddenly he heard his children calling. They'd lost a ball and while Bruno helped them look for it he lost track of his young son Gianfranco.

When he finally spotted the boy, Gianfranco was kneeling at the entrance to the grotto, hands clasped, whispering as if in a trance. "Beautiful lady! Beautiful lady!"

When Bruno's daughter Isola rushed to the boy's side, she too fell on her knees. *Beautiful lady!* Isola was in another world. Angry and confused, Bruno called to an older son, Carlo, who also fell to his knees when he looked into the grotto. Bruno tried to lift his daughter with all his strength but couldn't budge her, and not knowing what else to do, he stormed into the grotto preparing to fight anyone who might be in there hypnotizing his children.

The grotto was empty. There was only the filth of immorality. He stood just behind his children and looked to Heaven. "My God, help us!"

Immediately he saw what looked like two pure, transparent hands that touched his face and seemed to remove something from his eyes. In the midst of darkness he saw a small light growing brighter and stronger—lighting up the entire grotto. A joy passed through every joint of his body, and suddenly where the grotto was brightest he witnessed a halo of golden light and a heavenly woman. She had black hair gathered at the top of her head, a green mantle cascading to her feet, and a brilliant white dress with a pink sash, her feet resting on a tufaceous rock.

She was kind and motherly, recalled Bruno, but her face was full of tranquil sorrow.

In her right hand was an ash-colored book and at her feet was a black cloth with a broken cross, which seemed to symbolize the priest's cassock, cast aside and despised by a secular society.

"I am she who is related to the Divine Trinity," she told Bruno. *"I am the Virgin of Revelation. You persecute me, and now it is time to stop! Come and be part of the holy fold which is the celestial court on earth. God's promise is unchangeable and will remain so. The nine First Fridays in honor of the Sacred Heart, which your faithful wife convinced you to observe before you entered upon the road of lies, has saved you."*

The Virgin gave Bruno a secret to take to the pope and warned that his friends would want him to believe the vision was satanic. Pray, she said, and beware of such doubts. She explained that *Hail Marys* said with love and faith were *"like golden arrows that go straight to the Sacred Heart of Jesus."* She pleaded for Christian unity, telling Bruno that there should be one flock and one shepherd.

During the apparition, which lasted an hour and twenty minutes, she also confirmed the reality of her assumption into Heaven. Then she stepped forward, took center stage of the grotto, bowed lightly, and disappeared into the wall.

The area was flooded with a sweet ethereal fragrance, a fragrance reminiscent of what was encountered at Fatima.

While Bruno was to endure severe trials in the coming days, including attacks by Satan that left him confused and in doubt, the veracity of his experience was established by authorized investigators and implicitly approved by the Church.

Born anew and saved from his spiritual enemies, Cornacchiola changed his name to Brother Maria Paolo and spent the rest of his life urging Christians to pray and avoid sins of the flesh, which were symbolized by the filth of the grotto's floor.

He also urged love for Mary.

Her mantle, he said, was a refuge "in the Hell that is breaking out in the world."

CHAPTER 11

Hints of Tribulation

The appearance of Mary as "the Virgin of Revelation" was noteworthy coming as it did at the halfway point of our century. From now on there would be the rising tide of apparitions, turning into a flood, that I mentioned in the first chapter. With each decade more hints would be given about the future, the momentum building as world events unfolded and the century began revealing its profound and disturbing mysteries.

Was Mary in apocalyptic attire because *Revelation*—or at least *part* of the Apocalypse—was going to be fulfilled during our generation? Would the new atomic bomb, two of which were dropped in Japan, turn out to be the long-awaited catastrophe? Did *Revelation* pertain to Fatima's Third Secret?

When pressed on the secret's contents, Lucia, the surviving Fatima visionary, was said to have blurted, "It's in the Gospel and Apocalypse. Read them!"

That Mary was pointing to the Book of *Revelation* was also indicated in the 1879 apparition at Knock, where she appeared with St. Joseph, St. John the Evangelist (who had a book), and a lamb above an altar—as there is the Lamb of God in *Revelation*. The Lamb is especially prominent in Chapter Six of the *Apocalypse* when He begins to open seven "seals" that hold the power to certain world events

68

which are to occur as part of what's called the Great Tribulation. According to John's prophecy, the first seal concerns a *"conqueror,"* the second *"conflict on earth,"* the third *"scarcity,"* the fourth *"widespread death,"* and the fifth is called *"the cry of the martyrs."* We've just seen how the U.S.S.R. instituted the largest religious persecution in history, creating more martyrs in a few decades than in all previous centuries together.

But all this, as well as the famines and world wars, seemed to be a prelude, an *indication* or sneak preview, of what was in the seals, as opposed to the actual and final *fulfillment* of the seals themselves. That fulfillment, the climactic opening of the seven seals, remained for the future, and to assuage God's anger and postpone His punishments both Jesus and Mary ordered a reparation that would include much more prayer (especially the Rosary); the new devotion of First Saturdays; the conversion of sinners; and personal sacrifice. At Lourdes she'd emphasized the same: penitence and prayer. It's a theme we'll see repeated with greater and greater urgency. Pray. Pray the Rosary. There was no getting around Heaven's plan of using Mary as an instrument; mankind was told to find refuge in her Immaculate Heart.

Most urgent had been the request of prayer for the Soviet Union, which, it was clear, would be the tool of chastisement if it was not converted. And for that conversion to occur, Lucia said, Russia had to be consecrated to the Immaculate Heart of Mary. The Virgin told Lucia back at Tuy in 1929 that *"the moment has come in which God asks the Holy Father in union with all the bishops of the world to make the consecration of Russia to my Immaculate Heart, promising to save it by this means."* When no action was forthcoming, Lucia said Jesus appeared to her saying, *"They did not heed My request. Like the King of France they will repent and do so, but it will be late. Russia will already have spread her errors throughout the world, causing wars and persecutions of the Church. The Holy Father will have much to suffer."*

According to Brother Frére Michel de la Sainte Trinité, a Fatima expert whose thick volumes provide seminal background on the historic apparition, Fatima's request for consecration was also conveyed to Rome by another Portuguese seer, Alexandrina Maria da Costa, whom I mention because she typifies a phenomenon we could call "peripheral reinforcement," whereby secondary and lesser known visionaries sprout up around the more famous apparitions as if to confirm, bolster, or add detail to them. Alexandrina too saw Jesus. Alexandrina too was told of the importance of consecrating the world to Mary's heart.

But neither her request nor that conveyed by Lucia struck a response at the Vatican. For whatever reasons, Pope Pius XI did not conduct such a consecration with *"all the bishops of the world"* and certainly did not specifically and publicly consecrate Russia. In 1939, soon after Pius XI's death, Jesus apparently spoke again to Lucia and told her to *"ask, ask again insistently for the promulgation of the Communion of Reparation in honor of the Immaculate Heart of Mary on the First Saturdays. The time is coming when the rigor of My Justice will punish the crimes of diverse nations. Some of them will be annihilated. At last the severity of My Justice will fall on those who want to destroy My Reign in souls."*

On October 31, 1942, in the midst of the Second World War, the new pope, Pius XII, consecrated the entire Church and world to Mary's heart, making a cloaked but unmistakable allusion to Russia, and the following December, on the Feast of the Immaculate Conception, he also consecrated the diocese of Rome. But there had still been no consecration focusing specifically on the Soviet Union, and in 1946, when historian William Thomas Walsh was allowed a rare interview with Lucia, she told him: "What Our Lady wants is that the pope and all the bishops in the world shall consecrate Russia to her Immaculate Heart on one special day. If this is done, she will convert Russia and there will be peace. If it is not done, the errors of Russia will spread through every country in the world."

While Lucia acknowledged that the Holy Father had already consecrated Russia by including it in the consecration of the world, "it has not been done in the form indicated by Our Lady," she said. "I do not know whether Our

Lady accepts it, done in this way, as complying with her promises.''

It was a difficult, nearly impossible situation that faced both popes, for singling out Russia in a major collegial event, with attendant international publicity, may well have provoked Stalin, who as it was had all but destroyed Russian Christianity. They also felt heat from the White House. The United States repeatedly lobbied the Vatican not to ruffle Soviet feathers, fearing another, even worse war.

As political leaders couldn't help but sense, Russia is an apocalyptical nation, and while Satan had achieved great success with the mayhem of Hitler and World War II, he had a larger plan in mind, and that was to destroy the entire planet. The altar of Pergamos was now in the Kremlin. Indeed, there are those like Frére Michel who go so far as to suggest that part of Hitler's satanic mission was to draw attention away from the larger threat posed by Russia.

While no one knows his full plan, Satan's aggresiveness was so apparent that the bishops of Spain took up the issue in a letter to the world. They specifically cited Communist-inspired posters in Bilbao that profaned Mary in ''bestial fashion'' and blasphemed against the Eucharist. ''The hatred against Jesus Christ and Our Lady has reached the point of paroxysm,'' the bishops fretted. ''The forms of profanation have been so incredible that they cannot be conceived of without presupposing a diabolical suggestion.''

A climax seemed to be in the wind, a growing confrontation in the spiritual world as well as the physical realm. God was watching to see how far the diabolism would go. He would watch and then when the diabolism spread too far He would act. At LaSalette the Virgin explained that she was here to hold back the arm of her Son, and it will soon become obvious that this is indeed her main task, the motherly mission of postponing and lessening chastisements. In granting secrets to visionaries like Lucia she was conveying the gravity of God's anger but at the same time rallying us to *prevent* major cataclysms. In 1944 Lucia wrote the Third Secret on a piece of paper, placed it in an envelope, and sealed it with wax. The secret was then given to Bishop da Silva of Leiria, who was told it should not be revealed to the public before 1960.

There were strong indications that the remaining Fatima secret pertained not to current events but to something major in the more distant future. When Lucia's stipulation for release in 1960 was made, that restriction only served to further incite the public's imagination, bolstering the idea that the end of the world, or at least the end times, awaited mankind later in the century. Lucia explained that after 1960 the secret would "appear clearer." A rumor spread that it foretold of Italian Communists kidnapping the pope, but neither that nor other equally imaginative rumors bore the slightest truth. The secret applied to the entire world, not just the Vatican and the pope; it wasn't even confined to Europe or America. When Walsh asked if Mary had said anything about the United States, Lucia gave him a startled glance, and then smiled bemusedly, as if to say that America might not be as important in the scheme of things as Americans imagined.

"Have you had any revelation from Our Lady about the end of the world?" persisted Walsh.

"I cannot answer that question," replied Lucia.

This much was known: the world was headed for some kind of tribulation, and by inference it went well beyond World War II and seemed pertinent to events at least as large in scope and possibly larger than what the world hitherto had experienced. It was something worse than World War II. It was worse than the Ukrainian genocide. It was there in the Apocalypse, perhaps amid the seals, and it would occur after 1960.

CHAPTER 12

"The Gates Are Opening"

While the Third Secret remained under lock and key, there was soon a veritable explosion of other alleged supernatural warnings. During the 1940s at least 35 noteworthy apparitions were reported. In their imagery, some were as apocalyptic as Knock and Three Fountains, while others were verbal extensions of Fatima and LaSalette, which again begged the question: Did the apocalyptic trappings mean the world was moving headlong toward catastrophe? Was something even more unpleasant than the genocides of Hitler and Stalin really awaiting us—something on a cosmic scale?

I have no idea how many of these apparitions are worthy of belief, but it *was* the Age of Mary, and just as a peripheral visionary arose in Portugal to back up Lucia's request for consecration, so too did apparitions arise in other parts of the world to repeat warnings. There was the Virgin, in rays of light above a church in Grinkalnes, Lithuania, or crowned with the stars of the apocalypse in Dalmatia. There she was in Bodennou, France, with a backdrop of stormy black clouds, or in Lublin, Poland, where a statue of her wept *blood* for two days. There was Mary appearing in Germany to a seer named Barbara Reuss, announcing that her hour—the hour of the woman clothed with the sun—was fast approaching.

73

She manifested herself in Ohio, Paris, Hungary, Spain, and Romania.

In the French village of Ile Bouchard she appeared to four children December 8-14, 1947, asking them to pray ardently for France, which she said was threatened by a Communist takeover.

It was all getting very intriguing but it also raised a red flag. How many of these visions were copycats of Lourdes and Fatima, the products of imagination? Worse, how many might be counterfeits perpetrated by Satan? Lurking always just out of sight, but keeping close track of every action by his Heaven-sent adversary, the devil sought to foil the attempts at warning and converting mankind. As fundamentalist Catholics and Protestants often caution—as the Bible itself emphasizes (*2 Cor.* 11:14)—Satan can readily masquerade as "an angel of light." We are told in *2 Thessalonians* 2:9 that during the great apostasy and coming of the lawless one there will be "all power, signs, and lying wonders." As Jesus Himself predicted (*Mark* 13:22), *"For false christs and false prophets will rise and show signs and wonders to deceive, if possible, even the elect."*

By the middle 1940s and early 1950s there were already indications that certain of the Marian apparitions were bogus—diabolical subterfuge or simple human fantasy. Out of the dozens reported, only the manifestation at Three Fountains met with Church recognition, and even famous ones were plagued by doubts and disputes. When I visited the main basilica in Montichiari, Italy, I was surprised to learn that the renowned *Rosa Mystica* apparitions which started there in 1947 were condemned by the local bishop, Bruno Foresti of Brescia, who in a formal declaration said the *Mystica* phenomena failed to "give good reasons for credibility" and that whoever promoted it "disturbs the faith of believers, inducing them to act contrary to the teachings of the Church."

I was surprised because the *Rosa Mystica* seemed like such a beautiful apparition, and statues fashioned after it were said to cry miraculous tears at locations throughout the world. A nurse named Pierina Gilli was the visionary, and her messages connected in a very direct way to Fatima, starting with the fact that the second apparition was on the same day of the year, June 13, as the second Fatima apparition.

Pierina claimed that apparitions occurred both in the hospital where she worked and at the Montichiari basilica. At her first manifestation Mary arrived in a mournful purplish dress and a white veil. She was visibly sad, her tears falling to the floor, her breast pierced by several swords. She said only three words. *"Prayer, penitence, expiation."*

Upon her second visit the Virgin was dressed far more cheerfully, with a white dress and in the place of the swords, red, white, and gold roses. "Please tell me who you are," pleaded Pierina.

"I am the Mother of Jesus and the Mother of all of you," the *Rosa Mystica* replied. She said the swords that had been in her heart represented a crisis in faith, including *"deadly"* sin among the religious and the loss of candidates for the priesthood. The roses she now wore represented prayer, sacrifice, and penitence. As at Lourdes Mary identified herself as the Immaculate Conception, and as at Fatima, she requested new devotions in reparation.

"My Divine Son Jesus has sent me here to bring a new Marian devotion for all male and female institutes, religious orders, and secular priests," she said during apparitions that continued for the rest of 1947. *"I promise those religious institutes, orders, and secular priests who venerate me in this special way my special protection, an increase of spiritual vocations, and great sanctity among the servants of God. I wish the 13th of each month to be celebrated as the day of Mary. On the twelve preceding days, special prayers of preparation should be said."*

Henceforth, the 13th of each month was to be celebrated as the day of Mary, while the other devotion was to include attendance at noontime Mass (or failing that, prayer at home) every year on December 8, feast of the Immaculate Conception. She pledged that whatever was asked during the hour would be granted if it was in accordance with God's will. As long as people prayed for sinners, said Mary, Christ would continue to be merciful. She was struggling to prolong the period of mercy. *"My Divine Son, tired of continuing offenses, wanted to act according to His justice, so I placed myself as a mediatrix between Him and the human race, especially the consecrated souls."*

The Lord, she said, had *"delayed a great judgment."* But for the mercy to continue she needed a dedicated flock who knew how to pray and do penance. *"Penance means acceptance of the little daily crosses and also doing one's work in the spirit of penance. In Fatima I spread the devotion to my Immaculate Heart. In Bonate* (a town near Bergamo where she appeared during World War II) *I tried to introduce this devotion into Christian families. Here in Montichiari I wish to be venerated as the Rosa Mystica, as already indicated so often, together with the devotion to my heart which must be specially practiced in religious institutes so that they may obtain more graces through my motherly heart."*

On December 7 Mary materialized with two children whom she identified to Pierina as Francisco and Jacinta, the deceased Fatima visionaries. *"They will help you in your trials and sufferings,"* said the Blessed Virgin. *"They, too, suffered. I wish from you the simplicity and goodness of these two children."*

It was the godly souls who had turned lukewarm that most offended Christ, said Mary, especially those who betrayed their vocation. *"By their great offenses, they brought punishment upon the Church—*as we experience it in our days—*but then the original spirit of their holy founders will blossom again."*

There was no question that the essence of her message was apocalpytical: *"Our Lord cannot any longer watch the many grievous sins against purity. He wants to send a flood of punishments. I have interceded that He may be merciful once more. Therefore, I ask for prayer and penance to atone for these sins."*

A *"flood of punishments."* The same message was coming out of an equally controversial apparition in Holland where Mary was said to appear as "Our Lady of All Nations," standing on a globe with a cross behind her. This series of apparitions also met with a negative reaction from the local clerics, and there did seem to be plenty of room for skepticism. The visionary was a woman in Amsterdam named Ida, and she saw every conceivable type of calamity: storms, waves, missiles, quakes, palace intrigue at the Vatican, and economic disasters. Such a profusion of doom made me wonder if Satan had a hand in the disarray of Ida's visions, yet I also had to wonder if their incomprehensibility was any greater than the incomprehensibility of the seven seals of *Revelation.*

"Let all the children of men, of all the countries in the world, be one!" said Our Lady of All Nations. *"Seek and ask only for the true Holy Spirit. I have come to tell this depraved and degenerated world, all of you unite. I will lead all the dispersed flock back to one fold."*

Ida saw a "strange war" and supposedly heard the Virgin warn of *"disaster upon disaster"* caused by phenomena of nature. In Russia she saw a "hellish light" that seemed to explode from the ground upwards. A prophecy of Chernobyl? She saw a hand of heavenly protection over the Ukraine, and things would go well for a while, said Mary, but then she pointed to a globe that looked like it was ready to burst. Indicating the sky eastward, where there were many stars, she said, *"That is where it will come from."*

A meteor? A comet? An asteroid?

Ida was later told natural disasters would overtake the world *"from north to south, south to west, and from west to east."* She saw a rent that ran diagonally across the earth. Great misery and distress, she was told, were *"imminent."* During an apparition on December 7, 1947, she saw thick clouds over Europe and titanic waves. *"They will first have to perish by the flood,"* the seer was told, which she was further informed would constitute the *"desolation."*

That seemed to fly in the face of *Genesis,* in which God tells Noah that *"never again shall all flesh be cut off by the waters of the flood; never again shall there be a flood to destroy the earth* (9:11)." But let's go on. There were also premonitions of political upheaval, currency crises, boycotts, and economic warfare. The apparition said Russia would try to deceive the other countries and Ida was shown a vision of "blue and white stripes intermingling and then stars. After that I see the sickle and hammer, but the hammer breaks away from the sickle and then all things whirl together. Then I see the crescent and the sun. These too commingle with the rest. And finally a sort of buck or mountain goat comes jumping through the lot. While all this is whirling around together, a circle appears on the left and through this the globe is turning. Now a big pointer appears and I hear the words, 'The hand of the sun dial is going in the opposite direction!' "

After that, in this apparition of December 26, 1947, Ida saw "something like a cigar or torpedo flying past me so rapidly that I can scarcely discern it. Its color seems to be of aluminum. All of a sudden I see it burst open." She added: "Then I see faces before me, swollen faces covered with dreadful ulcers, as if it were a kind of leprosy."

Was the breaking apart of the hammer and sickle a reference to the eventual break up of the Soviet Union? Was the goat Satan trotting through the former Soviet republics—Latvia, Ukraine, Georgia—and stirring up ethnic animosities? Was a nuclear warhead represented by the "aluminum torpedo?"

Ida saw Jerusalem surrounded by battles and a "sword hanging over Europe and the East." She saw the multitudes in the East—presumably Asia—and heard Our Lady say, *These he will rouse. . . A great disaster will occur; that will startle them. The Baltic is full. You do not see that.* " She saw the Chinese crossing a line and an insurrection in Manchuria.

There were also warnings concerning the southern flanks of Communist Europe. Ida was given visions of the Balkan region, which would include Bulgaria and Yugoslavia. "There is a war," Ida said during the vision. "They are fighting again. The Lady says, *Child, there will be a fierce struggle. We have not seen the end of this struggle yet. Economic disasters will come. The empire of England is tottering.* ' "

While there was the promise that *Japan will be converted,* " Ida saw a heavy cloud over India. There were also clouds over St. Peter's. She saw the pope and above him the word "VIOLENCE." There would be political warfare within the Vatican, Mary warned, and in what can only be described as an especially symbolic vision, Ida heard Our Lady say, *Look,* " and saw a wolf standing before the Virgin to her left. Then a wolf or dog holding a torch in its mouth stood straight in front of her. Beside it was a lioness, and to the extreme right a large falcon or eagle.

The *"other spirit,"* said Mary, was *"infiltrating with dreadful success."* There was a mingling of red and white clouds. She told the seer that realism and humanism were becoming the new paganism and that the diabolical attack was no longer directed against nations so much as *"the mind of man."* Righteousness and brotherly love were sorely lacking, she observed, deploring, again, the *"degeneration of mankind."*

Ida was also allowed a glimpse of what Mary described as a *"spiritual battle that is being carried on all over the world. . . much worse than the actual wars now being waged, because it is undermining mankind."* On June 9, 1946, the Dutch seer saw Mary step to one side, and from the other direction demons approached.

All Christians needed to unite, Mary said during a 1948 apparition, because *"the gates are opening."*

The gate was open and a wolf was at the door.

CHAPTER 13

A Shower of Roses

Three knocks. A hoarse voice. A foul odor.

At a Carmelite convent an hour south of Manila, novice Teresita Castillo was under demonic attack. It was July 31, 1948, in the far-off Philippines. Satan was trying to chase her from the sisterhood. As a calling card he left behind sooty inhuman footprints.

Most of all the demon may have been trying to forestall or even prevent an appearance by the Virgin Mary, for on August 18, after several more attacks (after appearing on the wall with fire around his head, and leaving the poor young woman with bruises and welts) the devil was gone, his place taken by a beautiful woman who was dressed in white and emitted a lovely fragrance.

It was not Satan. The devil was very different. There was no longer the echoing voice and the burnt odor.

"Do not fear, my daughter. He who loves above all things has sent me."

Soon the other sisters, watching Teresita in profound ecstasy, discarded their skepticism. Mary also favored the prioress, Mother Cecilia, with interior locutions, and other nuns witnessed the miraculous materialization of rose petals. For three months Teresita continued to experience a sweet, unearthly, and motherly presence, speaking with the Virgin near a vine in the garden. Soon the entire convent, then the city, then the archipelago were caught up in the phenomena, Heaven's own calling card. Hundreds and thousands gathered near the convent. The town was Lipa, scene of a horrible massacre during the war, and as if to erase those scars, Heaven granted the nation witness to beautiful and extraordinary events, including figures in the clouds and rose petals that fell from the sky with likenesses of Jesus on them. Looking upward in astonishment, crowds of Filipinos, crowds that had overnight grown to baseball-stadium proportions, claimed to see the petals materialize out of thin air, and when the bishop visited the convent, intent on bringing a halt to the "hoax," a shower of petals fell on him as he entered the convent.

I thought of Fatima and the time a crowd there too saw roses fall from the sky, but at Fatima they were ethereal roses that vanished before they touched the earth, while here they were tangible flower petals, red, yellow, orange, anxiously gathered as souvenirs; and when botanists analyzed them they concluded that the petals were of a variety known only to Russia, which is nearly two thousand miles to the north.

During the apparitions a strange blue bird fluttered about and the nearest vine whipsawed as vigorously as the bush at Lourdes. Like Lucia, Teresita was administered Holy Communion by an angel, and as the petals fell, onlookers also reported that a statue sculpted according to Teresita's description of the Virgin and holding a rosary moved its mouth and hands as if reciting the beads. The sun pulsed, and many were cured of infirmities. Calling herself the mediatrix (or female mediator) of grace, Mary imparted the gentle words, *"Pray, my child. The people do not heed my words. Tell my daughters that there will be persecutions, unrest, and bloodshed in your country. The enemy of the Church will try to destroy the faith which Jesus established and died for. The Church will suffer much. Pray for the conversion of sinners throughout the world. Pray for those who rejected me and those who do not believe and trust me. Spread the meaning of the Rosary, because this will be the instrument for peace throughout the world. Tell the people that the Rosary must be said with devotion. Propagate the devotion to my Immaculate Heart. Do penance for priests and nuns. But be not afraid, for the love of my Son will soften the hardest of hearts and my motherly love will be their strength to crush the enemies of God. What I ask here is the same I asked at Fatima.''*

There were secrets, but Teresita guarded them jealously for the next forty years. "I'll tell you this much," she said to a journalist. "One (of the secrets) is for China, not Russia."

I was struck by the mention of China in an apparition occurring at just about the same time that Ida was hearing messages in Amsterdam about Manchuria. On December 10, 1950, the Dutch visionary was shown Formosa and Korea and told by Mary that there would be *"periods of tranquility, which, however, do not last. The Eastern nations have been aroused by an ideology that does not believe in the Son.''* That ideology was threatening to spill across Asia, even down to the Philippines, and certain of its errors, especially the distorted promulgation of Darwinism, already were entrenched in the West, which was worshiping at the throne of DNA. In this expanding and godless environment the events in the Philippines seemed like a welcome little proof of the supernatural, not so much a calling card as a wake-up call.

It was what the Church needed: a rallying point against not just atheism but also the hedonism sweeping the world and especially the Philippines' big brother, America, where a magazine called *Playboy* was in the offing and where Hollywood, featuring Marilyn Monroe, had become the new Babylon, exporting lust in the same way that Moscow exported godlessness. By the early 1950s television was replacing the family hearth, and even in the Philippines authorities had to be disconcerted over the disrespect with which the Church, now thought to be an archaic institution, was suddenly held. With Soviet tanks soon to crush East Berlin, and already entrenched in Czechoslovakia, it seemed only a matter of time before Russia's philosophy of atheism would spread like its military hardware. North Korea, turned into a Communist state by China and Russia, invaded South Korea, and in the Philippines that was far too close for comfort.

In this era where science and militarism declared them-

selves the only truth, I would have thought the Church,
once it determined that there was no fraud or demonism,
would embrace an event like Lipa for what it was: God
sending us flowers and gently nudging us away from fanatical materialism—a materialism that took different forms
but was in many ways growing as vehement in the Philippines and West as it was in Beijing and Moscow. These
were strange times, however, and the Church, perhaps
wary about charges of superstitiousness, decided that there
was no room in such modern times for Teresita's apparitions and set about crushing the apparition, ordering the
burning of any diaries associated with Teresita, disposal
of rose petals, and destruction of the statue. Boxes of letters
and other records of the apparitions were burned. And the
bishop, who approved of Lipa after his personal encounter
with the rose petals, was stripped of his administrative
powers in the early 1950s, ostensibly for "poor accounting
practices," his equally favorable auxiliary bishop also
removed and banished to a different diocese. Meanwhile
Mother Cecilia, the prioress, was transferred to another
convent and given the chores of a scullery maid.

Church interrogators tried to intimidate Teresita into
signing a false confession, a statement saying the apparitions were a fabrication intended to bring her personal
attention; and when the befuddled and terrorized young
postulant found the strength to refuse, she was confronted
by an angry psychologist-priest who made motions as if
ready to throw an ashtray at her.

The repression was orchestrated by the papal nuncio in
Manila, at whose direction a committee of Filipino bishops
was convened, hastily concluding that the Lipa events were
not of a supernatural nature, their own verdict signed without even interviewing the visionary, who was also seques-
tered at a different convent and forbidden, as were the other
nuns, to speak of the 1948 happenings. While the committee of bishops appeared unanimous in their conclusion that
Lipa was fraudulent, several of them confessed before they
died that they too had been coerced, signing the negative
"findings" only under threat of excommunication.

I wondered if this was what the Virgin meant when she
warned of what Lucia described as the "diabolical dis-

orientation'' invading the world, ''deceiving souls'' and sowing confusion in ''many persons who occupy positions of responsibility.'' Confusion is Satan's hallmark, the first indication of his presence. The Church, it appeared, was encountering Pope Pius X's worst nightmare—the infiltration of ''partisans of error'' into its ''very bosom,'' where they would be ''the more mischievous the less they keep in the open.''

There was always room for skepticism, but at Lipa certain authorities, bowing to the pressure of a new and scientific world—a world that had now all but totally discarded spirituality in favor of biology and psychology—took scientific methodology to the extreme, all but erasing an event that captivated an entire nation and gave evidence, it seemed, that their Church was based on truth and the living presence of God. *"To my daughter who does not believe,"* Mary had said, referring during the apparitions to one stubborn nun, *"I do not oblige you to believe. But do not block nor debase my sacred place, nor despise my words."*

Aerial view of LaSalette, France.

The grotto at Lourdes, France.

The Miraculous Medal. Front and back.

Bernadette Soubirous.

The incorrupt body of St. Bernadette in the convent of St. Gildard, Nevers, France.

The church at the apparition site in Knock, Ireland.

Behind the Iron Curtain, churches were
mercilessly demolished or closed.

The chapel presently standing at the apparition site at Zaravanystya, Ukraine.

The apparition site at Beauraing, Belgium.

The widespread escalation of hatred, famine, drought and disease during the twentieth century.

Loli, Conchita, Jacinta and Maria Cruz
of Garabandal, Spain in ecstasy.

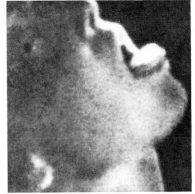

St. Michael the Archangel administered communion
to the girls. On one miraculous occasion
the host was visible.

World War II brought about new technological advances with these benefits for mankind.

The stigmatist, Padre Pio.

The grotto at Tre Fontaine, Italy.

Our Lady appearing to enormous crowds in Zeitun, Egypt. She was photographed on the rooftops of the coptic cathedral.

*Fr. Stefano Gobbi of Milan, Italy with the
Pilgrim Virgin of Fatima statue.*

A wooden statue of Our Lady weeps in Akita, Japan.

Stigmatist Mirna Nazour of Damascus, Syria
with her icon that exudes oil.

CHAPTER 14

The Ladder to Heaven

You could smell the sulphur. You could feel the diabolical contention. It was Satan, diluting authentic apparitions with false visionaries, persecuting the real seers, blinding newsmen to the events, and sowing confusion within the Church—confusion and negativism.

In Rome the saintly pope, Pius XII, pressured by world events and the "modernism" within his own Church, knew that even if the world was no longer suffering the overt turmoil of Nazism, it had never been headed on a more precarious course. Bombs! Atomic bombs! Godless Russia! The Americans were lighting up the Nevada desert with nuclear tests and the Soviets were developing a satellite called Sputnik.

"If my requests are heeded, Russia will be converted, and there will be peace," said the Virgin of Fatima. *"If not, she will spread her errors throughout the world, causing wars and persecutions of the Church. The good will be martyred, the Holy Father will have much to suffer; various nations will be annihilated . . ."*

Though he hadn't read the Third Secret, Pius knew of the central message, and in fact told one visitor that "the pope's thinking is contained in the messages of Fatima." He was a Marian pope, and Mary's splendid little coincidences surrounded him. A pilgrim statue of the Fatima

101

Virgin arrived in Rome on October 29, 1950 and the next day Pius XII, meeting with more than 400 bishops and cardinals, announced his intention to define the dogma of the Assumption. That courageous decision involved the rare invocation of papal infallibility, but he felt certain that Providence had led him to declare that Mary was assumed bodily, not just spiritually, into Heaven. Signs in the sky seemed to bear him out. On this same day, the eighth anniversary of the consecration of the world to Mary's Immaculate Heart, with the Fatima statue at the church of Casaletto, immediately behind the Vatican gardens, Pius took his usual walk in the gardens around four o'clock, strolling up to the esplanade of Lourdes, when it happened.

"At a certain moment," he recalled, "having lifted my eyes above the papers I had in my hand, I was struck by a phenomenon I had never seen before. The sun, which was fairly high, looked like a pale yellow opaque globe completely surrounded by a luminous halo, which nevertheless did not prevent me at all from staring attentively at the sun without the slightest discomfort. A very light cloud was before it.

"The opaque globe began moving outward, slowly turning over upon itself, and going from left to right and vice-versa. But within the globe very strong movements could be seen in all clarity and without interruption. The same phenomenon repeated itself on the following day, October 31," the pope wrote in a note to one of his cardinals.

On November 1, the actual day for definition of the new dogma, more than half a million pilgrims crowded St. Peter's Square. As Sister M. Pascalina Lehnert recounted, " A deep blue sky extended above the cupola of St. Peter's. Beside the sun one could also see the crescent of the moon, just above the cross of the cupola! How was this possible? The others saw it and were astonished: 'who is this...fair as the moon, beautiful as the sun...!' we recite on Prime of that day. Already it was most extraordinary that the day was so warm and so clear, and this crescent of the moon over the cupola of Michelangelo at this hour of the feast created the effect of a wonderful symbol."

Nor was that the end of it. The pope saw the solar miracle again on the day he formally proclaimed the new dogma and once more on the octave of the feast. When he made inquiries at the Vatican Observatory he was told no one there had observed anything similar in the skies of autumnal Rome.

It's clear to me that Pius XII was not behind any Church mishandling of apparitions, and he had reacted strongly against the progressive "intelligentsia" when they tried to get him to say something contrary about Fatima. The only statements he had to make were positive. "Tell your religious to continue working with the greatest enthusiasm promoting the cult of Our Lady of the Rosary of Fatima," he said to the master general of the Dominicans.

But there was great resistance to Mary within the Church's liberal factions, especially among "progressives" who apparently were convinced that supernatural events did not exist in the modern world. They ignored apparitions that were proliferating across their own Italy, virtually at the Vatican's doorsteps, in the same way Mary's manifestations had proliferated across France. She was appearing in Cisterna, Casacicchio, Arluno, and particularly in the province of Savona, at Balestrino, where, starting October 4, 1949, events swirled around a girl named Caterina Richero, who experienced at least 120 apparitions through the 1950s and 1960s. The messages were astonishingly similar in both power and brevity to those that later came from Medjugorje, Yugoslavia.

She even greeted them with the same, *"Dear children."*

The Virgin of Balestrino explained that *"in suffering is the ladder that brings you to Heaven for those who are able to bear it with resignation"* and that *"without prayer you can't do anything."* Instead of working at night, she wanted the people of Balestrino to recite the Rosary. With prayer, especially the Rosary, she told them *"you can even win over your enemy."* The graces asked of Heaven are considered *"according to the degree of merit,"* she said. *"Pray so much, to the point where the enemy will not be able to enter your hearts."*

She asked that the people pray *"that all the sinners will be converted and will be able to merit a day in the reign of His glory."* It was important, she told Caterina, to *"remain close to Him."* The day on which Christ would *"manifest"* was *"near,"* and she wanted the lives of her children *"pure as snow."* She urged devotion to Christ in the Eucharist. *"Jesus wants to save you as His own,"* the Virgin said on June 5, 1956. *"Prepare yourselves with prayer and penance."*

She urged the sacrament of Confession, and repeating her constant theme, warned that there *"is too much sin in the world"* and that *"My Son Jesus is very disgusted,"* adding on February 5, 1954, that *"He wants to send a punishment, but I, His mother, will try to find a way to keep you under my mantle."*

The Third World War, she said in 1951, is *"still far away."* Good deeds would be rewarded, said Our Lady of Balestrino, *"but if you continue to do bad deeds there could be a terrible punishment on this land."*

The time had come to appreciate and meditate upon Christ's Mercy. This was what the Lord had repeatedly emphasized to Sister Faustina. Mercy, mercy, mercy. Sinners were to embrace it, and the pure souls were to adore God for His clemency. The grace of Divine Mercy was especially available to those who recited a chaplet He gave to Sister Faustina, widely known as the Chaplet of Divine Mercy. Those who trusted in His Mercy received invaluable grace. *"For the sake of your love, I withhold the just chastisements, which mankind has deserved,"* He told Sister Faustina. *"A single act of pure love pleases Me more than a thousand imperfect prayers. One of your sighs of love atones for many offenses with which the godless overwhelm Me. The smallest act of virtue has unlimited value in My eyes because of your great love for Me."*

All mankind was to recognize His Mercy as *"a sign of the end times."* For it is followed by His Justice.

Was anyone listening? Was anyone aware of those messages, or the apparitions reported elsewhere—in Denver, where Mary was seen in 1950 by a 15-year-old girl, weeping and arms crossed over her heavy heart?

Did anyone know that in 1952 she appeared to a Jesuit in India—Father Louis M. Shouriah—asking devotion to that same "sorrowful heart?"

And had any word gotten out of the equally moving appearances inside the U.S.S.R.?

Seredne! Had anyone heard of Seredne? Does anyone in the West know of Seredne still?

Seredne was another miracle in the Ukraine, a nation which one day would provide the final nail in the Soviet Union's coffin, leading to the final break up of that hammer and sickle. Please pay close attention to the happenings in Ukraine. It will also figure into the outbreak of apparitions in the 1980s and 1990s and may figure into the future of our world.

Bordered on the west by Poland and Czechoslovakia and the north by Russia, the Ukraine was hidden behind the titans of Communism, and the faithful there (Orthodox, Catholics, Baptists) clung to their beliefs in a nearly supernatural display of courage. By 1950 all the Catholic dioceses in the Ukraine were liquidated but still the people met clandestinely in remote chapels that the Communists, while obliterating their dioceses, had not yet gotten around to destroying.

Such was the case at Seredne, where a striking visitation took place on December 20, 1953. To be exact it occurred in a nearby village called Dubovytsya. This is in the Ivano-Frankivske region of Ukraine, where Stalinists slaughtered thousands of helpless peasants and piled them into mass graves.

In a vision during Mass, a woman named Hanya saw the hill of Seredne and a spot where there had been small wells of clear water—just as there were miraculous wells at the shrines of Zarvanystya and Hrushiw. Hanya saw it all vividly, even though she'd never visited the hill.

As her vision continued the Virgin Mary appeared and began to speak:

"My daughter, my daughter, my daughter, you see what a fullness of grace I possess. But I have no one to give my graces to, for there are so many daughters and sons who have turned away from me...I wanted to obtain a great forgiveness for poor sinners, for disaster is upon us as in the times of Noah. Not by flood but by fire will the destruction come. An immense flood of fire shall destroy nations

for sinning before God. Since the beginning of the world,
there has never been such a fall as there is today. This is
the kingdom of Satan. Rome is in danger of being
destroyed, the pope of being killed. Rome must be renewed
and raised through the hill of Seredne. The sinful world
with its sinful people is in desperate need of renewal."

Did the fire mentioned to Hanya relate in any way to the
meteorites warned about at Amsterdam, or the "aluminum
torpedo?" Were future punishments what caused a plaster
statue of Mary (a statue fashioned after the Fatima Virgin,
with thorns and flame around the heart) to shed tears in
Syracuse, Sicily, on August 29, 1953, tears proven in a
laboratory to be human? Was Seredne connected to both
the weeping statue and the Third Secret of Fatima?

Four years after Seredne, the Fatima secret, still sealed
in a double envelope, finally found its way to the Vatican.
For some reason Pius XII, like the bishop of Leiria, chose
not to study its tantalizing contents—perhaps deciding to
wait like everyone else for 1960, when it was to be made
public. It was placed in a little wooden safe in the papal
apartment, bearing the inscription *Secretum Sancti Officti,*
or "Secret of the Holy Office."

On February 19, 1958, Ida, waiting in Holland for a sign
that her apparitions were authentic and not of the devil,
received a message that the pope would die at the beginning of October. She jotted it down, sealed it just as Lucia
had sealed her own secret, and gave it to her spiritual
director, a priest named Frehe. On October 9, 1958, Pius
XII did indeed meet his death.

The new pope was Angelo Giuseppe Roncalli, a jovial,
bustling figure who took the name John XXIII. He was 78
and would reign for only five years. While Pope John XXIII
read the Third Secret a year into his term, by then hints
of its contents had already spread by way of an extraordinary interview that Lucia gave to Father Augustine Fuentes
on December 26, 1957. During the conversation Lucia
informed the priest that Mary was "very sad because no
one has paid any attention to her message, neither the good
nor the bad." Lucia described the punishment from Heaven
as "imminent" and said God was going to chastise the

world "in a terrible manner," repeating the warning that Russia would one day be the instrument of chastisement if it was not converted, and that many nations would disappear from the face of the earth. The devil, said Lucia, "is in the mood for engaging in a decisive battle." He was especially after those planning on entering the priesthood. He was making them delay or cancel their entrance into the religious vocation, while among the laypeople Satan was removing all enthusiasm for sacrifices and dedication to God.

"Father," she told Fuentes, "the Most Holy Virgin did not tell me that we are in the last times of the world but she made me understand this for three reasons.

"The first reason is because she told me that the devil is in the mood for engaging in a decisive battle against the Virgin. And a decisive battle is the final battle where one side will be victorious and the other side will suffer defeat. Hence from now on we must choose sides. Either we are for God or we are for the devil. There is no other possibility.

"The second reason is because she said to my cousins as well as to myself that God is giving two last remedies to the world. These are the Holy Rosary and Devotion to the Immaculate Heart of Mary. These are the last two remedies, which signify that there will be no others.

"The third reason is because in the plans of Divine Providence, God always before He is about to chastise the world exhausts all other remedies. Now, when He sees that the world pays no attention whatsoever, then, as we say in our imperfect manner of speaking, He offers us with a certain trepidation the last means of salvation, His Most Holy Mother. It is with a certain trepidation because if you despise and repulse this ultimate means we will not have any more forgiveness from Heaven because we will have committed a sin which the Gospel calls the sin against the Holy Spirit...Let us remember that Jesus Christ is a very good Son and that He does not permit that we offend and despise His Most Holy Mother."

While the secret remained under wraps, waiting for release at the beginning of the next decade, Mary, persisting in her attempts to rally the faithful behind the Iron Curtain, as well as give hints of what a chastisement might entail, descended, it was claimed, upon Turzovka, Czechoslovakia. It was 1958, the hundredth anniversary of Lourdes, and Czechoslovakia had been a Western-style republic until the Communist coup turned it into a permanent puppet of Moscow.

In a mountainous part of its north-central region, not far from the Ukraine and Poland, was the village of Vysoka, and in that vicinity the hamlet of Turzovka—just 3,000 or so souls, about the size of Hrushiw. Our Lady appeared on a mountain called Okrouhla, which, like LaSalette, was rounded at the top, having at its summit a pine that served as a hidden shrine, decorated with an icon of Our Lady of Perpetual Help.

On June 1 Mary appeared on Okrouhla to a 40-year-old forester named Matous Lasuta who'd been praying before the icon when, suddenly, the trees disappeared and in their place was an exquisite, unworldly garden. In that surreal garden was a woman who fit the description of the Virgin of Lourdes.

Matous struggled with the sight before him, glancing around to see where the pines had gone. But instead, as in a movie, he saw a vision of the globe. Earth. Earth and all the nations. There were spots of various coloration on the map, some green, some yellow, similar to visions of the Dutch woman Ida. He was made to understand that the green was good and the yellow denoted countries marked for destruction owing to their sinful behavior. The yellow moved like a wave, invading and expanding in one country after another, until it had infected all the lands. Then he saw powerful explosions bursting over both the land and seas. He saw leaves fall and burst into flames when they reached the ground, which was soon entirely afire. The vision lasted three hours. *"Matous,"* said Mary, *"what you have seen, make it known to the world."* She pointed across the trees and when the woodcutter looked he saw Heaven descending to the earth. In that splendor was Christ. When the Mother of God left, Matous, trembling, saw a rosary left in the grass.

According to Lasuta, Mary said mankind could expect the future to hold terrible floods and "other misfortunes through the elements." There would be earthquakes and even mountains would move. The air would be filled with demonlike forms that symbolized sin—terrifying humanity.

Then nature will calm down, according to *Vers Demain,* a publication that wrote about the events, "and a bright spot will appear—but the world will not be recognizable. Everything will be destroyed. It will be difficult to find life and living beings. God will punish the wicked and those who will have blasphemed Him."

Two-thirds of mankind would be gone.

That was a heap of bad news but there was also some that was encouraging. According to Matous, the Virgin said that *"all my children will receive and carry the sign of the cross on their foreheads. This sign only my chosen ones will see. These chosen ones will be instructed by my angels how to conduct themselves. My faithful will be without any kind of fear during the most difficult hours."*

According to *Vers Demain,* that apparition was followed by half a dozen others. "On July first, the Blessed Virgin showed Lasuta how the chastisement could be avoided or made lighter through prayer, the Rosary, and penance," said this publication. "The prayer can hold off the justice of God, but such prayer has to come from the heart, not proceed only from the intellect, and it must not be said absentmindedly. And to the prayer must be added good works. These good works must not consist in a bare distribution of food, clothing, or money, but the gifts must be accompanied by encouraging words, a smile, a friendly glance. As for penance, it must consist above all in abstaining from evil and in doing good."

While the bishop, Monsignor Netzey, at first prohibited visits to the site, he later revoked his prohibition, which should have made life easier for Matous but for one fact: this was a Communist country. Before the apparitions ended, Matous was arrested by Communist Party police and thrown in jail. Submitting him to several trials, the prosecutors and judge tried to get Matous to recant his story, and when Matous refused, the judge got flustered and adjourned to a further session. Matous was declared insane and confined to a hospital near Sillein, a humiliation he was to suffer for ten months. He spent the next year at home before he was arrested again and sentenced to three years. When they tried to take his mugshot, however, an image of the Virgin of Fatima kept appearing.

Though the Communists chopped down the pine tree, villagers pounded a cross in its place and hundreds visited it, erecting altars and statues. Sixteen times the Communists came and destroyed the little shrine and yet pilgrims continued to flow up the mountain. As usual, a miraculous spring supplied healing waters, discovered when a villager named Jaroslav Zavalenka had a dream in which a woman told him where to dig. It reminded me of a similar dream that caused residents of Hrushiw in the Ukraine to clean up the healing well there, which had been desecrated by a Communist hooligan, Yustyna Kon, a century before.

But this wasn't just a healing well. When water from the Turzovka spring froze, exquisite pictures and etchings formed in the ice, images of the Virgin and Jesus, or of a monstrance radiating light. In one glass was the portrait of Mary standing on a rock, in others a lamb or such other symbols. "In the glass of Mrs. Agnes Konecna a picture formed of the Most Blessed Virgin Mary," reported *Vers Demain*. "The picture was surrounded by ice. She took the glass to show it in the office of the J.Z.D.; all the officials shook their head. They let the water thaw out, then refreeze. Again a picture appeared, a chalice with a Host."

Mary also manifested, it seems, in flesh-and-blood form. We don't know the date, but on a bus traversing the stretch from Cadec to Turzovka, a strange peasant woman approached the driver for a ticket, drawing the stares of passengers who studied her bare feet and the rosary hanging from her belt. When the driver asked where she was going, the woman replied, *"Turzovka."*

The driver took a ticket from his book and handed it to the woman, but she didn't have the money to pay for it. An elderly man quickly offered to donate the fare, but the woman declined, telling him he had three children at home and needed the money himself.

How did she know that? It was true: money was tight and there were three children he was caring for.

When the driver himself said he would pay the fare, the

woman turned to him and with equal accuracy stated that he too needed his money because he planned to get married. The passengers, befuddled, continued to stare and she was asked for her identification card. The woman turned to the driver and told him he had it in his coat pocket.

The driver, who knew he hadn't taken her card, looked at her with surprise but found his hand groping in his pocket anyway. The only card in there was a holy card of the Blessed Virgin.

When he looked up, the passenger was gone.

Up at the mountain, where Mary had appeared in ethereal splendor, and where the sun turned and spun off colors, as at Fatima and Montichiari, the Virgin continued to indicate future events. There would be, she'd told Lasuta, rolling thunder, freezing nights, trembling of the earth. She seemed to be referring to *Revelation* when she said, *"The angels who are entrusted with the work of destruction are ready, but the wrath of God can be stayed by praying the Rosary, by penance, and by the sinners' repentance."*

Was she not pointing to John's great prophecy? Was she not alluding to the Seven Angels of the Apocalypse? Was she not referring to the sealing of foreheads in *Revelation* Chapter 7, which is in the midst of the Seven Seals?

We've discussed five of the Seven Seals that are a part of the Great Tribulation, whereby there is famine, conflict, widespread death, and the cry of the martyrs. The remaining two, the sixth and seventh, include "Cosmic Disturbances" and the tossing to earth of a censer filled with fire, which is a prelude to the "Seven Trumpets."

When the first angel sounds his trumpet in John's prophecy, there is "hail and fire, mingled with blood." A third of the trees are burned up, says *Apocalypse* 8:7. And all the green grass set afire. The second angel? When he sounds his trumpet (8:8) something like a great burning mountain is thrown into the sea, "and a third of the sea became blood." The third angel: "And a great star fell from Heaven, burning like a torch, and it fell on a third of the rivers and on the springs of water; and the name of the star is Wormwood; and a third of the waters became wormwood; and many men died from the water, because it was made bitter (8:11)." The fourth: a third of the stars darkened, and a third of the day. The fifth is opening of the bottomless pit, and release of a smoke that will darken the sun. With it will come a new swarm of demons, commanded to attack "only those men who do not have the seal of God on their foreheads (9:4)."

Those without the seal would be tormented for five months, as by a scorpion.

"In those days men will seek death and will not find it; they will desire to die, and death will flee from them (9:6)."

Upon the sounding of the sixth angel a third of mankind will be killed. There will be an army numbering 200 million. Their breastplates will be red. They will spread plagues.

When those who do not die still don't repent of their "sorceries or their sexual immorality," yet another angel will arrive with a rainbow around his head, his feet like pillars of fire.

Then will come the thunder.

CHAPTER 15

Behind the Iron Curtain

The stories coming out of the Communist countries were tremendously absorbing, for nowhere was the spiritual battlefield as conspicuous. I'm convinced if we looked into the matter we'd see that while the nations behind the Iron Curtain were experiencing the most horrific forms of repression, they were also the recipients of special glimpses of the supernatural.

By this time the Polish nun Sister Faustina was deceased, but her many communications with Mary and Christ continued to resonate in the quiet circles of East European Christianity, granting insights both into the working of God's judgments and the spiritual preparation of the soul. Whatever was raging around the victims of Communism, it was nothing compared to what was raging within human souls. In the very first chapter, I said we were going to assume that demons exist and view historical events and trends in light of potential evil influence. Mostly we have focused on the rage of Satan embodied in world leaders and philosophers. But we should know this as well: the evil spirit has access to each and every one of us, and also affects *our* thoughts and actions. It is a continual spiritual warfare, and life on earth is one huge test. When we take the easy way—the way often set before us by Satan as a temptation, focusing only on money, physical gratification, and worldly comfort—we risk an unfortunate situation upon death.

In one vision Sister Faustina was summoned to the judgment seat of God. There she stood alone before the Lord Jesus. Suddenly she saw the complete condition of her soul as God sees it. "I could clearly see all that is displeasing to God," said Faustina. "I did not know that even the smallest transgressions will have to be accounted for. What a moment! Who can describe it? To stand before the Thrice-Holy God!"

Another time, claimed Sister Faustina, her guardian angel appeared and told her to follow him. "In a moment I was in a misty place full of fire in which there was a great crowd of suffering souls. They were praying fervently, but to no avail, for themselves; only we can come to their aid. The flames which were burning them did not touch me at all. My guardian angel did not leave me for an instant. I asked these souls what their greatest suffering was. They answered me in one voice that their greatest torment was longing for God. I saw Our Lady visiting the souls in Purgatory. The souls call her 'The Star of the Sea.' She brings them refreshment. I wanted to talk with them some more, but my guardian angel beckoned me to leave. We went out of that prison of suffering. (I heard an interior voice) which said, *'My Mercy does not want this, but justice demands it.'* "

As if to explain the tribulation of Communist countries, the nun related how suffering is sent as purification and to make us more like Jesus. Even those with scarlet sins can approach God and receive forgiveness. The prayer most pleasing to the Lord, conveyed Sister Faustina, is prayer, as at Fatima, which asks for the conversion of sinners.

"One day Jesus told me that He would cause a chastisement to fall upon the most beautiful city in our country (probably Warsaw)," Sister Faustina wrote. "This chastisement would be that with which God had punished Sodom and Gomorrah. I saw the great wrath of God and a shudder pierced my heart. I prayed in silence. After a moment, Jesus said to me, *'My child, unite yourself closely to Me during the sacrifice and offer My Blood and My Wounds to*

My Father in expiation for the sins of that city. Repeat this without interruption throughout the entire Holy Mass. Do this for seven days.' On the seventh day I saw Jesus in a bright cloud and began to beg Him to look upon the city and upon our whole country. Jesus looked down graciously. When I saw the kindness of Jesus, I began to beg His blessing. Immediately Jesus said, *'For your sake I bless the entire country.' "*

But God's anger always hung like the sword of Damocles. In her room one night, Sister Faustina saw an angel identified as the executor of Divine Wrath. "He was clothed in a dazzling robe, his face gloriously bright, a cloud beneath his feet," said the nun. "From the cloud, bolts of thunder and flashes of lightning were springing into his hands; and from his hand they were going forth, and only then were they striking the earth. When I saw this sign of Divine Wrath which was about to strike the earth, and in particular a certain place, which for good reasons I cannot name, I began to implore the angel to hold off for a few moments, and the world would do penance. But my plea was a mere nothing in the face of the Divine Anger. Just then I saw the Most Holy Trinity. The greatness of Its Majesty pierced me deeply, and I did not dare to repeat my entreaties. At that very moment I felt in my soul the power of Jesus' Grace, which dwells in my soul. When I became conscious of this Grace, I was instantly snatched up before the throne of God. Oh, how great is Our Lord and God and how incomprehensible His holiness! I will make no attempt to describe this greatness, because before long we shall all see Him as He is. I found myself pleading with God for the world with words heard interiorly. As I was praying in this manner, I saw the angel's helplessness: he could not carry out the just punishment which was rightly due for sins. Never before had I prayed with such inner power as I did then."

The prayer of a humble and loving soul disarms heavenly anger, Faustina was told, and draws down an ocean of blessings.

The world needed mercy. The Mercy of Christ. The mercy to keep at bay even worse punishments than were already befalling Russia and the Communist countries. God wanted mercy to be preached, exhorted, worshipped, honored, and glorified. A focus on Christ's Mercy, a true contemplation of His kindness, and meditation on the wounds of His Passion, were the means of rescue and deliverance. Prayers beseeching that mercy were given to Sister Faustina, and I will present them in the last chapter. The prayers are said on rosary beads, including this refrain that should be recited over and again to God: *"For the sake of His sorrowful Passion, have mercy on us and on the whole world."* So important is the concept of mercy that I feel impelled to recommend all readers to write the Marian Helpers in Stockbridge, Massachusetts, 01263, and order her entire diary, which is full of invaluable spiritual insight.

"Let the greatest sinners place their trust in My Mercy," said the Lord. *"They have the right before others to trust in the abyss of My Mercy. My daughter, write about My Mercy toward tormented souls. Souls that make an appeal to My Mercy delight Me. To such souls I grant even more graces than they ask. I cannot punish even the greatest sinner if he makes an appeal to My Compassion, but on the contrary, I justify him in My unfathomable and inscrutable Mercy. Write: before I come as a just Judge, I first open wide the door of My Mercy."*

Those who trust in His goodness are assured of a permanent income on which to live. The duty is to trust completely in His goodness, and His Duty is to give all His people what they need, even the most oppressed. He made Himself dependent on our trust. The greater the trust, the greater God's generosity.

Everyone should have a picture of Jesus as Divine Mercy, the nun was instructed: the picture of Jesus with rays from His heart. *"I promise that the soul that will venerate this image will not perish,"* the Lord told Sister Faustina. *"I also promise victory over its enemies already here on earth, especially at the hour of death. I Myself will defend it as My own Glory."*

Besides stressing His Mercy, Christ was there in Poland to instruct Europe, and the world, about spiritual warfare. Sister Faustina saw the battle before her own avid eyes.

"Suddenly I heard a noise and the words: 'When you leave, we will destroy you. Do not torture us.' I glanced around and saw many ugly monsters. So I mentally made the sign of the cross and they disappeared immediately. How terribly ugly Satan is! The poor damned souls that have to keep him company! Just the sight of him is more disgusting than all the torments of Hell!"

The Evil One came by to plant fear. He came by to instill anxiety and doubt. He arrived to tell her Christ was contradicting Himself. He said she should not encourage sinners to trust in God's Mercy, because they deserve punishment. He told Sister Faustina she should pray only for herself.

"Despite the peace in my soul, I fight a continuous battle with the enemy of my soul," wrote the Polish mystic. "More and more, I am discovering his traps, and the battle flares up anew. During interludes of calm I exercise myself and keep watch, lest the enemy find me unprepared. And when I see his great fury, I stay inside the stronghold; that is, the Most Sacred Heart of Jesus."

As Jesus told her, *"You give me great glory today by fighting so faithfully. Let it be confirmed and engraved on your heart that I am always with you, even if you don't feel My Presence at the time of battle."*

Intense was the struggle, even among the innocent and young. In Hungary, at a school where children were being indoctrinated into Communism, the teacher challenged her students, who were a bit too religious for her taste, to call on God and see if He'd respond. God, she told the crestfallen youngsters, was no more real than Little Bo Peep. In the same way Little Bo Peep wouldn't show up if they called, neither could God, because He existed only in fairytales.

The teacher, a Miss Gertrude, was especially intent on breaking down a girl named Angela, who despite all the atheistic propaganda still received daily Communion. Miss Gertrude had Angela stand outside the classroom and then told the others to call for her. When they did, naturally, Angela came back into the room.

"So you see, dear children, that someone who exists comes when you call him," explained the brilliant and lucid Miss Gertrude. "If he does not exist, he would not be able to come. Are there any children in class who still believe in the infant Jesus?"

A few hands raised meekly and self-consciously into the air.

Miss Gertrude, so goes the story, stiffened her back. It wasn't the response she wanted. "Then I want you all to cry out together, 'Infant Jesus, come.'"

I'm not sure what year this took place, but according to the parish priest, these Hungarian children, who remembered their catechism, suddenly jumped to their feet and, led by Angela, cried out in unison. "Come, Infant Jesus!"

There was an agonizing silence as their teacher surveyed them icily.

They cried again, defiant, loud enough to vibrate the windows. "Come, Infant Jesus!"

And at that moment, very gently, the door began to creak open.

The sun streaming through the windows seemed to focus on the door and as it did the light grew in strength until it became a globe of fire. In the globe these children claimed to see a ravishingly beautiful infant.

The Child didn't speak, only smiled.

It was a globe like the luminous globe at Fatima.

After a short while the sublime Infant disappeared, the globe of light faded, and the door gently closed, leaving the teacher in a state of mind that we can only guess was one of acute befuddlement.

Does that sound like a cute fable? Is it nothing more than an example of wishful thinking—East European folklore?

It comes to us from the indefatigable Frére Michel. There are hundreds of similar accounts. Some of the best are from the Carpathian Mountains in the Ukraine. When I worked with the Ukrainian visionary Josyp Terelya, he had a whole diary of incidents that seemed to indicate supernatural intercession. Believers drew solace from little miracles while the atheists seemed often to suffer peculiar accidents and untoward fates. In Czechoslovakia, according to *Vers Demain,* a man who burned down an altar at a Marian shrine was killed by a thunderstorm on his way home, while another vandal, this time a woman at the same shrine near the Polish border, died within a couple months of destroying two other altars.

I don't know the veracity of every detail, but I do believe in a good number of such paranormal "coincidences." The bottom line is that those who persecuted Christians seemed to have all the immediate victories but in the end their lives rotted like fallen fruit. Those who took a hammer to the statues and icons—paid to do so by the local Communists—died agonizing deaths or found their limbs paralyzed after strange accidents.

Like France, the Ukraine has a rich Christian tradition and consecrated itself to the Mother of God in 1037 under the direction of Yaroslas the Wise. Historically dominated by its northern neighbor, Russia, the Ukraine was soon to endure a repression and persecution as great as any in history. And in Hrushiw (also spelled Hrushiv or Hrushow), between Lviv and Drohobych, on the right bank of the Bystrytsia River, a drama that served as an indicator of the evil times was beginning to unfold.

Founded in the 12th century, Hrushiw is a poor peasant village with ducks, pigs, thick gray mud, and kerchiefed peasant women laboring past the pastures with their long crooked walking sticks. Some 3,561 humble souls reside there, and the hamlet, about eleven miles northeast of Drohobych, near the train station of Dobrovljany, had a long and fascinating history of supernatural events.

It's said that Our Lady first appeared at Hrushiw 350 years ago, when local wars were being fought across this terrain that one day would be conquered by Russia and sucked into the southern flanks of the Soviet Union. I wasn't able to confirm many of the historical details, but there seems to be a consensus that a luxurious willow tree marked the spot of the Virgin's apparitions. An icon of Mary was hung in the tree around 1806, an icon that never seemed to fade with weather or age, and a spring of water erupted from a hollow in the willow, leading pilgrims to come, light candles by the well, and drink the miraculous waters. Eventually a little chapel was constructed over the well in what is known as the Krasna area of town.

None of that was to the liking of the local caretakers, or *feraltery,* who came by with whips to chase the pilgrims away. When the devout kept arriving, seeking supernatural cures, the *feraltery* took a different tact and decided to physically destroy the sacred spot. In 1840 or thereabouts the *feraltery* hired the local hoodlum Yustyma Kon to vandalize the park, cutting its trees with an axe and strewing rubbish. The miraculous well was destroyed—polluted with garbage and covered. The icon was taken down from the tree and hidden in the fearful village.

Those of you who don't believe in the existence of Satan are asked to explain why sacred objects and sacred places were so specifically and viciously targeted.

Around 1855 a plague of cholera had descended on Hrushiw as if in retribution for destruction of the miraculous well. "Everywhere there was sorrow and crying," according to one historical account. "People got drunk, others died of fear or wandered in despair around the villages and looked like walking corpses. In this time of misfortune there were found devout people who begged the Almighty for protection. All of a sudden a thought came upon everyone: 'This is why the Lord God is punishing us, because we permitted this holy place to be desecrated. Let us renew this place and the Lord will remove this terrible punishment.'"

As I alluded, a woman heard Mary's voice in a dream. *"My daughter, death is awaiting you too, but I want you to live. I beg you to clean the desecrated well, and have a Mass celebrated in dedication to Our Lord, so that death will cease throughout the village."*

Donations were quickly solicited and during 1856 the people bought an old chapel from the nearby village of Dorozh, which was planning a new church. The wood walls were hurriedly erected around the miraculous well and the icon of Our Lady was taken out of hiding and placed in the chapel. As the story goes, Hrushiw's epidemic came to a screeching halt. The chapel was called Most Blessed Trinity because in a vision before the chapel's construction someone had seen three tongues of flame— apparitional candles—burning above the well. In another dream a saintly village woman supposedly had seen Our Lady of Perpetual Help, who asked that the chapel be built. Apparitions of Mary had been reported on many occasions in Hrushiw's history. She was seen as a beauty in Jewish dress and villagers also heard the melodious sound of invisible bells.

There were also miracles in the bucolic countryside of Austria, which in the 1950s looked like it was going to go the way of Czechoslovakia—dominated by the red scourge of Communism. In 1954 Vyascheslav Molotov, the Soviet foreign minister, demanded that Austria agree to retain Russian troops in the country. Whenever this happened anywhere else, that country fell under total Soviet oppression.

But the Austrians resorted to a secret weapon known as the Rosary. By 1954—a special Marian year—Austria had organized a Rosary crusade with 450,000 members. They'd also prayed before (not *to*) a pilgrim statue from Fatima. In 1955, on special request by the chancellor, Dr. Julius Raab, the Rosary Crusade began reciting its prayers 24 hours a day. Shortly afterward Moscow invited a delegation from Austria to discuss the military situation and on May 13, 1955—anniversary of the Blessed Virgin's first apparition at Fatima—Russia agreed to withdraw from Austria, signing a peace treaty with Raab!

Can you think of any other situation in the days before Gorbachev when Communism, once planted in a nation's soil, suddenly took up and voluntarily left that territory?

For some reason these and other faith-building stories, including documented accounts of apparitions, failed to reach most Catholic ears. Ignored too was the writing of Sister Faustina. In Western sermons there was nearly no mention of the miraculous, and perhaps one reason was prudence and caution.

But it was also the outcome of a humanistic society. Priests were considered superstitious as it was and didn't welcome further ostracization.

Yet throughout the late 1950s, strange events continued to haunt the skeptics. Much of the phenomena seemed related to one particular pilgrim statue from Fatima. The sun danced and spun when it was displayed, and doves seemed to follow it everywhere. When it was brought to San Giovanni Rotundo, Italy, Padre Pio, the most celebrated mystic of our times, felt a "force" surge through him and was miraculously cured of what had been diagnosed as a respiratory cancer. There were also more solar prodigies. It was reported by one priest, a French Dominican, that the great miracle of Fatima was repeated at least three times in 1959, and again in Portugal at the conclusion of a ceremony for a monument of Christ the King. A servite of Our Lady of Fatima, Maria Candida Lucas Reis e Silva, testified that she saw the sun "covered by a little blood-red colored cloud, which later disappeared; I observed again the same movement of the sun and the same absence of a glare on the disc, which became more and more impressive when seen through binoculars."

Eventually the sun was sheathed by a bright yellow cloud that spread through the atmosphere, engulfing the onlookers.

Yet reporters who were there decided not to mention it in their news accounts.

Once more, such anecdotes are conveyed to us by Frére Michel. According to Brother Michel, Pope John XXIII, faced with the directive that the Third Secret should be revealed in 1960, finally read Lucia's notes in August of 1959 at the papal retreat of Castel Gandolfo. Having done so, however, and having shared portions of it with those in his immediate entourage, Pope John decided not to publicly release it, preferring to leave the issue to his successors. "This does not concern the years of my pontificate," the pope supposedly commented.

Instead, John wrote a personal note, attached it to the secret, took the envelope back to the Vatican, and kept it on the writing table in his bedroom until his death in 1963.

According to one press communique from Portugal, reliable sources at Vatican City said the secret might never be revealed. "Faced with the pressure that has been placed on the Vatican, some wanting the letter to be opened and made known to the world, others, on the supposition that it may contain alarming prophecies, desiring that its publication be withheld, the same Vatican circles declare that the Vatican has decided not to make public Sister Lucy's letter, and to continue keeping it rigorously sealed."

The new bishop of Leiria, who is thought to have been privy to at least portions of the secret text, was soon to comment that "Fatima has not yet said its last word." Clearly, its predictions were of events still in the future. But the bishop remained cryptic, warning about exaggerated guesswork. Fatima, he said, did not justify "the prophets of imaginary world catastrophes. Fatima cannot be reduced to sensational prophecies of frightening wars." It was something he described as "a great deal more serious than all that."

CHAPTER 16

A State of Confusion

There were now less than four decades left in the century, and up another rounded summit, in northern Spain, once more in the pines, among humble peasantry, occurred a remarkable series of events that would again touch Church nerves.

In some ways it was the most remarkable that we've encountered thus far, and perhaps many of you have heard of it. It wasn't as famous as Lourdes or Fatima, nor even Rue du Bac, yet it excited the imagination nearly as much as Fatima's Third Secret.

I'm speaking of San Sebastian de Garabandal, a hamlet 2,000 feet up in the Cantabrian Mountains, rather like a Spanish version of LaSalette, arrived at from the south on harrowing roads that pass sheer contrasting ramparts as majestic and colorful as anything in the Rockies. Easier access is from the city of Santander 55 miles to the northeast. In this tiny village where running water flows only an hour or so a day and where the horse remains a viable means of transportation, there occurred a series of events that seemed to announce the coming of the chastisements indicated at Fatima and Seredne.

From July 2, 1961 to November 13, 1965, one or more of four girls from Garabandal—Mary Loli, Conchita, Maria Cruz, and Jacinta—saw the Virgin Mary nearly every day and sometimes more than once a day for *an estimated total of 2,000 apparitions,* the frequency unprecendented in the annals of Mariology. Its parallels to Fatima, and for that matter to any number of previous apparitions, were enthralling. Once more, peasant children; once more, on the side of a mountain; once more, a clap of thunder. And like Cova da Iria, the Garabandal apparitions were preceded by a visit from an angel.

This was June 18, 1961. The angel, according to Conchita, appeared as "a very beautiful figure, surrounded by a great light that did not dazzle my eyes." The entity was subsequently identified as the archangel Michael. Was it the same angel whom Lucia had seen at Fatima, identifying himself as the "Guardian Angel of Portugal" and "Angel of Peace?" Was the same great heavenly force arriving in north-central Spain to prepare the way for Mary in a country that, like Portugal, had gone through civil strife and was battling the forces of Communism and Masonry?

On July 2 the Blessed Virgin appeared with Michael and a second angel who looked like Michael's twin. Mary was dressed in a white robe with a blue mantle and a crown of golden stars. There was a brown Scapular on her right arm and her hair was deep nut-brown, parted at the center. Her face was long, with a delicate nose, her mouth pretty and thin. She looked to be about 18 and presented herself as Our Lady of Mount Carmel—the way she appeared seven centuries before in giving St. Simon Stock the first Scapular, and also the way she presented herself at the final Fatima apparition.

Nearby a square of fire framed a triangle with an eye at the center and cryptic lettering. There was also a chalice and into it fell drops of blood or tears. Our Lady spoke to them of a coming punishment and in a sad low tone said, *"The cup is already filling."*

In the following days, months, and finally years, Conchita, Mary Loli, Maria Cruz, and Jacinta experienced startling ecstasies. As if drawn by an invisible force, they'd rush to the top of the mountain by way of a stony sunken path and encounter the Virgin among a cluster of nine pines. Mary kissed objects they handed her and often the children, deep in ecstasy, would fall to the hard ground but without experiencing so much as a bruise or scratch.

Often they ran down the path *backwards,* their feet miraculously maneuvering over rocks and stones, eyes bulging, their heads craned far back. When they stopped and began to converse with the apparition they sometimes became so heavy that men in the crowd couldn't lift them. Other times their bodies seemed to be in a state of partial levitation. On July 18, 1962, the archangel Michael gave Conchita Communion, and film taken of this miracle showed the Host suddenly materializing on her tongue while dozens watched in astonishment. The large white wafer appeared in her mouth as she stared at an entity no one else could see.

I must admit that some of the characteristics of Garabandal have bothered me. The contortions of the girls, their craned necks and bulging eyes, may have been a cultural quirk, for I saw the same strange posture with visionaries in other Spanish-speaking countries. But it made some wonder if Satan was behind the apparitions, or at the least whether he appeared on occasion. I also wondered about the triangle with the eye, for while this is said to be a symbol of the Divine indwelling, and is seen in European church art (as well as on the American dollar bill), it's also a symbol used in Masonry. More than anything I was concerned with doubts the visionaries and their relatives expressed. Although, in time, her fears would be relieved, Conchita's own mother was convinced at one point that the apparitions were "absolutely false" or at least "did not come from God."

There was a state of confusion. From the outset Mary warned the girls that they would experience a number of trials and sufferings, including the nagging doubts about what they had seen. Two years after the first apparition they began to tell their parents they weren't sure anymore if it was Mary. Most dubious was Maria Cruz, who during some ecstasies seemed to be looking at a spot away from where the other three were staring. "No, I did not see the Virgin," she announced in March of 1963.

When Maria Cruz said this, according to one witness, her monotonous tone seemed to come from another world.

"At the very beginning of the apparitions, the Blessed Virgin told the four of us that we were going to contradict each other," Conchita recalled in her diary. "But interiorly we knew that the angel and the Blessed Virgin had appeared to us, because they had brought to our souls a peace, a deep joy, and a great desire to love them more than ever with all our hearts. I don't know why we doubted a little. It was a kind of doubt that seemed to come from the devil who wanted to make us disavow the Virgin."

From the outset the Chancery of Santander, which oversees Garabandal, issued warnings about the apparitions, including a declaration advising clergy to "abstain from going to Garabandal" until a committee completed a study of the case. On October 27, 1961, the Bishop of Santander issued a second statement saying there was "no proof that the said apparitions, visions, locutions, or revelations can so far be presented as true and authentic." While it was "too early" to give a final verdict, the Church emphasized that Garabandal's supernaturality had not been affirmed and today the matter remains in limbo, neither approved nor condemned.

Here's how Mary Loli, who now lives in Haverhill, Massachusetts, answers questions about the episode, including questions concerning secret warnings, a great miracle, and chastisements, which we'll be looking at in the next chapter.

I insert my entire interview with her to give you a sense of both the problem with this incident and at the same time its fascinating details:

Q: Did you ever count how many times you saw the Virgin Mary?

A. No, I didn't. For one year it was almost every day, at least for one year, and sometimes more than one time (a day).

Q: You saw her hundreds of times.

A: I guess so. Quite a few times (giggles).

Q: When was the last time?

A: The day I don't remember. The date I don't remember.

Q: Looking back now, do you have any doubt whatsoever that you saw the Virgin Mary?

A: Well, I don't remember very clear and it seems like

it happened to somebody else sometimes. It's so many years ago.

Q: But you don't doubt it?

A: (giggles) I don't know. I don't know.

Q: You're still not sure of it?

A: It's hard for me to explain, really. I don't know. I don't think too often about it and my life is not based on what happened to me. I just try to lead a good Christian life but without thinking about what happened.

Q: Before the apparitions did you have dreams of seeing angels or anything like that?

A: In a dream one time I did. I just remember it was an old broken-down house and I saw an angel calling me. But I don't remember how old I was.

Q: Tell me a little more about the angel who appeared at Garabandal before the Virgin appeared. Was he young?

A: Yeah, like a young child, nine years old.

Q: What did he wear, blue?

A: Yes. Like a blue tunic.

Q: How did he make you feel?

A: I don't remember exactly how I felt. Everything was messed up in my mind. I was a little scared because we had been stealing apples. I was scared we were going to be reprimanded.

Q: Have you been visited by the angel since?

A: No.

Q: Did the angel have wings?

A: Yes.

Q: Were they wings to fly, or just appendages out of the back?

A: Like out of the back, colored, like pink.

Q: You're sure it was Michael?

A: Well, because we asked.

Q: And he said Michael?

A: Yes.

Q: Were there rays of light coming from the Virgin?

A: It was very bright. It was night but it seemed like day. Because everything was very bright.

Q: Did you ever see her feet?

A: No.

Q: And her dress, was it always white?

A: Yeah, and a blue mantle.

Q: Did it ever look different?

A: She came one time and she was dressed in brown.

Q: Was that a special occasion?

A: I don't remember.

Q: Her face. Did it look like anyone you've ever seen in life, or on TV, or in the movies? Was she beautiful like that or how?

A: No. I (don't) think like anybody. It's so hard for me to explain about that because it's not clear in my mind.

Q: Did you ever see a picture of the Virgin of Guadalupe?

A: Yes.

Q: Did that look like Our Lady?

A: I don't know. I really haven't tried to compare.

Q: Is there a statue you've ever seen that looks like her?

A: No. I've seen some pretty statues, but I don't remember any like that.

Q: Did you see the pyramid that was framed with fire?

A: With an eye in it, yes. I don't remember much about it.

Q: It was next to her?

A: I think so.

Q: Do you remember seeing a chalice with blood dripping in it?

A: Yes.

Q: Was it a gold chalice?

A: Yes.

Q: Was it above her? Was she holding it?

A: I don't know for sure.

Q: And the crown. When she gave you her crown to hold: Did it have jewels?

A: It was like the stars, like 12 stars.

Q: Were they just stars?

A: Just stars, bright and shining. It didn't feel like anything. I could not feel to touch. It was like my hand couldn't go any further than where she was. It was like glass—but you didn't touch nothing. I can't explain it.

Q: And holding Jesus was the same thing?

A: Yes.

Q: Did he have any particular color of hair?

A: Brown hair.

Q: Dark skin?

A: Not very dark, but a little tan.

Q: And the color of his eyes?

A: Brown. Brown eyes.

Q: I read that sometimes when you four were seeing the Virgin it looked like you were frightened or sad because sad things were being said. Can you tell me any of the sad things that were said?

A: Well, about the punishments. I cannot really remember exactly. I just remember it was about punishment—that if the world did not change there would be a very big punishment.

Q: I believe you said the Virgin wasn't really there in body, but she was there.

A: I just know there was not feeling when I was touching. I don't know what that signifies. (Conchita described the feeling to me as like touching a "force field.")

Q: Do you go to Mass every day?

A: I do try to go to Mass every day.

Q: Loli, do you think the times are more evil now than back in the 1960s when you had the apparitions of Our Lady?

A: Well, I was not too aware of the world at the time, but I will say that ten or 15 years ago it wasn't as bad as it is today. I think it's terrible today.

Q: What bothers you the most about the world and the United States?

A: To me it's people have no sense of wrong or right, no conscience. They're thinking everything is okay. When I hear people talk on shows on TV and radio, my blood pressure goes up, just the way they talk about abortion, about morality—it's just, I don't know. It blows my mind out. It's terrifying. I have a son who was away in school for a while with the Legionaries of Christ, an order, he's 16 and back now, and it's almost like he's going into the world because he was 13 when he left and I'm so terrified—so terrified—seeing him go out. People have no morals and it's scary.

Q: What do you think of rock stars, such as Madonna?

A: I have seen very little of her, but one day I happened to pass through channels and I saw something that was horrible to me—somebody in a cage or something, rosaries or something. I just put it off because to me it was like evil. Terrible. And one of my kids says, 'I like that song,' and I say, 'You no listen to it because it is evil to me the way she tries to do things.'

Q: Talking about the fact that the world seems to be more evil than ten or 15 years ago, do you think the chastisement is near?

A: I feel God has to do something for things to change. It doesn't look like people are turning to God. In the media there are not many good things.

Q: Are you surprised it's taken so long for anything to happen? Did you think one of the warnings or the chastisement would happen before now?

A: Well with the warning I know what year it's supposed to happen. About chastisement, I—I was so young.

Q: Are world events suprising you? Was there any world event recently that looked like the beginning of chastisement to you? In Russia or Iraq?

A: I don't know. A punishment is supposed to be something very horrible, in the whole world.

Q: So you still think something is going to happen?

A: That's my feeling from the way I see the world. There has to be a big change.

Q: Loli, I know you can't reveal anything that's secret, but I have some general questions. You said you knew the year of the warning. That time has not passed yet?

A: No.

Q: Some others who've seen the Virgin claim this decade is going to be decisive. The 1990s are going to be very important. Do you agree?

A: Ah, I really don't know. I suppose. Even the pope is asked to pray very hard to the Blessed Mother for the whole world to change, as the millennium comes to an end.

Q: You have children. Are you fearful for them, considering the chastisements that are coming?

A: I think I am more afraid for the way the world is. I don't want to see them suffer, but for me there would be a bigger suffering to see them go bad, get influenced in the world. They're probably going to have to suffer for standing up for their religion and beliefs, which they do. Even though they go to Catholic school the children laugh at them because they don't watch those bad TV shows or different things. I think for them there will be suffering

little by little, but it is better than them being influenced.
I pray to God about it.

Q: Now, you know the chastisement?

A: I saw some of it.

Q: And it's not like anything we've seen yet?

A: No.

Q: Has Satan or a demon ever troubled you?

A: I don't know. In a dream I saw a demon. It happened more than one time. It was to do with the devil being around trying to destroy our family.

Q: Have you ever seen any saints in dreams or visions?

A: Ah, no, not that I can remember.

Q: Of any apparitions around the world, which seems the most interesting?

A: I don't know. I haven't thought too much about it.

Q: Were you told what the miracle is?

A: Not that I remember.

Q: Last question: If I were 60 years old, would I live long enough to see this 'warning'?

A: That's a trick question! (laughing)

Q: Well, you're going to live to see the warning, right?

A: Well, I hope so. (laughing)

Q: So life is normal for you. You don't spend all day thinking about this.

A: No. I did hear about other things, and from people who call. But I don't have a lot of time to read.

Q: You're a busy mother.

A: I have to drive every day at least four hours.

Q: Are evil institutions about to lose power?

A: I don't know. I hope God does something soon. Actually I look forward to it, even a punishment, something for the world to change. It's going to take something directly from God, for the world to change. It's not only this country. I go back to Spain and such a drastic change. It's terrible. The morals are way down. People don't go to church too much anymore and you don't hear much about God anymore, and the morality is horrendous, worse even than over here. Terrible. People think it's nothing.

Q: The devil is having a field day.

A: Yes, all over the world.

Q: Were you ever given a vision of Hell, Heaven, or Purgatory?

A: No. Not that I can remember.

Q: What do you think of Medjugorje, where the Virgin is said to still appear?

A: I've read a lot and heard a lot of Medjugorje, but not a book, and I don't know what to think.

Q: At Medjugorje they said this century had been given to the devil. Did you ever hear that?

A: No.

Q: If you had a message to give to America, what would it be?

A: Go back to God and base our life in God.

CHAPTER 17

An Asteroid?

That said, let's get to the meat of Garabandal, the stark messages about the future. During the apparitions Mary discussed three major upcoming events: a warning that would come from God, a great miracle, and a chastisement that sounded like the Great Tribulation. The girls were given a preview of such a chastisement in 1962 and during the apparition they too shrieked in terror.

We start with the Warning, since that comes first. Sometime within the lifespans of the visionaries, who were born around 1950, there supposedly will be a large event sent by God as an omen to mankind. The Warning will precede the great Miracle and the terrible Chastisement—like acts in a drama. If the visionaries live out a normal life, it means this warning will occur sometime between now and the year 2025. When I asked if the 1990s were the critical decade, Conchita, like Mary Loli, seemed unsure, but Jacinta, who wasn't told the exact year, guessed that the end of the 1990s will be pivotal. "It can be considered a very difficult decade because of the bad morality of the world," she said. "Because of that it can be the decisive decade."

While details of the Warning's actual nature are a secret, the visionaries have made a number of comments that give us a sense of it. According to Jacinta the event "will be seen in the air everywhere in the world and immediately (will be) transmitted into the interior of our souls. It will last a short time (in Loli's opinion just a few minutes) but it will seem like a long while because of its effect within us. It will be for the good of our souls and then we'll feel a great love for our heavenly parents and ask forgiveness for all our sins."

The allusion to something in the sky is interesting in light of the clues provided by Conchita, who also saw it as a cosmic event, "like two stars...that crash and make a lot of noise, and a lot of light...but they don't fall. It's not going to hurt us but we're going to see it and, in that moment, we're going to see our consciences."

The Warning itself will not kill us, said Conchita, but some people may die from the shock of it.

When it comes, said Conchita, "you will know we have opened up the end of time." She said the Virgin announced this event "by a word beginning with 'A.'" She said it will be "like a punishment, for the just and wicked alike. For the just, to bring them closer to God, and for the wicked to announce to them that time is running out, and that these are the last warnings."

Nobody, said Conchita, could prevent the Warning from coming. "It is a certainty, although I do not know the day or anything about the date." Everything will stand still for a few seconds, adds Mary Loli, even planes in the sky.

Conchita maintained that the Warning will be visible throughout the entire world, "in whatever place anyone might be," and "will be like a revelation of our sins, and it will be seen and experienced equally by believers and non-believers and people of any religion whatsoever." It will be like a purification before the Miracle, and "is a sort of catastrophe. It will make us think of the dead, that is, we would prefer to be dead than to experience the Warning." The Warning will not be explained by science, she asserts, but will be both seen and felt.

"The most important thing about that day is that everyone in the whole world will see a sign, a grace, or a punishment within themselves—in other words, a warning," she told one interviewer in 1973. "They will find themselves all alone in the world no matter where they are at the time, alone with their conscience right before God. They will then see all their sins and what their sins have caused. We will all feel it differently because it will depend on our conscience. The Warning will be very personal, therefore, we will all react differently to it. The most important thing will be to recognize our own sins and the bad consequences of them. You will have a different view of the Warning than me because your sins are different from mine.''

The phenomenon will not cause physical damage, continued Conchita, ''but will horrify us because at that very moment we will see our souls and the harm we have done. It will be as though we were in agony but we will not die by its effects but perhaps we will die of fright or shock to see ourselves...No one will have doubts of it being from God, and of it not being human...We must always be prepared with our souls in peace and not tie ourselves down so much to this world...''

Loli added that it will seem as if, for a few moments, the world is coming to a standstill, but so absorbing will be the experience that few will take note of their surroundings. Loli saw persecution of believers, and the pope in hiding, and then: silence as the Warning takes place. Elaborating on the events leading up to the Warning, Jacinta saw a persecution or invasion by Communists and was told to pray that this be avoided. Whether that ''invasion'' has been averted is anyone's guess. The important message was to make sacrifices, spend time before the Blessed Sacrament, and daily recite the Rosary.

Immediately I thought of the seals in *Revelation*. The seventh is ''cosmic disturbances,'' and ''A'' could stand for ''asteroid.'' In Amsterdam Ida warned of comets and pointed to stars in the east. Within 12 months of the Warning, according to Loli, will come the next major event, the Miracle. Conchita will reveal the date eight days before. She already knows when it will happen, which means she was coy with me or that she doesn't agree with Loli that the Warning and Miracle will be within a year of each other. ''What I am allowed to say,'' she told another inquirer, ''is that (the Miracle) will coincide with an event in the Church, and with the feast of a saint who is a martyr of the Holy Eucharist. It will be at half-past eight (2:30 p.m. Eastern Standard Time) on a Thursday evening. It will be visible to everybody in the village and on the surrounding mountainsides. The sick who are present will be cured and the incredulous will believe. It will be the greatest miracle that Jesus has worked for the world. There will not remain the slightest doubt that it comes from God and is for the good of mankind. In the pine grove, a sign of the Miracle will be left forever. It will be possible to film and televise it."

"We'd be able to film it," added Conchita, "but not feel the Miracle when we touched it. It could be compared to rays of light or a 'pillar of smoke'—in that it could be seen but not felt—and yet will really be neither."

I wondered if it related to the prophecies of Sister Maria Faustina, who in the 1930s said before Judgment Day there would be a period of mercy and "a sign in the heavens and over the earth." Maybe the sun was going to do something peculiar in the same way that sunspot activity was suspected as causing the "northern lights" which had terrified much of Europe—including Spain—just before Hitler annexed Austria. I thought of something like the aurora borealis, but the Garabandalites seemed to be speaking of a sign that will be localized and permanent. It will happen in either March, April, or May, on or between the eighth and 16th of the month, on the Thursday which falls on the martyr's feast day. Conchita told others that the Church event coinciding with the Miracle will be a rare happening such as definition of a new dogma.

Those who closely follow Garabandal, and give it credence, discuss the possibility that the martyr is Saint Pancras, whose feast will occur on May 12 in 1994. They also mention Saint Stanislaus, bishop of Kracow, whose feast will occur on a Thursday in 1996. Conchita added that the martyr had been "a boy who was carrying Holy Communion to persecuted Christians," and so Saint Tarcisius comes to mind. But his feast is August 15 and besides being outside of the March-May time frame, August 15 is the Feast of the Assumption, and the Virgin had stipulated, said Conchita, that the great Miracle will not occur on one of Mary's own feasts.

Whenever it *does* occur, the visionaries promise, it will be seen by looking above the cluster of pine trees. During an interior locution Conchita asked the Lord about the Warning and Miracle and He said that they will be *"to convert the whole world."* If that fails, if there is no major conversion, the Miracle will be followed by the great Chastisement.

Such a scenario sounded like it fit with Fatima, as if the Spanish visionaries had been granted insight into the Third Secret. It also brought to mind visions that occurred in the years immediately preceding Garabandal to an American nun, Sister Mildred May Neuzil of Rome City, Indiana, who first saw Mary in 1956 as Our Lady of Lourdes and then as "Our Lady of America," at times with the triangle and eye, standing on a globe, her right foot on a crescent moon, her left foot stepping on the snout of a small, ugly, fire-breathing dragon. She had roses on both feet, which flashed back to the *Rosa Mystica,* and in messages that were granted a Church imprimatur, the Virgin was asking for greater sacrifices from her flock to again forestall punishments that, it seemed to me, were originally scheduled to follow World War II and then postponed again in the 1950s and now the early 1960s. *"The pleadings of my heart have held back the Divine Justice about to descend on an ungrateful and sinful generation,"* Mary told her.

But four years before the first apparition at Garabandal, Our Lady warned Sister Mildred that mankind continued to risk *"the fires of untold punishment."* Without adequate human response, including self denial, Mary's intercession could not continue indefinitely. It was as if the small flocks formed by apparitions such as Fatima, Lourdes, Rue du Bac, LaSalette, Seredne, Zarvanystya, Knock, and Beauraing, along with the prayers of faithful everywhere, had stayed the Hand of the Father several times now. Honoring Mary's pleas, Jesus and the Eternal Father had delayed such punishment after the war but now, at Garabandal, Heaven was setting before mankind a specific program of Warning, Miracle, and Chastisement, a program that met with a new and explicit deadline.

The Chastisement, said Conchita, will be "very, very

great, in keeping with what we deserve." This would be the last act in the play, and like all last acts it will be the most important. It would be better for little children to die a natural death, she added, "than to die of the punishment." The girl had seen previews of it, and it was a thing never before seen on earth, more fearful "than anything we can imagine." She further described it as "far worse than if we were enveloped in fire. Worse than if we had fire above us, and fire beneath." She didn't know how much time will elapse between the Miracle and the terrible punishment, but unlike the irrevocable Warning, the Chastisement is conditional. It can be lessened by prayer, repentance, adoration of the Blessed Sacrament, and the Rosary.

There seemed to be occasional confusion between what belonged to the Warning and what belonged to the Chastisement, but from what I could gather there will come a time when a terrific wave of heat will strike and no motor will be able to operate, presumably because of massive electromagnetic interference. The world would seem motionless, perhaps knocked for a moment out of orbit. A real doomsday scenario. It sounded like science fiction, and had Garabandal not been so isolated, and the girls so uneducated and unworldly, with access not even to television let alone current American movies when they were young, I would have suspected them of borrowing from *The Day the Earth Stood Still.* Desperate to quench their thirst, people will seek water but in many places it will have evaporated. Gone mad, survivors will seek to kill each other, and people will throw themselves in the few lakes and seas that do have water.

On June 18, 1965, as sort of a final message, the Virgin sent this through the Archangel Michael: *"As my message of the 18th of October has not been complied with, and as it has not been made known to the world, I am now telling you that this is the last one. Previously, the cup was filling. Now, it is brimming over. Many priests are following the road to perdition, and with them they are taking many more souls. Ever less importance is being given to the Holy Eucharist. We should turn the wrath of God away from us by our own efforts. If you ask His forgiveness with a sincere heart, He will pardon you. I, your Mother, through the intercession of St. Michael the Archangel, wish to tell you that you should make amends. You are now being given the last warnings. I love you very much, and I do not want your condemnation. Ask us sincerely and we shall grant your plea. You must make more sacrifices. Reflect on the Passion of Jesus."*

It seemed too fantastic, and I wondered again if Satan was at work (hoping to diminish the credibility of all apparitions) or if it was an unknown trick of the collective subconscious; yet there is a quality to certain of the messages, such as the angel's last warning, that rings a note of authenticity, and in case it *is* true, we can't afford to ignore the description of the Chastisement.

It wasn't the end of the world, but it was so horrible that one of the Garabandal visionaries asked the Virgin to take all the young children before it happens. The Virgin replied that by the time it comes the children would be adults, and she gave one more clue as to the time table. "The Blessed Virgin," Conchita informed interrogators, "said in 1962 that there will be only two more popes after Paul VI."

CHAPTER 18

A False Light?

It was said that before he died, Padre Pio was given a vision of what the Great Miracle would be. If so he never said anything on the record about it, but the famous mystic was certainly bothered, even horrified, by the glimpses he himself had of the future. Once, when asked what lay ahead, Pio replied, "Can't you see that the world is catching on fire?"

Although there's no definitive way of telling, Padre Pio's attitude toward Garabandal seems to have been positive. The Franciscan stigmatist received Conchita at a private audience in 1966 and advised one man, a traveler from the United States, to visit Garabandal but to use "prudence." Asked on another occasion about its authenticity, he answered curtly, "How many times must she appear there to be believed?" Handed a book about Garabandal, Padre Pio gazed fixedly at the cover and as though by chance opened to the page with the last message—the cup-overflowing message of June 18, 1965. He then closed the book and blessed it.

If nothing else, Pio would have agreed with Conchita that the world, as she told one reporter, had gone *"al diablo"*—to the devil. Padre Pio was deeply saddened by the societal trends (miniskirts, pornography, the Pill) and he was especially disgusted by television. He feared it would destroy family life, and he advised everyone he knew not to buy one. He was also negative about motion pictures. When the subject of movies was raised Padre Pio would blurt, "The devil's in it!"

It was the 1960s. A spirit of revolution was in the air like no spirit since the great French uprising at the end of the 18th century. And who was the king of rebellion but Satan?

Turmoil and lack of faith ran rampant. Thanks to a strange and bitter woman named Madylyn O'Hair, school prayer was out and atheism, or at least agnosticism, was in. It was the decade during which *Time* would run a cover story asking, "IS GOD DEAD?" Never before had there been quite such a crisis of faith! God didn't fit with free sex or the new technology, and spiritual experiences were replaced by artificial ecstasies. If the Fifties paved the way with its billboards extolling liquor and cigarettes, that was just a foretaste of the drug abuse which lay immediately ahead. Suddenly there was the sweet musky aroma of marijuana everywhere, along with peyote buttons, mescaline, THC, and LSD.

It was the decade of Leary and Woodstock and a musical explosion unlike anything ever seen—music that may in some instances have been of deep satanic origin. There was Hendrix, complaining that he was possessed, and Jagger singing a song called *Sympathy for the Devil*. (Mick himself was given the nickname "His Satanic Majesty.")

Everything was going electrical, and the order of society itself seemed threatened. Hippies. Communes. And a nasty war in Vietnam. The Church of Satan was founded in San Francisco, and a photograph of its high priest, Anton LaVey, would find its way onto the cover of a bestselling rock album. Jayne Mansfield fell under LaVey's spell and was decapitated in a bizarre car accident. In America, Marx and Freud were the new standard while traditional values, including church, were chucked out the window onto streets filled with war protesters, Hell's Angels, and Black Panthers.

The decade of "love." The decade of drugs. If there was any parallel for the large-scale use of pot, it was back when the Indians smoked peyote (and for that matter tobacco) as a ritual to induce communication with gods and elemental spirits.

Drugs and sex: the staples of black magic, now being done on a massive scale. Drugs, sex, and alchemy: the creation and irresponsible dumping of new, cancer-causing chemicals that put one in mind of ancient German poison rituals and witchcraft.

DDT and other chlorinated poisons were now everywhere—in our water, in our food, in our body fat. One day they would cause Love Canal and depletion of the ozone layer. Was it paranoic to start weaving all these negatives into a supernatural conspiracy?

Manson. Son of Man. Was Satan mimicking and reversing Christ's title through the killer of Sharon Tate?

Was there any connection between the fate she met and her husband's last film, *Rosemary's Baby?*

Were moviemakers detecting a growing unseen force when they released *The Exorcist?*

Were the Beatles expressing a subconscious yearning, a cry in the night, when they sang *Lady Madonna* and *Let it Be?*

I don't have to run down everything that occurred during that tortuous decade. It was the beginning of the end of sexual standards, it was the age of the street criminal, with crimes of violence skyrocketing, and it was as close as we'd come to nuclear war with Russia. The Garabandal years, after all, were also the dangerous Kennedy years. For one week in 1962 it appeared the United States and Soviet Union would go to war over missile sites in Cuba and *that* would definitely have caused fire from the sky.

Many of those who gained renown during the Sixties, and for that matter the rest of the century, were inspired and anointed by the prince of our world, Lucifer. If you think I'm reaching when I connect the preceding items into a web of actual metaphysical evil, consider the following anecdote from Vincent Bugliosi, prosecutor in the Manson case. "Midway through the arraignment I looked at my watch," he wrote. "It had stopped. Odd. It was the first time I could remember that happening. Then I noticed that Manson was staring at me, a slight grin on his face.''

Much of the cultural muck came out of Greenwich Village and Berkeley, which were also centers of witchcraft. Yet at the height of his crudest and most blatant manifestations, the devil managed to elude the blame, considered by our intellectuals as just a harmless cartoon, a mythical, nearly comical figure. In one television commercial a man even dressed as the devil to sell potato chips.

No surprise, then, that during the Sixties, visionaries like Conchita found it rough going. There was resistance everywhere. The Church, or at least the local bishop, felt the apparitions could be due to "a condition of health conducive to ecstatic trances." In other words, temporary insanity. Opponents of Garabandal tried everything they could to prevent Conchita from going to Rome, and she felt Satan prowling all around her. "Pray for me a lot," she begged one priest, "because I'm quite certain the devil is always beside me."

Lucifer was also having a go at Padre Pio, whose battles with evil were legendary. On July 5, 1964, a possessed woman from near Bergamo was brought to the friary for exorcism and during that rite, according to one biographer, the woman screamed in an unnatural tone: "Pio, we will see you tonight!"

And that night the other monks heard terrific crashes coming from the old priest's cell.

When they got there Pio was sprawled on the floor. He'd been attacked, he said, by large devils "who had the hooves of Lucifer to beat me with." His face was swollen and discolored, his shoulders horribly bruised. A gash above his eyes required five stitches. He was bleeding from the forehead and nose.

Oddly enough, however, there was a pillow under his head, his only comfort. When asked how the pillow got there, Pio responded weakly, "The Madonna."

The next day, according to biographer C. Bernard Ruffin, the exorcism began anew and the demon spoke again. "Last night I was up to see the old man upstairs," roared the possessed woman. "I hate him so much because he is a fountain of faith. I would have done more, except the Lady in White stopped me.''

Around this time, not long after the first appearances at Garabandal, Mary was seen weeping in an apparition at Janonis in the parish of Skiemonys, Lithuania, another Soviet republic where religion had been banned and churches closed. She appeared on July 13 and 14, 1962, to an 18-year-old girl named Ramute Macvyte-Mapiukaite. There wasn't much of a message. During the first apparition Mary was silent, and the next night she spoke for just a few minutes. "I asked, 'When will you again appear?' '' recalled Ramute, "and holy Mary said, *'I will not appear here again. I will appear in Egypt with two angels.'* ''

In northern Italy, just south of Piacenza, not far from Montichiari, a stout uneducated woman from the village of San Damiano had an experience that was strange even in the annals of mystical phenomena. Rosa Quattrini was the mother of three children and was lying in bed gravely ill with perforated peritonitis when, one September day, on the feast of the archangel Michael, a strange peasant lady knocked at her door.

The woman was about 25, more blonde than brunette, wearing a poor bluish-gray dress and kerchief, unnaturally beautiful. She sought alms for candles that would be placed in Padre Pio's sanctuary.

Although there was just about no money in the house, Rosa agreed to make a donation. It was noon and when the church bells sounded the visitor told her to stand up, which Rosa, in her condition, found impossible.

The young woman reached for Rosa with both hands, sending a shock through the farm woman. Suddenly Rosa was able to get up and standing there they recited *Aves, Paters,* and *Glorias* in honor of Christ's wounds. After each cycle of prayer the stranger placed her hands on Rosa's painful abdomen and when they were finished praying the stomach wounds felt much better.

Then the visitor asked an elderly aunt named Adele to fetch a glass of water. The stranger dropped a dried olive leaf, a small piece of blessed candle, and three grains of earth from the Holy Land in it. She told Rosa to drink it at five in the morning, coinciding with the beginning of Padre Pio's early Mass, and when Rosa did she was permanently healed.

The following spring Rosa joined a pilgrimage to San Giovanni Rotundo as a way of expressing gratitude for the cure. While praying in the plaza at Padre Pio's church she heard a woman call to her by name. Immediately she recognized her as the woman who'd visited her the previous autumn. "Yes, I know you," said Rosa. "You were at my house. You are the one who miraculously cured me!"

Rosa told the stranger that she knew she was the Madonna but that "you have not wanted me to say it before now."

The lady answered, *"Yes, I am the Madonna of Consolation of the Afflicted."*

On Friday, October 16, 1964, while praying after the noon bells, Rosa heard another voice, this time from an invisible source, directing her to the vineyard next to her home. *"Come, come, I am waiting for you!"* As she approached the yard this voice grew sweeter and Rosa beheld a beautiful light. Rosa sat near a second trellis and made the sign of the cross with her rosary, and looking upward spotted a cloud descending with stars of gold and silver. She also saw rose petals falling. A red globe of light materialized on a pear tree and the white cloud vanished. Suddenly Mary was there, wearing a white cloak and blue gown with a white sash. Rays of light radiated from the palms of Mary's hands, as on the Miraculous Medal.

"Listen, my daughter. I have come from afar to announce to the world that it is necessary to pray, to pray much, for Jesus can no longer carry the cross. You must help Him carry it. I want all to be saved, the good and the bad. I am the Mother of Love and the Mother of all. You are my children. I want to save you all. If people do not pray, there will be great calamities."

As at most apparitional locations, the messages and warnings were buttressed with paranormal evidence. The pear tree burst into blossom late in September, and witnesses saw the sun spin and whirl. A year later a miraculous spring was discovered and many were healed. Pilgrims took hundreds of photographs laden with inexplicable images of the pope, of the Virgin in a streaming sun, of globes of light, and of seemingly paranormal cloud formations. Rosa's apparitions were to continue every Friday until her death 17 years later.

Of all the apparitional sites I've visited, San Damiano might justify the most caution. There is about San Damiano today a contentious and heavy air, and whether this is caused by those who have assumed control of the apparitional site, or because the apparition was not good to begin with, I know only that for me it lacked the peace and easiness of most Marian shrines. Moreover, some of the miraculous photos display erratic streams of neonlike light similar to what's been photographed at a condemned site in Bayside, New York.

Was San Damiano a "false light?" Bishop Umberto Malchiodo of Piacenza thought so and issued his first negative opinion on September 7, 1965. He requested the faithful to refrain from going there and repeated his position in 1966. There were deeply troubling aspects of San Damiano, including an alleged message from Mary that called it "sacrilegious" for Catholics to receive Communion in their hands. Such a statement was bound to cause division and disorientation among the faithful, and it was a clear contradiction of the Holy Father. In 1968 the Vatican sent a statement throughout Europe saying that San Damiano was "not worthy of confidence." There was also a district attorney's investigation to see if Mama Rosa, as she was known, was bilking pilgrims.

Despite such resistance Rosa continued to hold court for those who crowded San Damiano during the weekly apparitions. Clouds continued to form strange shapes, the sun continued to dance, miraculous images continued to appear in photographs, and Mama Rosa continued to convey alleged messages.

"When you see the fire and the whole world burning up, what will become of you who have not listened to my motherly words," Our Lady of San Damiano supposedly said in 1968.

"Many cities will disappear. . . The devil is loose in every part of the world. . . Take courage because the hours of sadness are coming and the hours of joy for those who

believed in my word. . . The Eternal Father is tired, tired, tired. He has freed the demon who is now working havoc and stealing very, very many souls, even those in high state if they do not understand anymore, and if they do not love. There is just pride and haughtiness. . .

"Don't worry about material things," Mary allegedly added in 1969. *"Be concerned with the salvation of souls. Pray, offer, suffer and be quiet. . . A night of great darkness will come with such obscurity that everyone will tremble. . . Sad hours are coming. . . And the doors are closing. . .*

"Your guardian angels will always be near you and defend you from the enemy because the enemy is working havoc. But you must be strong. If you have Jesus in your hearts and your weapon in your hands, the rosary, I will not abandon you. . . Often call St. Michael. He is your guardian angel. . . Make the First Saturdays of the month. . . The demon is working and is carrying on his battle since the Eternal Father has left him free as a result of your wanting to do things yourself.

"I cry so much. I have tears of blood which have been brought out by the sight of so many of my children on the brink of the pit. . . Be prepared (for) the great day of sadness when the Eternal Father does not want to draw back His power and His hand."

Unless, as had been the case in the 1950s and 1960s, there was a pardon, said Mary, *"the Eternal Father will act in justice three times."*

Was that the Warning, the Miracle, and the great Chastisement?

In May of 1965, back up in Czechoslovakia, where the phenomena continued at the mountain near Turzovka, more than a thousand pilgrims were witness to what they called their own great miracle. It lasted 15 minutes. On two sides of the sky was a brilliant luminosity and in the middle a huge heart. On one side Mary was seen and on the other Jesus near a large red cross.

The warning from Turzovka continued to haunt everyone who heard and believed it: that mankind was heading for a punishment worse than the fire which destroyed Gomorrah, a chastisement that would reduce the population of humans by two-thirds. Mankind could expect the future to hold *"misfortunes through the elements."* There would be earthquakes and even mountains would move. The air would be filled with demonlike forms. Devils would be allowed to torment us for our sins.

"Then nature will calm down," reported Matous Lasuta, "and a bright spot will appear—but the world will not be recognizable. Everything will be destroyed. It will be difficult to find life and living beings. God will punish the wicked and those who have blasphemed Him."

Meanwhile, miraculous images continued to crystallize in glasses of icewater from the well. On January 24 an image of the mountain crystallized in one particular glass and above it was a clock. The people took this new miracle as a sign that God's justice was approaching. While we should always bear in mind that our time is not God's time—that a day to God might be a thousand years to us— there seemed to be a real message in that ice, for the hands of the clock showed five minutes to twelve.

CHAPTER 19

The Third Secret?

By now the public was supposed to know the contents of Mary's Third Secret, but neither John XXIII nor Paul VI saw fit to release it.

By the mid-1960s, however, parts of the secret, or rather *purported* parts of the secret, were said to have been "exposed" in the European media, particularly a German weekly called *Neues Europa,* which published what it claimed was a large excerpt in 1963. The mysterious Fatima message had been obtained, claimed this publication, from diplomatic sources in Washington, London, and Moscow. According to *Neues Europa,* Pope Paul had sent the passage to John Kennedy and Nikita Khrushchev in hopes it would shock them into slowing the arms race. Soon after, pointed out the publication, an atomic test ban treaty was announced.

Did the Third Secret have to do with nuclear warfare? Did it relate to the wars foreseen in Amsterdam and Hrushiw? The natural diasters of Turzovka? The fire of Seredne and Garabandal?

In other words, did it spell out the great Chastisement, the punishment so often mentioned by visionaries since the 19th century, the dark times foretold since the days of the Miraculous Medal?

I'm personally skeptical that *Neues Europa* got its hands on the actual secret. It's easy to spot an immediate inconsistency. At the very beginning of the text *Neues Europa* quoted Mary as referring to October 13, 1917 as the day she revealed the secret when in fact it was given to Lucia three months earlier, on July 13, 1917. According to Frére Michel, Lucia herself, in a subsequent conversation with the bishop of Leiria, told him that such reports, spreading gloom and sensationalism, were "an invention" that "had nothing to do with the contents of the message." At a meeting in Rome years later, Alfredo Cardinal Ottaviani, then prefect of the Sacred Congregation for the Doctrine of the Faith, also denied that the secret had been circulated outside of Vatican City. "You can be quite sure," asserted the cardinal, "that the true secret has been kept in such a way that nobody has cast their eyes upon it."

What *Neues Europa* claimed, on October 15, 1963, was that a great punishment was coming to mankind in the second half of our century and the punishment would involve a "big, big war" and that "fire and smoke will fall from the sky and the waters of the oceans will be turned to steam—hurling their foam towards the sky, and all that is standing will be overthrown. Millions and more millions of men will lose their lives from one hour to the next, and those who remain living at that moment will envy those who are dead. There will be tribulation wherever the eye can see and misery over the earth and desolation in all countries."

Half of mankind, claimed the *Neues Europa* "secret," would be killed in a matter of hours.

While it's true that, in the first two secrets, Our Lady mentioned that certain nations would be *"annihilated"* if Russia was not converted, and while it's also true that visionaries at other apparitions would soon describe scenes similar to the *Neues Europa* "secret"—with boiling seas and Heaven-sent fire—many of those who have closely studied the circumstances surrounding Lucia's final secret believe that it pertains to matters of the Church, not natural disasters or wars. In other words, the final secret may entirely concern problems within Christianity and a nearly universal falling away from the faith. This chastisement, in short, would be a spiritual chastisement.

Was an apostasy—an abandonment of the Church— coming? Had it already started? Was that why Sister Lucia said it would be *"mas claro"*—clearer—after 1960?

The last message at Fatima, said Leiria Bishop Alberto Cosme do Amaral, "speaks neither of atomic bombs nor nuclear warheads, nor Pershing Missiles nor SS-20s. Its contents concern only our faith. To identify the secret with catastrophic announcements or with a nuclear holocaust is to deform the meaning of the message. The loss of faith of a continent is worse than the annihilation of a nation; and it is true that faith is continually diminishing in Europe."

Another Fatima authority, Father Joaquin Maria Alonso, added that "the content of the unpublished part of the secret does not refer to new wars or political upheavals, but to happenings of a religious and intra-Church character, which of their nature are still more grave."

Did it have to do with pastoral negligence? Or, as Father Alonso also wondered, deficiencies in the Church's upper hierarchy?

"There will also come a time of the hardest trials for the Church," said one part of the *Neues Europa* secret that some give credibility. "Cardinals will be against cardinals, and bishops against bishops. Satan will put himself in their midst. In Rome, also, there will be big changes. What is rotten will fall, and what will fall must not be maintained. The Church will be darkened and the world plunged into confusion...The time of times is coming and the end of all ends, if mankind is not converted and if this conversion does not come from above, from the directors of the world and the directors of the Church. But woe, woe if this conversion does not come about and if all remains as it is, nay, if all becomes even worse."

Lucia herself declared in 1957 that her mission was not to indicate physical punishments, which were sure to come if the world did not repent, but more importantly to indicate "the imminent danger we are in of losing our souls for all eternity if we remain obstinate in sin."

As Frére Michel, who conducted exhaustive reviews of letters and speeches delivered by those who *had* seen the secret, or had contact with Lucia, added, "The final secret of Our Lady predicts neither the end of the world nor atomic war: it concerns our faith...and more precisely the loss of this faith."

If so it bears similarities to those parts of the LaSalette messages that dealt with problems in the ministry as well as the general abandonment of faith. There would be a terrible crisis in the Church, said the Virgin of LaSalette in 1846, and civil governments would seek to abolish religious principles, making way for humanism and atheism—a prediction that seemed to anticipate the abolition of such public rituals as school prayer. Sinners would be introduced into religious orders, and members of religious orders, including bishops, would break away from the *"true religion."* The sins of those consecrated to God called out for *"vengeance."*

Was that why it has never been released? It pertained to matters of the Church? It had to do with internal strife over matters like those raised by the Second Vatican Council? Or was the meaning broader? Did it predict a great apostasy? A general falling away from the faith? Is that why Lucia had said it would become clearer during the sorry Sixties, when tens of millions replaced prayer with drugs or TV and God was suddenly declared "dead?" Did the secret depict the rise of agnosticism, the empty pews, the frightening decline in priestly vocations?

Was that what Pope John XXIII was referring to when he described the secret as predicting "very grave matters?"

There is certainly reason to believe that Lucia saw the struggle between Mary and Satan within the context of Church affairs—and that she was quite preoccupied with that warfare. The devil, she lamented, had focused much of his assault against the Rosary, which she described as the prayer, after the holy liturgy itself, "most apt for preserving the faith in souls."

Although evidence abounded that the Rosary is a most effective shield against demonic attack—an instrument, even, of profound deliverance—critics asserted that it is a repetitious prayer which overly glorifies Mary and diverts attention from Christ. They spoke as if the Mother of Jesus was some pagan goddess, and this itself, this strange new assertion that gained such currency during our century, was a diabolical calumny. One recites the Rosary while meditating on Jesus' time on earth. How could a meditation on the life and death of Christ Jesus, a meditation while repeating the Our Father, Hail Mary, and Gloria, suffer such a negative depiction but by the inspiration of Satan— who sought every means of halting the devotion?

"It is easy to recognize the ruse of the devil and his followers, who want to lead souls away from God by leading them away from prayer," Lucia later wrote. "The devil is very clever and looks for our weak points so as to attack us. If we are not diligent and attentive in obtaining strength from God, we will fall, for our times are very evil and we are very weak."

In Lucia's opinion the confusion inspired by attacks on the Rosary was part of the "diabolical disorientation" we've reported.

If that was the crux of the Third Secret—a loss of faith and deepening division among Christians, with serious misunderstandings and confusion—we have already seen how it took root in the Sixties, the decade during which Lucia wanted the secret revealed. We have also talked about how the churches emptied and atheism sprouted while the concert halls, featuring His Satanic Majesty, filled. Anyone who lived through those times knows that there were moments when it seemed like religion, all religion, would be permanently relegated to the dustbin of superstition.

Yet there was something about Lucia's comments that made it seem the secret also pertained to matters beyond the Church. If we remember, she had told Father Fuentes that the Virgin implied "we are living in the last times of the world." As Frére Michel points out, "she is not talking about the 'end of the world' properly speaking, which is identified with the return of Christ in glory for the last judgment. This indicates only that we are entering the last great period of the world's history, without being able to judge how long it will last."

Lucia herself never excluded the possibility of the secret

relating, however obliquely, to the return of Jesus. In fact, when pressed on the matter, Lucia made reference to the Book of Revelation, and *Revelation* implies the affairs not just of the Church but of the entire world. According to Frére Michel, Lucia even referred to specific passages from the *Apocalypse*—Chapters 8 and 13. If *Revelation* Chapter 8 is part of the secret, it is grave indeed. We've already gone over the essentials of this portion of the Apocalypse. It discusses the Lamb opening the seals: noises, thundering, and an earthquake; hail and fire, mingled with blood; a third of the vegetation burned up; a star falling from the heavens; the water turned bitter, to "wormwood;" the sea transformed into blood; a great mountain thrown into the ocean; and darkness, terrible darkness. "Woe, woe, woe to the inhabitants of the earth," says *Revelation* 8:13, with words similar to those of LaSalette.

As for *Revelation* Chapter 13, this is entitled "The Beast from the Sea." The beast, who is given power by the dragon, has ten horns and ten crowns and is empowered to make war with the saints and overcome them. He is given authority over every tribe, tongue, and nation. All the world follows this demonic manifestation, whose reign lasts for more than three years.

Then a *second* beast rises, this time from the land, and deceives the inhabitants of earth with great signs, including *fire* that comes down from Heaven. His number is 666.

Is the Third Secret, beyond mapping out problems in the Church, also, then, an allusion to the coming of war, geological disturbances, and the Anti-Christ? If so it is indeed an extension and affirmation of the secrets of LaSalette. Let's recall a few passages from that prophecy, in which Mary warned that God would one day strike *"in an unprecedented way."* At the first blow of God's thundering sword, said Mary, *"the mountains and all nature will tremble in terror, for the disorders and crimes of men have pierced the vault of the heavens."* She said the earth would become *"desert-like,"* that *"nature is asking for vengeance because of man, and she trembles with dread at what must happen to the earth stained with crime."* A forerunner of the Anti-Christ would arrive, warned the LaSalette apparition, *"with his troops gathered from several nations."* He would *"fight against the true Christ, the only Savior of the world. He will shed much blood and will want to annihilate the worship of God to make himself looked upon as God. The earth will be struck by calamities of all kinds (in addition to plague and famine, which will be widespread). There will be a series of wars until the last war, which will then be fought by the ten kings of the Anti-Christ, all of whom will have one and the same plan and will be the only rulers of the world."*

Were the ten kings the ten crowns of the beast?

In language strikingly reminiscent of Turzovka, Our Lady of LaSalette said that *"water and fire will give the earth's globe convulsions and terrible earthquakes which will swallow up mountains and cities."* Water and fire. Water, fire, and war. *"There will be bloody wars and famines and plagues and infectious diseases,"* said LaSalette. *"It will rain with a fearful hail... There will be thunderstorms which will shake cities, earthquakes which will swallow up countries... The fire of Heaven will fall and consume three cities... Here is the king of kings of darkness, here is the Beast with his subjects, calling himself savior of the world."*

CHAPTER 20

"Many Will Die"

Either the LaSalette visionaries, as well as those from places such as Turzovka and Garabandal, had simply served up rehashed biblical prophecy—plagiarizing *Revelation*—or parts of John's prophecy were about to be fulfilled.

In Russia, where few if any messages from foreign apparitions could penetrate, diminishing the possibility of copycats, there were similar apocalyptic visions. On February 12, 1970, in the deepest and darkest corner of the Soviet prison system, a bulgy-eyed skeleton of a man named Josyp Terelya was trying to get some sleep when his cell, number 21, was illumined by a brilliant light. Terelya, a Ukrainian Catholic activist who'd been jailed since the age of 19, at first thought that it might be the moon. But it wasn't quite like any lunar light and the moon didn't shine into Special Corpus Two of Vladimir Prison.

It was a living, breathing illumination next to his spare bunk, and Terelya wondered if he was hallucinating. In the light appeared a pleasant young woman with dark blue eyes. She wore a pale blue veil that was almost azure— summer clothing despite the cold dampness of the cell. In her right hand was a rosary. "She was like a huge jewel in the shimmering light," Terelya later told me. "Majestic beyond words. My mind was so directed that I accepted her without question. Softly but firmly she spoke to me."

The apparitional woman told Terelya that he had traversed four paths of his life and was beginning the fifth. She told him he must forgive the Communists even though they'd stolen his youth and ruined the Church he so dearly loved, the Catholic Church of Ukraine. Then she addressed issues of international interest:

"I have shed many tears. Many people are denying the future life. They are denying my Son. Around us is a very intense intolerance. Russia continues to remain in darkness and error and to spread hatred for Christ the King. Until people sincerely repent and accept the love of my Son, there will not be peace because peace comes only where there is justice."

According to Terelya she told him to look to the right, and there he saw a misty screen. "I saw fire," said Terelya. "I saw fire and tanks and I knew there would be war between Russia and some other country."

The woman vanished but the light remained about ten more minutes before it too disappeared, receding into a ball and then a point of light that blinked out, leaving him alone again in the dreariness of Vladimir prison.

Two years later, on February 12, 1972, Mary returned again to Terelya, this time to save his life. He'd been placed in a freeze cell and was so cold he couldn't even move his mouth. The Communists were trying to kill him for circulating Catholic literature and other "counter-revolutionary" propaganda.

Suddenly Terelya became aware of an intense flash in the cell, and while he couldn't open his eyes, he heard what sounded like footsteps. There was also an inexplicable feeling of warmth. Against his eyelids was what felt like the palm of a woman's hand. When the hand lifted Terelya was able to open his eyes, and there was the same apparition he'd seen in 1970, this time dressed as a Carpathian mountain woman, with a heavily plaited blue dress and a fringed kerchief. *"You called to me,"* she said. *"And I have come."*

I repeat this story from a book I helped Josyp write, *Witness* (Riehle Foundation), because it's one of the most dramatic Marian apparitions on record. So warm was the cell, and so noticeable was the light, that guards were later alerted and prison officials, accompanied by doctors and psychologists, struggled to rationalize what had happened—how Terelya had lived, and how the freeze cell had suddenly become so warm. They investigated the matter for months.

But before the guards saw the light and barged into the cell Terelya spoke with the apparitional woman for an extended period of time. And she elaborated on the messages about Russia and the world.

"She drew me into prophetic visions," said Terelya. "The wall melted and instead of the freeze cell I saw tremendous, real-life images materialize before my eyes."

While in 1970 such visions had been cloaked in a mist, this time they were as clear and real, noted Terelya, as on television. *"Now, look,"* she said, in a way that reminds us of Matous Lasuta in Turzovka and Ida's visions in Amsterdam.

Terelya saw a map, and parts of it were burning. It was Russia—fires erupting in Russia—and adjacent countries were also involved. Were these adjacent countries the republics such as Lithuania, Georgia, Byelorussia, and Ukraine—poor, tattered Ukraine—which subsequently declared their independence and formed their own nations?

There were flames in various parts of the world, and Terelya also saw a river that looked like the Amur, which separates eastern Russia from China. He saw tanks and fire throughout Siberia.

The tanks, said Terelya, were Chinese.

"Before the year 2000, Russia will be at war," claimed Terelya. "There will be an awful fiery war for 12 years. Many will die."

I don't know what to make of Terelya's personal prophecies, which often sound unlikely, and we can call to question whether he was hallucinating, since he *was* under the strain of prison and in this circumstance about to die. We should also keep in mind that the Ukraine is famous for its superstition and folklore. Josyp is an emotional man who doubtlessly has been affected by his prison years, and he often goes off on tangents or loses his temper, which doesn't aid his credibility.

But few who have spoken to him at length doubt that he has had deeply mystical experiences, and some of his prophecies, as will become apparent in later chapters, have actually materialized in suprising detail. Fewer still question his conviction and courage. In the U.S.S.R. the Church—Orthodox, Protestant, and Catholic alike—was all but a memory. Khrushchev had already implemented a huge anti-religious campaign, closing not only Catholic churches but also two-thirds of the Orthodox structures, and the Church wasn't faring much better under Leonid Brezhnev. All told perhaps as many as 50,000 churches were or would soon be closed, demolished, or converted to secular use among denominations in all the republics of the vast empire.

Those churches and religious institutions that remained open were closely watched by the KGB. The secret police went so far as to replace a metropolitan of the Orthodox church—an archbishop—with a man suspected as being an undercover KGB agent named Viryukin. The KGB was infiltrating the very helm of what was left of the Russian Church! Was this not a spectacular fulfillment of the seemingly outlandish prophecies at LaSalette, predicting demonic influence at the top of the hierarchy?

More remarkable still, in 1974 the religious division of the Latvian KGB put radioactive tracers on paper sold to Baptists so agents using helicopters equipped with sensors could track a hideout where the Baptists were printing New Testaments!

Clearly, the persecutions warned about for decades and centuries, the persecutions mentioned in the Gospels, the persecutions that for all we knew heralded the latter times, were not some ephemeral fear but were already being realized to a large and brutal extent in the Soviet Union.

So obvious was the satanic undertone of Communism (so obvious was it to Church leaders, at any rate) that Ukrainian Metropolitan Andrew Sheptytsky requested Rome to order prayers of exorcism.

Throughout the U.S.S.R. were reports of UFOs and perhaps these were, as *2 Thessalonians* 2:9 warns, "the work-

ing of Satan, with all power, signs, and lying wonders."
At the beginning of September in 1970 a fiery UFO was
spotted south of Lake Issyk-Kul in Kirghizia, while in
Romania and Bulgaria flying objects shaped like triangles
or pyramids had been spotted.

The U.S.S.R. was also in the midst of an occult revolution. An entire book was written about the psychic discoveries there, witches who could see blindfolded and
practitioners of psychokinesis. In 1978 I obtained a U.S.
Defense Intelligence Agency report that included the feats
of Nina Kulagina, who was filmed causing objects such
as matches, glasses, and cigarettes to skitter across kitchen
tables through sheer "power of the mind."

But the greatest manifestation of occult force was in the
religious persecutions conducted by the Soviets. Lucky
were those who lived through their prison sentences. Pastor Georgii Vins, executive secretary of Churches of the
Evangelical Christians and Baptists, was arrested in 1974
and sentenced to ten years of prison and internal exile,
while Borys Zdorovets, who had already served seven
years, was sentenced in 1973 to another three years of
severe regime camp and seven years of exile for organizing
a Baptist prayer meeting in the forest. In Stryi, Father
Bernard V. Mitskevych, a Roman Catholic, was arrested
in 1973 for fixing a dilapidated church building. As
Ukrainian Cardinal Josyf Slipyj put it, "The cross of persecution borne together has given rise to a true ecumenism
which, purified by uncompromising confession of the faith
and the blood of martyrs, reaches down to the most fundamental principle of the Gospel: to seek what is of God
and not what is of men. For Catholics and Orthodox, Baptists and other denominations suffer in the same way for
Christ's sake."

In the long-battered and always persecuted Ukraine,
Communists had threatened on several occasions to
destroy or at least shut down one of the most famous
monasteries in the world, the huge complex at Pochaiv.
It was left standing only because the Soviets feared international repercussions, or perhaps because there was a
heavenly intervention.

It wouldn't surprise many of those who know the history of Pochaiv if the intervention had indeed been supernatural. Located on a mountain several hours east of Lviv, Pochaiv was the site of an apparition way back in 1198. A monk saw a pillar of fire and when the flame died down Mary appeared. In 1240 the Tartars destroyed Pochaiv but it was rebuilt and a miraculous icon was brought there in 1559 from Greece. There was a healing spring and a footprint in rock said to have been left by the Virgin. In 1675 Pochaiv was threatened with destruction not only by the Tartars but also Turks, but as they began their mass assault the sky was said to have opened and Mary was seen in a huge illumination, accompanied by a throng of angels. She spread her mantle over the church and monastery.

While Pochaiv survived, the famous shrine at Zarvanystya (pronounced *zar-van-eetza*) had been closed and damaged, its miraculous icon hauled away when the Communists came rumbling into town. This icon dated to the 12th century and legend has it that a monk discovered the icon while he was hiding from the same Tartars. Sleeping near a brook, he had a dream in which the Mother of God appeared with another host of angels. When the monk awoke the next morning he noticed an odd bright light near the brook and approaching it discovered the radiant icon—a picture of Mary and the infant Jesus. So powerful was the experience that he had a chapel built there.

Now it was the Communists playing the part of Tartars. Despite a 24-hour watch by the villagers, Soviet militiamen had marched into Zarvanystya and carried off its precious icon. On the same day that the icon was confiscated, however, an absolutely identical image of Our Lady was seen reflected in a spring underneath the chapel.

"Everyone saw the face of the Madonna in the water, marked with the deepest sadness," noted one chronicler.

Eighty miles or so away, the little chapel at Hrushiw, where Mary appeared in 1914, was all but forgotten, boarded-up by the triumphant, arrogant Communists.

Deprived of religion, the peasants wandered by their

precious refuge, in permanent trauma.

Gone from view were the embroidered cloths and precious trellis.

Gone from view was Hrushiw's own miraculous icon.

KGB Perm Camp in Ukraine.

CHAPTER 21

Michael and the Dragon

These were incredible times, and the Blessed Virgin Mary was calling for Christian unity. Only a strong brotherhood would halt the assault. That message was repeated in a tremendous fashion from 1968 to 1973, when she appeared above a church called Saint Mary's in the Middle East. This time it was far from a Catholic setting. The church belonged to the Orthodox—the Coptic Orthodox—and was situated, of all places, in Zeitun, Egypt, a suburb of Cairo.

Mary, in the land of the pyramids. Mary, in a center of Islam! Mary, above a church that was located near the historic and holy area known as the Mataria—where she, Joseph, and the Christ Child had come to rest after fleeing into Egypt to escape the despot Herod.

It was an exceedingly important apparition, witnessed by at least a million Egyptians (more people than any known supernatural event in history) and yet the Western press, hostile to spirituality in general and Christianity in particular, all but totally ignored it. Hundreds of thousands saw her! Bishops saw her! Scholars and government leaders saw her!

But in America: a few blurbs in a newspaper or two, and

that was the end of it; they were too busy writing about hot pants, the Chicago Seven, and a political burglary.

This was the apparition predicted in Lithuania. It had also been foreseen back in 1918, when Mary appeared in a dream to a devout Egyptian named Khalil and told him to build a church on his land. If he did, she said, she'd return in fifty years to bless it.

Khalil did as he was told, and exactly five decades after, on April 2, 1968, at about 8:30 p.m., several woman pedestrians and a group of Moslem workmen, checking into a transit garage, noticed movement up on the dome of the church Khalil had built.

"While I was signing in the attendant's book at the garage, I heard some people shouting in the streets," recalled Farouk Mohammed Atwa. "I ran to them. I saw a lady dressed in white on the church dome at the north. I shouted to her, 'Be careful! Take care! Wait!'"

Atwa and his colleagues thought the woman, who was kneeling at the cross on top of the dome, was ready to commit suicide. "Lady, don't jump! Don't jump!" A rescue team was summoned but as the pedestrians watched they realized something very extraordinary about the woman. Despite the smooth, sloping dome, she was able to perfectly maintain her balance. When they called to her, the woman stood. As the newspaper *Watani* later reported, "They all saw her dressed as if in a bright gown of light in a view similar to that associated with the Virgin Mary. One of the women gave out a very long *'Za gha ruta'* (cry of joy). Involuntarily she then cried out, *'Setena Mariam,'* which means, 'Our Lady, Mary.' The woman began pleading for the Lady's blessings."

Atwa gawked at the ephemeral woman and pointed toward her with his finger, which was bandaged because of gangrene and scheduled to be amputated the next day. The woman, he thought to himself, resembled a nun. Suddenly a small flock of white doves—or at least lights that looked like doves—materialized out of thin air and hovered around Mary's head. They weren't really birds. They flitted instead of flying. And their wings didn't move.

The apparition faded after a few moments, leaving Atwa and the others speechless.

Who was it on the roof?

The next morning, when Atwa went to have his operation, the doctor was astonished to see that Atwa's finger had completely healed.

The apparition returned a week later and soon was seen up to three times a week, generally at night, on occasion visible for hours. Huge crowds formed around the church, growing larger with each subsequent evening as word spread and as Mary continued to appear to the throngs. Authorities searched a 15-mile radius for any electrical devices that might be used to project the image but soon they too were convinced that a transcendental event was occurring. Even former President Abdul Nasser found himself among the witnesses. "The official investigations have been carried out with the result that it has been considered an undeniable fact that the Blessed Virgin Mary has been appearing on Zeitun Church in a clear and bright luminous body seen by all present in front of the church, whether Christian or Moslem," said a report issued by the General Information and Complaints Department.

While most nights there were 5,000 to 10,000 people around St. Mary's, at times the crowds swelled to an estimated 250,000. The transit garage was removed to accommodate the masses, and for the first time in Egyptian history, Catholics, Orthodox, and Moslems prayed together in public. The Moslems chanted from the Koran. *"Mary, God has chosen thee. And purified thee; He has chosen thee. Above all women."*

Witnesses saw Mary emerge from a blinding globe of light, most frequently above the northeast dome, which was situated over the church's main altar. Sometimes she was only a vague image in the tall pattern of light; other times her face seemed huge, larger than life and resembling an Eastern icon. There were also occasions when she looked like a real-life human who just happened to be able to stroll atop the domes without the slightest loss of balance. Looking to the crowds, she would wave with an olive branch at the people and bow to them. Often she struck the pose of the Miraculous Medal, light streaming from her hands. Smaller lights flew past her like meteorites.

Especially unique to the Zeitun apparition was the incense. Huge billows of purplish-red smoke with a fragrant odor would rise from the church, as by a million censers. Sometimes Mary's likeness formed in the smoke.

"In every place incense shall be offered to My name (Mal. 11)."

Incense is also mentioned in the Book of Revelation—again, Chapter 8.

The main message seemed to be ecumenism, and included among the witnesses was the spokesman for the Protestant churches in Egypt. As they watched, the Virgin, in shimmering dress, with halo, often turned her head in the direction of Russia. The glow around her was golden, and silent lightning came from a cloud that blanketed the area.

Sometimes she appeared only once a week, sometimes for only minutes. Sometimes nothing at all happened, or the onlookers spotted just a vague light or falling star. But often her apparitions lasted for long periods.

The Orthodox patriarch, Kryollis VI, quickly formed a commission and one of its members, Bishop Athanasius of Beni Souieff, reported that on the night he personally went there, April 29: "Some clouds covered the dome, when something like fluorescent lamps began to illumine the sky. Suddenly there she was standing in full figure. I stood there and tried to distinguish the face and features. I can say there was something about the eyes and mouth, but I could not make out the features. That continued until about ten minutes before five. The apparition then began to grow fainter, little by little. The light gave way to a cloud, bright at first, then less and less bright until it disappeared."

On other occasions she arrived with a blinding explosion of light, in a long white robe and a veil of bluish-white. The stunned spectators could see her garments swaying in the warm night breeze. Sometimes clouds like thick fog would roll toward St. Mary's as if funneling through the streets and absorbing the fragrant incense. Members of the Church commission witnessed the apparition for eighty minutes, and on May 5, just a month after the main phenomena began, the patriarch announced that the apparitions were authentic and of God.

"In making this statement the Patriarchate declares with every faith, with deep joy, and with overflowing thanks to the heavenly grace, that the Virgin Mary, the Mother of Light, has appeared clearly and steadily on many different nights," said the official statement. "May God make this a sign of peace for the world."

To some she became known as the "Queen of Peace," to others the "Mother of Light." For a while the phenomena were nearly a nightly happening, but as time passed Mary appeared less frequently. Toward the end, in 1973, she came only to individuals. Her light show was over. The longest appearances I could find were the nights of May 4-5 and June 8-9, 1968, when, according to one devotional pamphlet, Mary was visible for about nine hours—from 8 p.m. until five in the morning! It took a while to soak in: week after week Moslems and Christians, believers and non-believers, Orthodox and Jews, were witness to an awesome spectacle in the middle of a densely populated suburb. It was on Egyptian TV. It filled columns in the local newspapers.

"It was a very personal blessing for everyone," says Pearl Zaki, a former Lutheran from Minnesota who had married an Egyptian professor and happened to be there for the apparitions. "Mary didn't speak in a way to give messages, but God put her there and people could see her. In the beginning everyone who was there could see her, from what I'm told, but later it was less clear and some could see her while others couldn't. It was an external vision. We were waiting and the heavens opened and in the light was the Virgin. It was as simple as that. How the light came, I can't explain it. It was like space opened up and she was there, on top of the big dome. She looked like a full-figured person in the light. When she moved you could see the back of her head. Sometimes she was in a halo of light, sometimes by herself. The second time I saw her—standing on the ground, gliding down from the church—her head bowed down and she moved into a wall and vanished."

Hundreds of apparitions. Some obvious, some barely perceptible. No direct messages but many symbols. Doves. Incense. An olive branch. There was a lot to mull over, including the fact that the Zeitun apparitions began just a few months after the Six-Day War, which had pitted Egypt, Syria, and Jordan against Israel. As foretold in the Bible, the Jews had recaptured Jerusalem during the brief conflict.

Coincidence? Two dissident Soviet scholars who heard about Zeitun worried about its implications. They wrote to the U.S.S.R. Congress that "the return to Jerusalem of the reborn Hebrew state was predicted by Jesus Christ as a sign 'of the end of the times of the pagans.'" Something extraordinary, they warned, "some extraordinary menace which encroaches upon humanity, must have induced the love of God, in a manner without precedent, to visit the sinful world."

Was Mary in Egypt because it too would one day play a part in the Great Chastisement? Would it again become the land of tribulation? And what of Jerusalem? It was already known that ten years before, Mary had appeared there, too—right in the Holy City where her Son was crucified. According to the Coptic Orthodox League of Jerusalem, Mary materialized in a room opposite the classrooms at the Coptic Orthodox patriarchate around mid-day on June 21, 1954, "fully dressed in white," like the later Zeitun apparition, and moving toward Saint Antonio's Church. Students cheered and followed her, gathering dirt and ash from where she stepped. News spread quickly, according to the league, and "thousands of people of all nationalities and sects rushed to the patriarchate to see the miracle. All responsible and official military and police personnel as well as heads of all churches in Jerusalem attended and authenticated her appearance."

Had that signaled a specific concern about Jerusalem and its role in the context of the Virgin's unfolding appearances elsewhere? In other words: were Jerusalem and Israel going to set the stage for the alleged Warning and Chastisement?

If so then the Egyptian apparitions also had great significance. Zeitun is too meaningful a place to have been chosen by coincidence—the place where Mary, Joseph, and Jesus had gone to escape persecution! Mary was returning to a route of escape and refuge, as if in fulfillment of *Reve-lation* 12:6: "Then the woman fled into the wilderness, where she has a place prepared by God . . ."

Revelation 12:6, we must remember, comes in the chapter about "a woman clothed with the sun."

Immediately after is 12:7—the war that breaks out between Michael and the dragon.

His Holiness, Pope Paul VI, with Bishop João
P. Venancio at Fatima with Sister Lucia at the
Fiftieth Anniversary celebration on May 13, 1967.

CHAPTER 22

The Road to Armageddon

Without uttering a word Mary was saying volumes about the Middle East and the future. There was even a connection to Fatima. For centuries Portugal had been occupied by the Moors, a Moslem tribe, and, in fact, Fatima itself had been *named* after the daughter of Mohammed. While overtly warning about Russia and how it would spread errors around the world, Mary also seemed to be nodding her head—barely noticeable—toward the Arab world, perhaps as both a clue to future secrets and as another plea for religious unity. The late Archbishop Fulton J. Sheen believed Mary wanted to be known as "Our Lady of Fatima" as a sign and a promise that the Moslems, who accept the virgin birth of Christ, would eventually accept His divinity as well. In the latter days, predicted Saint Louis Marie Grignon de Montfort, the Moslems would be converted to Christianity.

There were potential pieces of evidence everywhere. The Zeitun apparitions certainly seemed related to Mideast tensions. The phenomena began just after the Six Day War and ended immediately before the outbreak of another confrontation between Jews and Arabs, the Yom Kippur War.

Was the Middle East, as suspected for so long, going to set the stage for that great battle of the end times, the battle

171

of Armageddon? In culling through the books of Daniel, Ezekiel, and Revelation, the Baptist theologian John F. Walvoord came to the conclusion that events will evolve something like this:

A "Mediterranean dictator" will rise with tremendous charisma, taking control of the area around the Mediterranean and fitting the description of the beast of *Revelation.*

Walvoord argues that Russia's loss of power and formation of a "new world order" will clear the way for him.

The dictator will seize control of a new, ten-nation European confederacy, and for three and a half years—the 42 months mentioned in *Revelation* 13:5—will seduce the world by masquerading as a brilliant, indeed ingenious, savior and prince of peace. He will be especially adept at using the media. After hypnotizing much of the world with his political skills he will move more openly into the field of religion, convincing many that he is not just a great governmental leader but also possessed of such spiritual force that he should be looked upon as godlike, a virtual deity. Using satanic power—the energy given him by the dragon, Satan—he will show great wonders and ruthlessly crush believers of the true Christ.

The reign of this evil leader will bring down God's wrath—the Great Tribulation. It will consist of many of the images that we've encountered in visions: warlike effects and great disturbances that will affect nature. According to Walvoord, "one catastrophe after another will afflict the earth." There will be changes in climate and large-scale fire caused either by problems with the earth's orbit around the sun or by a nuclear incident.

These are included in *Revelation's* seven trumpets of disaster.

"Brief though it may be, the three and a half years of the Great Tribulation include the most awful times of catastrophe and destruction that the world has ever known," argues Walvoord. "The new world dictator's blasphemy, disregard of God, hatred of the people of God, and murder of countless believers in Christ will bring down the terrible Divine judgments described in *Revelation* 6-18. Catastrophe after catastrophe will follow as the Great Tribulation unfolds."

Here's where Egypt and Jerusalem come in. According to Walvoord's reading of the Bible, major segments of mankind will rebel against the wondrous world dictator, the Anti-Christ, and a great army from Africa, which would include Egypt, will attack from the south while Russia and other armies descend on the Holy Land from the north. While he will be able to drive back the first attempts at revolt, he will next encounter an advancing horde of 200 million (*Rev.* 9:16), which could only mean Chinese. Of course, other nations too will join in.

We are now at Armageddon. But in Walvoord's theory the world will be stopped in awe by a great shaking of the earth and the Second Coming of Jesus.

Such a scenario raises a new flock of questions: Was Mary saying the same thing and trying to tie together the loose ends? Was she warning about the Tribulation and Armageddon? Or as a few anti-Catholics would have it, was she herself a counterfeit perpetrated by Satan, trying to unite religions to make it easier for an anti-christ or *the* Anti-Christ to assume control and power?

We know only that appearing in Egypt meant something new, and that 'something' had to possess unusual significance. More people saw her here at Zeitun than at any other known site of apparition. Hundreds of thousands. Maybe millions. Mary, in the land of tribulation and chastisements!

I'll leave this particular topic for now with what Saint Nilus, an Egyptian martyr condemned to the quarries of Palestine and burned alive, prophesied in the fourth century. As the advent of the Anti-Christ drew near, said Nilus, the mind of man would be darkened with passions of the flesh. Ungodliness and iniquity would rule. There would be no respect for parents and love would become extinct. Immorality would rule supreme. Lying and greed would reach their zenith, as would fornication, adultery, homosexuality, theft, and homicide. Faith would dwindle to nothing. Then the Anti-Christ would assume control of the earth, according to Nilus, working his lying signs and wonders. He would give mankind evil wisdom to invent ways of speaking "one to another from one part of the earth to the other." Like birds men would fly in the sky and like fish penetrate the depths of the sea. Humanity would live in material comfort but that comfort itself would be a satanic deception.

Then God, seeing the destruction of the human race, would shorten the days of deception, lest even the elect be hoodwinked; and suddenly, said Nilus, a two-edged sword would appear, destroying those who followed the deceiver.

CHAPTER 23

'Those Who Will Be Saved'

"Many men in this world afflict the Lord," Mary told a nun, Sister Agnes Sasagawa. *"I desire souls to console Him to soften the anger of the Heavenly Father. I wish, with my Son, for souls who will by their suffering and their poverty enact reparation for the sinners and ingrates. In order that the world might know His anger, the Heavenly Father is preparing to inflict a great chastisement on all mankind."*
There it was, right to the point, Mary, speaking to Sister Agnes during a visit to the chapel of a convent on the hill of Yuzawadai in Akita, Japan. The Virgin was now in the Far East! It was 1973, a few short years since Zeitun, and the nun, who belonged to the Institute of the Handmaids of the Eucharist, was an infirm woman who'd often experienced visitations from angels. They spoke to her and even led her to the chapel, as the angel had led Catherine of Rue du Bac. Praying before the Blessed Sacrament, Sister Agnes would see smoke and flames envelope the altar, a smoke like the incense at Zeitun, or there would be brilliant rays of light, the light of Jesus, like the light that illuminated the chapel where Lucia prayed and received messages in Tuy.

There was also a statue on the premises, a statue fashioned after the "Our Lord of All Peoples" apparitions that

Ida witnessed in Amsterdam. Carved from wood, the Virgin stood on the globe with a cross behind her. On occasion a brilliant light would surround the statue, and blood flowed inexplicably from one of the hands.

A voice, a sweet indescribable voice, like a prayer, seemed to issue from Our Lady of All Peoples; Sister Agnes could hear it even though she was clinically deaf. On Saturday, October 13, Mary's voice spoke an important message:

"As I told you, if men do not repent and better themselves, the Father will inflict a terrible punishment on all of humanity. It will be a punishment greater than the Deluge, such as one will never have seen before. Fire will fall from the sky and will wipe out a great part of humanity, the good as well as the bad, sparing neither priests nor faithful. The survivors will find themselves so desolate that they will envy the dead. The only weapons which will remain for you will be the Rosary and the Sign left by my Son. Each day recite the prayers of the Rosary. With the Rosary, pray for the pope, the bishops, and the priests.

"The work of the devil will infiltrate even into the Church in such a way that one will see cardinals opposing cardinals, bishops against other bishops. The priests who venerate me will be scorned and opposed by their confreres. . . churches and altars sacked; the Church will be full of those who accept compromises and the demon will press many priests and consecrated souls to leave the service of the Lord.

"The demon will be especially implacable against souls consecrated to God. The thought of the loss of so many souls is the cause of my sadness. If sins increase in number and gravity, there will no longer be pardon for them.

"Pray very much the prayers of the Rosary. I alone am able still to save you from the calamities which approach. Those who place their confidence in me will be saved."

Besides exuding blood, the wood statue in Japan also shed tears on 101 occasions. Pay special attention to this apparition; it has been approved by the local bishop. And it made me take a second look at the "false" Third Secret of Fatima quoted by *Neues Europa* a decade before. Either Sister Agnes had read the "false" secret and was regurgitating it, or the secret wasn't false after all. For the *Neues Europa* message of 1963 used some of the very same words: a great punishment, worse than the Flood, cardinal against cardinal, "bishop against bishops," Satan in their very midst.

Was it Heaven sending us another notice, was the Holy Spirit indeed employing Mary as a special mediatrix for special times, until her Son came back, or was this a hoax and, worse, idolatry, the devil in a statue, trying to beguile a handful of devout nuns in a lonely convent?

I don't think the devil was in the statue. It sounded more like he was outside trying to keep Sister Agnes *away.* One evening, August 4, she was headed to pray when something or *someone* grabbed her shoulder and pulled her backward. When she turned the nun saw a horrible dark shadow leaning over her. She tried to free herself but the demon held her with such strength that all she could do was plead for the Virgin.

"Hail Mary! Guardian angel...Save me!"

An angel appeared, and the evil force immediately left.

Sister Agnes was caught in the huge cosmic battle, and evil was flourishing everywhere. The 1970s were a decade in which the devil would increasingly display physical manifestations. If you thought the 19th century was a cesspool of occultism, it was nothing compared to the 1970s, a decade in which books about parapsychology would crowd library shelves, movies turned increasingly demonic, millions sought spiritual bliss with yoga or other irreligious meditations, classes on mind control spread across America, psychic phenomena were demonstrated in our very classrooms, and even scientists, usually averse to *anything* spiritual, took an interest in the "spoon-bender" Uri Geller, who could also "read" minds and who, it is claimed, was once miraculously "teleported" from Manhattan to Ossining, New York—a distance of more than thirty miles. He was the new D. D. Home. Hundreds of others levitated tables, pushed glasses like the Russian Nina Kulagina, affected random event generators, or psychically healed.

Yet one more time the words of LaSalette, like an echo: People would be *"transported from one place to another"* by evil spirits and *"in all places there will be extraordinary wonders, because true faith has died and a false light shines on the world."* Our Lady said churches would be built to serve demons, and besides the most obvious example—the Church of Satan—there were also Spiritualist churches where "ministers" went into trances and, channeling, spoke to the deceased. It was the parapsychology of the 1970s that gave birth to the New Age movement.

"On occasion, the dead will take on the form of righteous souls, and be brought back to life, preaching another Gospel contrary to that of the true Jesus Christ."

At LaSalette, the Virgin also told Melanie that evil books would be abundant, but few would have predicted that they would all but completely chase Christian works from the bookstores. America's shelves were now teeming with astrology, palm reading, hypnotism, pyramid power, mediumship, earth worship, reincarnation, and Carlos Castaneda. Whole sections of bookstores were dedicated to the occult. As far as fiction, the bestsellers usually inspired fear of the devil (instead of fear of God) and usually concluded with dark winning over light. Anything with a "religious theme" was rejected by agents and editors.

While it is healthy to reserve a certain wariness of demonic forces, and it is certainly better to recognize evil than be blinded to its existence, we should never become obsessed about it or fearful, for that gives it all the more power. As Lucia once asked, "Is God less powerful than the devil? It is necessary to go forward without fear and without trepidation. God is with us, and He will be victorious."

Yet that's what all the books and movies were trying to do: engender shivers of fear. Or sensuality. Suddenly there wasn't a bestselling novel or popular movie that, under the pretense of art, didn't exhibit coarse dialogue or sexual acts—preferably acts of adultery. Those were the *conventional* movies. The X-rated ones, of course, were much worse. In the 1970s, marriage became a quaint relic. People

lived with each other. It was a clever way of legitimizing
fornication, and an equally good way of thumbing a nose
at the Church. All it took was a birth-control pill, and if
that didn't work, an abortion. In 1973, the year the statue
of Mary at Akita shed tears, the U.S. Supreme Court, in
what will one day be seen as the most sinister disorientation in the history of jurisprudence, legalized the killing
of the unborn child.

The floodgates were opened. Within twenty years 4,200
babies were being slaughtered every day in the U.S. alone,
while ten million a year were aborted in the Soviet Union,
and China enacted a policy of compulsory abortion for
women with too many children.

A great victory this was for the proteges of Margaret
Sanger. If illicit "lovemaking" was a mass sex ritual, what
was abortion but a massive and unrecognized blood ritual?
A new *holocaustein?* There was even a coven of witches
in California who, as I recall, used aborted fetuses for their
black masses.

No wonder statues of the Madonna, statues of Fatima and
the *Rosa Mystica,* cried blood and tears. The devil was
absolutely rampant, his infestations hidden in the psy-
chiatric jargon I mentioned before—"neurosis" and "multiple personality."

Neurosis was a first indicator; multiple personality was
outright possession.

Obsession, oppression, depression, possession.

The devil was patient when it came to taking control of
a personality.

At Fontanelle, Italy, a suburb of Montichiari where the
Rosa Mystica apparitions had recommenced, a possessed
woman near the miraculous well howlod like a dug and
spat at the statue of Our Lady. "You...You!" she
screamed. "Because of you and your...I am damned! Just
because of you!"

When a priest witnessing this blasphemy lifted his hand
and made a cross on the back of the woman, she reeled
around and sticking out her tongue began to laugh hide-
ously. "You are only a few by now," she said to the priest.
"Nobody will believe you any more, but they believe me!
We are legion. You've made it easy for us as in no other

age. It's your fault that we gained so much power! The youth are already ours! Thanks to you! We are legion! We are legion!"

There was plenty of *Rosa Mystica* phenomena after the initial 1947 apparitions. Although still disapproved by local authorities, Pierina Gilli had started seeing Mary again in 1966, and in the skies near Montichiari were supernatural symbols: A small group of pilgrims were witness to a dark area that formed in the afternoon sky and at the right side of it they saw a crown of 12 stars.

"By now we discerned in the distance a small faint disk which became noticeably bigger and came toward us," said one eyewitness. "It became red with beautiful shades and was then shaken to and fro like a lantern in a storm. It arrived at the edge of the clouds and seemed to fall down. Frightened, we all knelt down and called on God for help. I thought the Last Judgment had come and my one thought was that my children might be saved. The sun stopped falling. It started rolling around on its axis like a wheel of fire, first to the right, then to the left, throwing huge flames of fire to the earth. The whole sky was red, an indescribable and frightening sight."

At 9:15 p.m. on January 30, 1975, Pierina was given another apparition of the Blessed Mother. *"The times are getting worse and worse,"* said Mary. *"A terrible danger is threatening. The Church too is in great danger. Things will get so bad that people will think all is lost."*

Later in the same mesage: *"As you can observe for yourself, human pride has resulted in confusing those in the highest offices of the Church. They wish to drive me, the mother, out of the Holy Church and tear me from the children's hearts."*

The following year Mary continued, *"For hundreds of years I have come down time and time again, in many places throughout the world. If, since my Assumption into Heaven, I had not returned frequently to the earth to gather my children around me, the world without my motherly and loving intervention would to a great extent have grown cold and dry toward the Lord."*

CHAPTER 24

An Interior Force

Mary's role as advocate of Jesus, and at the same time as *our* advocate, staving off the punishments, was very much a theme in messages granted to a tough, rotund Italian priest, Father Stefano Gobbi, who was praying in a chapel built at the spot of the Fatima apparitions when he experienced "an interior force."

During the following twenty years Mary would speak regularly to Gobbi not in apparition but as a "voice" in his heart and consciousness. Such locutions are subject to great question, since a voice can easily be a trick of the subconscious, but there is a real power and coherence in certain of Father Gobbi's messages, and if he is truly hearing the Madonna's voice, we are indeed in those days immediately preceding the fulfillment of *Revelation*.

I say that because the voice Gobbi hears confirmed that atheism is the "red dragon" spoken about in the Apocalypse and that the current times do indeed present us with the confrontation between the woman clothed with the sun and the dragon.

Mary's messages are a battle cry and a disclosure of our spiritual state. Night had now fallen upon the world, she lamented to Gobbi. It was the time of Satan's greatest triumph. There were even people attacking the purity of

Jesus—*"such a horrible and satanic blasphemy that all Heaven is, as it were, dismayed and incredulous!* For that and other reasons, a *"tremendous and now inevitable storm"* was about to break upon humanity; the *"demon of corruption, the spirit of lust, has seduced all the nations of the world! Not one of them is any longer preserved."*

Our Blessed Mother also lamented that Satan would *"make every effort to remove me further from the hearts of my faithful, in order to keep me even more obscured in the Church. He is now engaging in the greatest battle against me, the decisive one, in which one of us two will be defeated forever."*

Because the demon of lust had *"contaminated everything,"* nothing could any longer hold back *"the hand of God's justice, which will soon be roused against Satan and his followers."* In ringing words nearly identical to those which would soon be spoken at Medjugorje, she declared that *"this is the hour of the power of darkness."*

Father Gobbi was 42 at the time of his first locution, a native of the lake region north of Milan, ordained in 1964 after working for a real estate and insurance company. His locutions were specifically addressed to priests whom Mary sought to form into a special cohort for her struggle. *"My angels have already begun the battle,"* she told Gobbi on October 24, 1975. *"At my order they are bringing these sons of mine together from all parts of the world."* It was the crucial role of these priests to *"live only for my Son Jesus, carrying out the Gospel to the letter,"* which would enable them to outweigh the faithless priests *"who no longer believe and yet they still remain in my Church, true wolves in sheep's clothing."*

Though Satan might rage against her cohort, she said he would not be able to touch a hair on the head of anyone consecrated to her.

The angels were being sent, she said, to keep them from the devil's snares.

But priests needed to pay more attention to the high praises of Christ and recital of the Rosary.

That was what Mary most desired, what she most persistently urged, what she always, always begged: *prayer.*

Prayer would defeat Satan. Prayer would help the Church through its Calvary. You couldn't pray too much. *"At Fatima, I pointed to my Immaculate Heart as a means for the salvation of all humanity,"* she said. *"I pointed out the way of return to God. But I was not listened to."* The First Saturday devotion never really caught on, and as for fasting and sacrifice, it was now even difficult to get Catholics to forsake meat on Fridays, let alone to fast on bread and water. On July 28, 1973, Mary told Gobbi that the time of apostasy—the great loss of faith emphasized at Fatima and mentioned long before by Paul in his Second Letter to the *Thessalonians*—was unfolding. Attendance at Mass continued to decrease, both in America and in strongholds such as France, where she'd made such an effort through apparitions, and priests were being seduced or discouraged by Satan. Enemies of the Church were seizing professorships in the seminaries and colleges, making them into what Pius X called "chairs of pestilence," and sin was justified and even extolled by academics, moviemakers, and the media. Laymen had stopped going to Confession and were told by certain religious sects that Confession, like devotion to Mary or the communion of saints, was an antiquated superstition. Many Christians had been made a "sport" by Satan, complained the Virgin, *"obscuring my place in the Church and obliterating me in souls!"*

Such an hour is the hour *"when the abomination of desolation is truly entering into the holy temple of God,"* said Mary. Even the pope, Paul VI, remarked in 1977 that after rereading the biblical accounts of the end times, "I attest that, at this time, some signs of this end are emerging." The Church had been forsaken, deprived of its inhabitants, desolated, the subject of apostasy, and as a result, mankind was approaching the brink of what Mary called *"the greatest storm in history."*

I was especially interested in Mary's use of the phrase *"abomination of desolation"* because the term is a codeword for the apocalypse and in *Thessalonians* comes before "the son of perdition," or Anti-Christ. "Let no one deceive you by any means, for that Day (the Second Coming) will not come unless the falling away comes first, and the man of sin is revealed, the son of perdition, who opposes and exalts himself above all that is called God or that is worshipped, so that he sits as God in the temple of God, showing himself that he is God," says Paul in *2 Thessalonians* 2:3-4. Precisely the same phrase is written in Chapter 12 of the Book of *Daniel,* which begins, "At that time Michael shall stand up, the great prince who stands watch over the sons of your people; and there shall be a time of trouble, such as never was since there was a nation." In *Matthew* (24:15) we're warned by Jesus Himself that *"when you see the 'abomination of desolation,' spoken of by Daniel the prophet, standing in the holy place, then let those who are in Judea flee to the mountains. Let him who is on the housetop not come down to take anything out of his house. And let him who is in the field not go back to get his clothes. . . For then there will be great tribulation, such as has not been since the beginning of the world until this time, no, nor ever shall be."*

When the abomination of desolation comes, when Satan finds himself in the temple itself, after the apostasy, the Great Chastisement cannot be far behind. Such times, repeated Mary, were fast approaching. She implied that the chastisements had already been postponed on at least two specific occasions because of the prayers of *"a few unknown souls,"* but more prayers were needed to stave off Divine retribution, and this, she explained, was the reason for her intervention, to form a cohort not just of priests but also, through the apparitions, of laymen who would pray to again put off or even shorten the hours of the coming trial. She was doing so out of love. She was acting as a mother. *"What is the rose if not the most beautiful symbol of love? That is why, from among all the flowers, I am called upon by you as the 'mystical rose.' "* Do not become uneasy, she said in 1975, *"if you find that movements inspired by souls to whom I have revealed myself are springing up here and there. On the contrary, all are part of my great plan."*

In 1975, on the Feast of the Immaculate Conception, the Virgin elaborated on her role, saying she'd been destined to *"give you my Son Jesus. And my Son Jesus has given*

*me to each one of you as your true mother... When, in
this last century, my adversary wanted to challenge me
and begin a struggle which, through the error of atheism,
would have seduced and deceived all humanity, from
Heaven I appeared upon earth as the Immaculate One to
comfort you, because it is, above all, my duty to fight and
to conquer the Evil One."*

He was the *"ancient serpent,"* the *"seducer and the
artificer of all evil,"* said Mary, and *"this is then the hour
when I will personally intervene."*

If Heaven's plan did not work, said Mary, then mankind
could shortly expect the great punishment. And if that
comes *"it will be only as an ultimate and solemn demand
for suffering to bring about the renewal of the world and
the salvation of so many poor children of mine."*

Recalling the words of Jesus in *Matthew* 24:15, Mary
made clear that the chastisement will indeed be a thing of
great and unexpected horror. It will be an *"upheaval,"* a
"purification," an hour of yet greater darkness, and it will
come, it seems, when Satan is celebrating a complete victory over the Church and the world. This is in basic agree-
ment with the theory set forth by Dr. Walvoord, who
believes the chastisements will arrive after the Anti-Christ
takes control. Mary told Gobbi that *"times of great
indescribable tribulation are in preparation. If men only
knew, perhaps they would repent!"*

The chastisements were put off during the 1950s, 1960s,
and now in the 1970s just as chastisement was delayed,
for a time, at Sodom and Gomorrah. But that couldn't go
on forever. The situation was fluid and subject to change,
and for that reason, Mary became piqued when there was
too much concentration on when the punishments would
begin. While the times for certain lesser events such as
"warnings" might be known beforehand, no one could
know, as Jesus says in *Matthew* 24:36, the day and hour
of the Great Tribulation, or at least the hour of His Second
Coming, which will be after the tribulation. *"Do not ask
me when this will take place, because I have already
initiated this triumph,"* Mary said to Gobbi on July 29,
1975, complaining the following September, *"There are
even some who, in my name, believe that they can indicate*

the dates of events and exact occurrences, and they forget that the hour and the moment are a secret hidden in the merciful fatherly Heart of God...And so I say to you, beloved sons, do not scrutinize the future; and thus neither anxiety nor discouragement will take hold of you! Live only in the present instant, in complete abandonment, close to my Immaculate Heart, the present instant which the love of the Heavenly Father puts at your disposal, my little children."

The point was that the focus should be on prayer and self-denial—*"nothing comes without pain,"* she said at Balestrino—because if we are right with God we have nothing to fear, while on the other hand, if we become obsessed with future punishments, we are in danger of distracting ourselves and falling into discouragement.

But no way was Mary telling us to ignore upcoming events, for she spoke at tremendous length on precisely this topic not only at the major apparitional sites but also to Gobbi. It was in fact one of Mary's major reasons for coming, to communicate the possibility of punishment, for if mankind knew what it was risking, she said, mankind might come back to its senses.

CHAPTER 25

Floods, Darkness, Fire

In apparitions throughout the 1970s Mary continued citing the future with increasing urgency.

Or at least that's what a number of mystics, stigmatists, and visionaries were saying. Time was short. Mary was showing visions of a barren desert strewn with corpses. The world was laid waste. *"The earth will tremble in a most frightful way and all humanity will stagger,"* she told Italian seer Elena Leonardi on April 1, 1976. *"An unforeseen fire will descend over the whole earth, and a great part of humanity will be destroyed."*

A "small Judgment" was on the way, according to another visionary, the Yugoslavian known simply as "Julka." The Lord had told her that he'd put off but had not abandoned His intention; the punishment would come suddenly.

A widow and mother of two children, Julka saw various stages of chastisement, starting with a strong warm wind and ten claps of thunder that would strike with such force they would shudder throughout the world. It was like a terrific hurricane. She also envisioned the air afire and a series of earthquakes.

"The whole atmosphere of the earth, from the ground to the sky, was a gigantic sheet of flame," according to Julka. After that the sun turned "red as blood" and a great

187

darkness rose like a mist. In that darkness came a bright
yellow light with Jesus enveloped in white clouds. *"As you
have seen, so it will be,"* He supposedly told Julka. *"I shall
come quickly and in splendor. All My creatures who survive the Great Tribulation will see Me."*

To four children in Heede, Germany, Jesus is said to have
proclaimed the same thing. *"Now I Myself am coming at
the last hour to warn and admonish mankind."* Here He
used the term "minor judgment" while in Putot-en-Auge,
France, a visionary named Madaleine who claimed to see
Christ and the archangel Michael referred to what was coming as "the Great Tribulation."

There were other indications that something big was up.
At Garabandal, forty pilgrims witnessed the sun spin in
1972. A couple years later, on June 12, 1974, a streak of
lightning was seen in Spain's northern sky, a strange red
band falling to the earth and changing into what looked
like a large, majestic "M."

Between 1947 and 1954 there had been at least a dozen
apparitional cases reported to Catholic authorities every
year, and since then, although no one has precise figures,
the number or at least the intensity seemed to be growing.
The 1970s *roared* spiritually. Mary was seeking to stem the
tide of chastisement, and had done so already.

"In the last times the Lord will especially spread the
renown of His mother," the Venerable Mary of Agreda
once said.

The power of Mary over the devils, added Saint Louis
de Montfort, would be "particularly outstanding in the last
period of time."

But the postponement of punishment couldn't wait forever. A mystic in Bonn, Germany, claimed in 1975 that
Christ spoke to her about abortion, referring to one clinic
as a *"pit of murder."* Meanwhile, in Pennsylvania a visionary saw endless rows of infantile faces.

"The Lord is not slack concerning His promise, as some
count slackness, but is longsuffering toward us, not willing
that any should perish but that all should come to repentance," says *2 Peter* 39:10. "But the day of the Lord will
come as a thief in the night, in which the heavens will pass
away with a great noise, and the elements will melt with

fervent heat; both the earth and the works that are in it will be burned up."

Fire! There was always talk of an inferno from the sky, along with the tremors, tidal waves, floods, poisoned water, blood-red seas, famines, wars, and revolutions. Mystics were especially keen on a trial by which mankind would be plunged into three days of horrifying and inexplicable darnkess.

According to Sister Faustina, Christ said, *"All light in the heavens will be extinguished, and there will be great darkness over the whole earth. Then the sign of the cross will be seen in the sky, and from the openings where the hands and the feet of the Savior were nailed will come forth great lights which will light up the earth for a period of time. This will take place shortly before the last day."*

The Blessed Mother told the Polish nun, *"I gave the Savior to the world. As for you, you have to speak to the world about His great Mercy and prepare the world for the Second Coming of Him Who will come, not as a merciful Savior, but as a just Judge. Oh, how terrible is that day! Determined is the day of Justice, the day of Divine Wrath. The angels tremble before it. Speak to souls about this great Mercy while it is still time for (granting) mercy. If you keep silent now, you will be answering for a great number of souls on that terrible day. Fear nothing. Be faithful to the end."*

Floods, darkness, fire—and also the Anti-Christ. In the 14th century, Saint John of the Cleft Rock quoted a prophecy to the effect that "twenty" centuries after the Incarnation of the Word, the Beast in its turn would become man. "About the year 2000 A.D., Anti-Christ will reveal himself to the world," said St. John.

Then there's the old English prophecy, found on a tombstone in Essex:

> When pictures look alive, with movements
> free,
> When ships like fish swim beneath the sea,
> When men outstripping birds can soar the
> sky,
> Then half the world deep drenched in blood
> shall die.

In the 1400s St. Francis of Paola predicted that a period would arrive with laxity in morals, ridicule of Christian simplicity, and a disregard for Church Canons. Those traits would spell "evil times, a century full of dangers and calamities." If what all the mystics were saying was remotely true, we are in for not just a rebuke but natural and artificial turmoil the likes of which are unrecorded in our history books—a tribulation worse even than anything invented by Hitler.

What was in preparation, Mary told Father Gobbi, *"is so extraordinary that its like has never happened since the creation of the world; that is why everything has already been predicted in the Bible."*

And what did the Old Testament say?

"A fire goes before Him, and burns up His enemies round about, His lightnings light the world; the earth sees and trembles," says *Psalms* 97:3-5.

"And it shall come to pass in all the land," says the Lord in *Zechariah* 13:8-9, *"that two-thirds in it shall be cut off and die, but one-third shall be left in it: I will bring one-third through the fire. . ."*

The tribulation by fire has its precedent in *Genesis* 19:24, where the Lord rains *"brimstone and fire"* on Sodom and Gomorrah.

Earthquakes? You can find those throughout the Old and New Testaments. "I looked when He opened the sixth seal," says *Revelation,* "and behold, there was a great earthquake; and the sun became black as sackcloth of hair, and the moon became like blood."

For behold, added Isaiah, "the Lord will come with fire. And with His chariots, like a whirlwind, to render His anger with fury, and His rebuke with flames of fire."

In *Zephaniah* we're warned that the "great day of the Lord" will be a day of wrath, a day of trouble and distress, "a day of darkness."

When God's Spirit is poured upon the earth, said the prophet Joel (2:28-31), sons and daughters would prophesy, young men would have visions, old men dreams. *"And I will show wonders in the heavens and in the earth: Blood and fire and pillars of smoke. The sun shall be turned into darkness, and the moon into blood, before the coming of the great and terrible day of the Lord."*

There were certainly signs in the skies, there were certainly a lot of "sons and daughters" prophesying, and at Zeitun there had been the requisite pillars of purplish-red smoke. The "two-thirds" mentioned by Zechariah was now turning up in modern predictions like those of the Czech woodcutter Matous Lasuta. Others varied slightly, estimating that three-quarters of the population would perish.

In fact, assuming it wasn't mere plagiarism, the similarities between ancient and current prophecies are rather startling. I'm especially taken by the prophecies that mention not just fire from the sky, but specifically a *blood-colored* luminosity. "The lightning will penetrate homes," said a stigmatist named Marie Julie Jahenny. "Red clouds like blood will cross the sky, the crash of thunder will shake the earth to its very core. The ocean will cast its foaming waves over the land, and the earth will be turned into a huge graveyard. The bodies of the wicked and of the righteous will cover the face of the earth. The famine that follows will be severe. All plantlife will be destroyed as well as three-fourths of the human race. This crisis will be sudden and the punishment will be worldwide."

To Mother Elena Aiello of Calabria, Italy, Our Blessed Mother was said to have forecast that *"clouds with lightning, flashes of fire in the sky, and a tempest of fire shall fall upon the world."*

The scourge, she said, would last roughly seventy hours.

While fire was the most frequent prophecy (mentioned too in the great message of LaSalette: *"fire will purge the earth"*), there was also the matter of darkness. At some point, presumedly before or after the flames, earth, according to dozens of visionaries, would be plunged into the three days of abnormal and petrifying darkness. Day would be as night. Night would be like a coal mine. "Nothing will be visible, and the air will be laden with pestilence which will claim mainly, but not only, the enemies of religion," said Blessed Anna Maria Taigi.

The darkness was a common theme with visionaries.

"During a darkness lasting three days the people given to evil will perish so that only one fourth of mankind will survive," said Sister Mary of Jesus Crucified, implying that the absence of light was part of the Chastisement. It would be *"the darkest hour,"* and suffering and anguish *"such as never before experienced"* were *"about to overtake mankind,"* Our Lady said to Sister Mildred.

The darkness, according to a nun in France known as "the Ecstatic of Tours," would come toward the end of events, after the earthquakes. In a revelation to Jeanne le Royer, Christ had supposedly indicated that there were two hours left before the sun would set for mankind—meaning two centuries.

That was in the 1700s.

Like Julka, mystics saw Jesus arriving to break the power of anti-christ and end the chastisements. But before His Second Coming, said Mary of Agreda, who lived in the 1600s, the Blessed Virgin Mary, more than ever, would shine in mercy, might, and grace in order to bring unbelievers into the faith. "The power of Mary in the latter days," she predicted, "will be very conspicuous."

CHAPTER 26

An Hour of Clemency

On the afternoon of October 12, 1975, a severely wounded Vietnamese soldier named Stephen Ho Ngoc Ahn, crippled and unable to talk, was silently reciting the Rosary when Mary appeared and said, *"Tomorrow is the anniversary of my appearance at Fatima. I will cure you so that you can walk and talk again."*

Ahn had been tortured by the Viet Cong, who not only beat him but administered injections causing total disability. For two months after the apparition he remained as he had been for years, paralyzed.

But Our Lady came to him again on December 21, and this time she addressed him by name and told Ahn to wheel himself into the yard so she could give him a sign. When he did the young soldier spotted a huge comet in the sky. It was like an immense star moving with majestic determination across the Asian skies, and Mary was in front of it, her crown shining with light.

The next day Ahn brought his foster sister to the yard, and she too saw the comet.

Just days later, on Christmas, Mary appeared to Ahn a third time while his family was at midnight Mass. She explained why he was still a cripple. *"On October 12, in order to test your faith, I promised to heal you, but although I did not do so, you always believed in me. Now, on December 28, at nine in the morning, I will make you walk and speak again at the Binh Loi Fatima Center. You must go there the evening before and stay with me all night."*

Although Ahn obtained permission from the center's director to pray through the night, a nun, lacking any written approval, refused to allow Ahn in, locking the doors. Despite that rebuttal Ahn started to pray the Rosary and at the end of the first decade he suddenly found himself inside the locked gates, surrounded by a blaze of light. In the light was Mary. Communist soldiers who were on guard outside the shrine saw this illumination and came running. It reminded me of the Josyp Terelya account at Vladimir Prison. But when the guards got to Ahn the light dimmed and only he could see it.

"Stephen, I am giving you these rosary beads," said Mary. *"Take them and try to say the Rosary and repent of your sins. Tomorrow at 9 a.m. I will heal you and you will walk and speak again. Are you happy to accept all the sufferings that will come to you because of it?"*

"Mother," Ahn replied on paper. "I am prepared to accept all the suffering from whatever source it comes if I will be able to walk and talk again so that the world will recognize your power."

The Blessed Virgin began to speak to Ahn about the neglect of Christ's Sacred Heart. *"These devotions have been almost forgotten, even by the religious,"* the apparition said. *"People no longer remember God and their Blessed Mother, Mary. If they don't repent of their sins and say the Rosary, the world will suffer great disasters. Children too will be innocent victims of these disasters."*

Soon the bells announcing five a.m. were ringing. Mary was gone and Ahn, to his puzzlement, found himself back outside the gates and dressed in the clean clothes he'd brought to wear at 9 a.m. Mass. After Communion he went to take a drink of water from a tank near Mary's statue, as she'd instructed him, when suddenly Mary appeared yet again and handed him the glass of water.

Ahn drank it with a fervid desire for healing and as Our Lady left he struggled to touch her clothes. "Mother!

Mother!'' he cried—speaking his first words in five years.

A few minutes later he was able to use his legs. With understandable elation he stood up and moved from his wheelchair.

On May 14, 1976, during another appearance, Mary repeated the message of Fatima. People must quickly turn to the Rosary, she said, and repent of their sins. Unless they accepted that message, a great disaster would befall the world such as had never been seen before. The following July the Virgin told Ahn she was especially sad about the moral state of priests and religious.

Unless sins were repented there would be an *"imminent disaster"* that would *"destroy mankind."*

As the 1970s, the "Me" decade, reached its culmination, the warnings from Mary were starting to sound shriller. A period of clemency, it seems, was again about to end.

To know why, we had only to look at America. Never before had there been such greed and self-centeredness. Wall Street was gearing up for the great splurge of junk bonds and corporate takeovers, which meant a quick buck for executives; and in industrial regions of the United States, corporations seeking other ways to fatten their profits dumped highly toxic pollutants anywhere that was cheap and convenient, to such an extent that only one major river system in the contiguous states—the Suwannee—was free of chlorinated hydrocarbons.

In Louisiana, near a contaminated bayou called Devil's Swamp, cattle were dying by the droves, while at other dumps black sludge seeped into basements like something out of the *Amityville Horror.*

Our religious tradition, the tradition upon which America was founded, was also being poisoned. Instead of mainline Christianity, young people sought spirituality in spontaneous and unaffiliated "churches." Brimming with spiritual pride, dynamic preachers and televangelists attacked the more established religions, repudiating the Virgin along with the Holy Sacraments.

Other young Christians sought answers in what became known as the "human potential movement." Psychology was reaching a fervor, and so was the influence of hypnosis, Eastern meditation, mental programming, and alpha training. While it was now illegal to pray or read the Bible at public schools, it *was* okay to lecture students on ESP and other occult phenomena.

The western hemisphere was being swept, to put it another way, by a surge of witchcraft and paganism. It wasn't precisely the type of paganism they had in ancient Greece, but it was paganism nonetheless. Television became our Coliseum. The youth were looking *inward* for the answers instead of *upward*. We talked to plants. We sent telepathic waves. We searched for the vibes of success. Women now competed with men, and the distinction between sexes blurred. Our trends and lifestyles were shaped by a small cadre of nonbelievers who wrote the scripts for prime-time television.

The television set became the great idol of our century, and our addiction to it made us superficial and deviant. Materialism dominated as never before. An epidemic of pride and egoism infected all segments of society. We were now too busy for anything but our careers; we were certainly too busy and important, too sophisticated, to get on our knees and pray.

So consumed was American society with itself, and so unwilling to make personal sacrifice, that the divorce and abortion rates exploded. An unborn child was unceremoniously "terminated" if it stood in the way of a career or was otherwise the least bit inconvenient.

Mary was coming because of our horrible, self-destructive pride. She needed prayer offerings. She needed humble people like Stephen Ho Ngoc Ahn to stop the chastisements. Victim souls. Prayer warriors. With each decade the major punishments loomed ever closer; the "star of the abyss" was waging war with the mark of Jesus; and the Holy Spirit's response was to step up the frequency of Mary's motherly and humbling appearances. *"What happens to the world depends upon those who live in it,"* she said in the Our Lady of America messages. *"There must be much more good than evil in order to prevent the holocaust that is so near approaching."*

On November 23, 1975, Pierina Gilli, the *Rosa Mystica* visionary, said the Virgin came to her and explained that *"the world ought to have been visited by a great judgment because of its hardening of sin"* but had been spared by prayers and other spiritual offerings. Once more, however, the cup was filling. Blessed Anna Taigi saw "black airships traversing the skies and covering the earth with fire and darkness."

Messages. More messages. Volumes! The trickle that had begun in 1830 and reached the strength of a stream at Fatima was now breaking into whitewater. As the time got closer, Heaven was sending more detailed prophecies just as God had sent more details to the Jews (see *Jeremiah*) before the Babylonian captivity.

There were any number of spectacular visions. Mystics saw demons flying in the night air, shouting blasphemies, or angels preparing the plagues. They saw terrifyingly huge tornadoes and households that shook and trembled during a hurricane. The Great Chastisement would happen, predicted the Ecstatic of Tours, "when everyone believes that peace is assured, when everyone least expects it."

According to the unusual impressions of a 19th century seer, Marie de la Faudaus, only blessed candles would give light during this horrible darkness. "Lightning will penetrate your houses, but it will not put out the blessed candles," she believed. "Neither wind nor storm nor earthquake will extinguish them."

What was it that could cause hurricanes and earth tremors, that could plunge the world into utter darkness?

Would the earth leave its orbit?

Was it nuclear "winter"? Symbolism?

Or was it all morbid fantasy?

The Vatican wasn't sure and maintained a discreet silence. These were complex times, and matters were only to grow all the more complicated. Along with all the other Christian denominations, Catholicism remained in a state of high confusion, shellshocked by what Pius X had called "the disastrous conditions of humanity at the present hour."

Yes, this was indeed an apostasy, perhaps the Great Apostasy. Mankind, in a mood of fantastic arrogance, continued to usurp the place of Creator. *We* controlled life and death. *We*, through medical technology, could perform miraculous cures. *We* knew the foundations of the universe. *We* could see into the next galaxy.

The arrogance of godless mankind, the "abomination of desolation," was already sitting in the sanctuary.

An abomination of desolation: when we see that, Jesus had warned (*Matthew* 24:15), we should flee to the mountains.

The falling away from faith could be called both an abomination and apostasy. And false prophets. Christ likewise said that before the Great Tribulation *"false christs and false prophets will rise and show great signs and wonders."*

There were false prophets in science and there were false prophets on college campuses and there were false prophets espousing both feminism and the playboy philosophy.

Were the gurus and yogis, the imams and Eastern mystics, the ayatollahs capturing world attention: were they too false prophets?

Demonic forces were taking over and working marvels. In India a wonderworker named Sai Baba materialized holy ash in his hands—made it appear out of nowhere—and promoted himself as a new messiah. Hundreds of thousands followed him, while others formed fanatical religious cults that brainwashed their members. In the emerging New Age movement, channelers were getting messages from entities like "Lord Maitreya," who advertised himself as the Second Coming.

This isn't some ridiculous game. This is demonism. The New Age movement is without God. *Man* becomes his own divinity, and that's heresy and apostasy.

If you really want to know the truth, the roots of the New Age harken back to Egyptian paganism and Masonic philosophies like those of the Golden Dawn. It's rooted in the principles of Aleister Crowley, the "Beast." Their strategy? Create a world government and a world religion based on principles of the New Age, and presto: the stage is set for a false messiah or the Anti-Christ. As Pius X said, apostasy is "the sign announcing the beginning of the last times, and that the Son of Perdition spoken of by the apostle might already be living here on earth."

CHAPTER 27

People of Light

In the hills overlooking Caracas, Venezuela, a matronly aristocrat, Maria Esperanza, could see not only the flickering metropolis but also the lights, the spiritual lights, of the earth. She is a mystic and visionary, one of the greatest alive (as phenomenal as anyone since Padre Pio), and she too saw potentially grave events in the future, especially if Russia didn't convert back to Christianity.

The Virgin had been in communication with Maria since her youth but was now coming in a new and special way. She called herself *"Mary, Reconciler of all Peoples and Nations,"* and she was trying to avoid clashes between the East and the West.

There were going to be difficult times in the Soviet Union, between the government and its people, she told Maria, and the world needed to consolidate itself through moral values. Sometime around 1992 and 1993 would begin the "time of times," the apocalyptic times, and "justice in the world" would begin.

It wasn't clear how such times were going to begin nor how long it will take "the time of times" to develop. It might be months or years before it is appreciated. Esperanza was tight with detail, uninterested in gossip, concentrating instead on the need for prayer and conversion. But in the twinkle of her wondrous brown eyes one could

199

nearly see the reflection of future trials—not the end of the world, not necessarily a world war, for Maria wasn't nearly as pessimistic as many visionaries, but difficult times, yes. She foresaw a poorly intentioned leader who would help make matters more difficult, and perhaps that leader would come to power in Russia, which she warned might act one day "in a surprise way."

Esperanza! One felt nearly as in song after meeting with Maria, her vigor contagious, her humility charming, her generosity pouring like clear water, a love that swept over her husband, her seven children, and anyone who came within range of her smile.

There were also the phenomena, the truly unfathomable phenomena. She was a stigmatist, suffering the wounds of Christ on Good Friday; she was known as a "reader of souls," like Pio himself; she was seen to transfigure during prayer, or to levitate during Mass; she possessed the perfumelike odor of sanctity; and many of her friends, professional types not given to nonsense, insisted that there had been instances when Maria bilocated, or seemed to be two places at once. She would be home, in plain sight of her family; at the same time she was seen at the home of a friend or acquaintance miles away.

Born in 1928, Maria had displayed tendencies toward the mystical since childhood. At age 12 she'd contracted bronchial pneumonia and despite a pessimistic prognosis made a miraculous recovery. Intent on a religious life, she'd joined a Franciscan order, but at the age of 26 Maria experienced an apparition of Saint Thérése of Lisieux, "the Little Flower," who told Maria her vocation would not be as a nun but as a wife and mother.

Two years later, on December 8, she was married in the chapel of the Immaculate Conception in St. Peter's Basilica.

Her husband, Geo, is Italian, and to speak with him today is to encounter an equally effervescent soul who has never quite gotten over the range of his wife's experiences. For starters, she had been told the very date, November 1, 1955, on which she would meet him, and since their marriage Geo had learned to accept the inexplicable: apparitions, prophecies, healings, and messages.

The stigmata had come to Maria as a young woman, while praying at Mass, and it was a gift straight from Heaven, a gift of suffering. "I was talking to Our Lady, and when I raised my eyes I saw Saint Thérése the Little Flower and she threw a rose to me," recalls Maria. "I was kneeling and jumped up to catch it, but I felt something stinging and saw blood coming out of my hand."

For years afterward Esperanza suffered Christ's wounds in her hands, feet, and side on Good Friday, the holes sizeable and daunting, observed even by skeptical physicians, who saw the wounds develop as she said the Stations of the Cross. More astonishing still, and most difficult to believe, were testimonies to the effect that on 14 occasions a rose—an actual flower, stem and all—had broken through the skin of her bosom and unfolded gloriously from her body.

If she was duping her friends she was also duping the local bishop. "Two doctors sent testimony saying a rose came out of her skin," said Bishop Pio Bello Ricardo of Los Teques. "There was a hole in the skin and a bruise and great suffering. The two physicians thought she was having a heart attack."

There were elements to Maria's mysticism that raised questions, as always there are questions, about where the phenomena were coming from. When relating messages from the Virgin, Maria's voice changed to one that was lower and sweeter, a "very curious" phenomenon, in the bishop's view, and a bit like channeling or spiritism, which infects many parts of South America.

But Pio Ricardo Bello, after personally interviewing two hundred people, including psychiatrists, psychologists, engineers, and lawyers who had experiences around Esperanza, was convinced not only in the supernatural authenticity but that the manifestations were surely "good, not evil."

The only "abnormality" the bishop found was a profound spirit of prayer—"very, very profound." Indeed, Maria had a chapel in her home, with a pew and altar. Her son-in-law Juan Carlos told me of coming downstairs in the middle of the night and seeing Maria transfigured, with a light around her. He also witnessed another phenomenon that occurred on occasion to Maria, the sudden and mysterious materialization of the Communion Host on her tongue, as if administered by Jesus or an unseen angel.

Dozens of witnesses talked about the bilocations. So physically inexplicable was this—being in two places at once!—that I wondered: Was this her guardian angel, taking on Maria's appearance to let people know that Maria was praying for them?

The same questions had dogged those attempting to understand Padre Pio, who Maria met under typically unusual circumstances. As the story goes, Pio had told some people that a young woman from Venezuela would be coming, and around that time Maria did indeed travel to San Giovanni Rotundo with some of Pio's "spiritual children." When the great priest came out of the confessional and saw her, he blurted, "Ah, Esperanza!" Recalls Geo: "We visited Pio many times. He called to her spiritually. One night we were in Rome and he told Maria he was waiting for her at San Giovanni Rotundo. It was ten at night but Maria told me to get a schedule for the trains."

During her conversations with Pio she told the Capuchin monk she had been given a dream about a little piece of holy land where the Blessed Virgin Mary would come, a parcel of property which would serve as a center of pilgrimage, especially for youth. She'd seen it in detail, and while she had no idea precisely where it was, Maria knew what it would look like. She saw farm equipment and a stream.

"From 1957 until 1974 we searched for this land in all of Venezuela," says Geo. "In 1974, in February, we heard about a farm and decided, let's see it. We called the guy in March and went to see it. When we arrived Maria said, 'We have to buy this farm.' In June we signed the contract. We purchased the land with Jesus Andrew, an engineer, and Jose Castellano, an attorney. We were glad to accomplish this as we had dreamt of this for many years. It corresponded exactly with a vision my wife had been given when she was a very young girl."

The land was about an hour and a half from Caracas, just beyond the last of the urban sprawl, in an impoverished area of aluminum shanties, banana farms, and tropical mountains. The area is known as Finca Betania, and it is 12 miles from the village of Cua, in the region of a river called Tuy—ironically the same name as the town in Spain where Fatima visionary Lucia dos Santos experienced visions.

Finca Betania is at the bottom of one of the small mountains, clouds hovering close to the forest, an old sugar mill setting on the "holy land." Although it wasn't apparent at first, there was a stream and waterfall on the property—and next to the cascade, a Lourdes grotto. "At first we didn't see the grotto but when we bought the land in 1974 we found it there hidden," recalls Geo. "It filled us with great surprise. We carved a little flatland out of the mountain."

That clearing became their sanctuary. They grew accustomed to visiting the farm on Saturdays, praying and taking care of the livestock. Then they went to Italy to care for Geo's ailing mother. After spending more than a year abroad, Maria said the Virgin was calling her to return to Caracas. *"You shall see me on the land you purchased,"* Mary told her.

It happened on March 25, 1976, the feast of the Annunciation. Maria, Geo, and a couple dozen friends were meditating on the life of Christ and reciting the Rosary in front of the grotto when suddenly the Virgin appeared. *"My child, I am giving you a piece of Heaven,"* Mary said. *"Lourdes. . . Betania in Venezuela. It is a place for everyone, not only Catholics. It is for all because there should be no class distinctions of nations and religions. This is your mother who gives herself as in Lourdes, Fatima, El Pilar in Zaragoza, Guanare* (a site of apparitions in Venezuela many decades before), *and as in so many other places where I still offer myself."*

It wasn't clear, due to problems in translation, if that message came before or after the first Betania apparition. The point is that Mary was beginning a mission to a special site in Venezuela, a site that would not only meet with the bishop's approval but would present the few foreign pilgrims who journeyed there a sweet tranquility such as could not be felt except at the most extraordinary sites like Medjugorje.

The grace was nearly palpable. According to Bishop Ricardo, Maria continued to experience apparitions during 1976 and the following two years. "Besides her, very few people have declared to have seen the apparition during that period; yet I received testimonies of people who had witnessed phenomena such as fog that comes away from the hill, brilliant light, intense fragrance of flowers, songs of an invisible choir, playing of lights, and movements with the sun."

A pious group was formed to pray at Betania on weekends and feast days. In 1984 the apparitions would reach a highwater mark, with dozens of others, and after that *hundreds* of others, seeing Mary. But that happened much later. What's important just now are the messages. Humanity, she told Maria Esperanza, was deteriorating due to *"the infiltrations of demagoguery, falseness, and social injustice."* It was important to save all God's children from *"the mocking and ridicule of the pharisees of these apocalyptic times."*

That meant brotherhood, Christian brotherhood, a reconciliation between all peoples. Accomplishing that would take silent meditation, prayer, and contemplation. The Hell that had risen within the human race *"has to be extinguished,"* Mary told Esperanza. Economics and material possessions had turned mankind cold and egotistical.

"Little children," she said, *"today, in these times, He, with me, wishes to renew consciences because mankind is currently abusing the graces received and is moving toward perdition, and if there is no change and improvement of life, he will succumb under fire, war, and death. We want to stop the evil that suffocates you; the evil of rebellion; and overcome the darkness of oppression by the enemy. This is why, again, in this century, my Divine Son arises, so that you will follow his steps, as a shepherd of souls, and obtain the alliance of peace among people, and preserve your hearts as clean temples."*

She also came *"to ease the burden of my sons and priests. It is they who in answer to my call will have to make my place chosen for these times of great calamities."*

I was beginning to lose count of the visionaries who have warned of "fire." Should we take it literally? The bishop

was of the opinion that visions from people such as Esperanza could be allegorical—that for instance an earthquake
"can be a real message but a symbolic vision of terrible
things surrounding the world." When I visited with her,
Maria declared simply that "things are going to happen"
in the near future. Each person, in her view, was a "being
of light," and as such obligated to fight for Christ. "The
power of God is so great that He has sent His own mother
to defy Satan." If we're filled with "spiritual health," she
said, the devil will flee.

We are beginning to live the chastisements now, she
said, and Maria foresaw "a very difficult and serious time"
when there will be "a revolution in general that will make
people rise up against injustice." There were many anti-
christs, she said; one was Saddam Hussein. An anti-christ
was always rooted in pride. The situation in the world was
going to improve, but not before certain trials. "The yellow
races will stand up, and that's very serious and I'm very
afraid, because they would like to take over the world,"
claimed Maria. "It's a very difficult time for humanity, but
man will survive. The justice is coming. A very hard
moment will come very soon—1992, 1993, 1994—1994,"
she told me. "But it will make us better people."

After that, said Maria, "Jesus will have a great surprise."
He is living "with His mother among us. We will see Him
in glory with rays of light. He will brighten the whole
world with His rays. The last messages are beautiful—it's
incredible the way He will come in glory."

CHAPTER 28

"Here Is the Remedy"

The great eruption of apparitions, the most spectacular since the Pentecost, was about to begin. Was it a time for optimism or pessimism?

It was certainly a time of supreme spiritual turbulence.

Not even the popes could agree on what was developing. While Pius XII, the pope who had witnessed the sun miracle, believed "the present hour is a dread phase foretold by Christ" and that darkness was "about to fall on the world," his successor, John XXIII, all but totally contradicted that viewpoint at the opening of the Second Vatican Council in 1962. "We feel we must disagree with those prophets of gloom, who are always forecasting disaster, as though the end of the world was at hand," he declared. "In the present order of things, Divine Providence is leading us to a new order of human relations which, by men's own efforts and even beyond their very expectations, are directed toward the fulfillment of God's superior and inscrutable designs."

This was not to say John didn't fear chastisements. Like Esperanza and Sister Elena Aiello, he felt Mary's mission was to suspend or lighten the punishments, and suspension implied only a postponement. But that didn't mean every dreadful prophecy should be accepted. Frightful events including the end of the world had been rumored

206

throughout history; it was the stuff of morbid and idle minds. In Fatima's own diocese the bishop railed against "the prophets of imaginary world catastrophes."

That was all well and good. It was refreshing to hear a measured tone. I too feel uncomfortable with melodramatic and implausible predictions. But if nothing else there was something bad afoot in the Church. There was something apocalyptic about our loss of belief. Only a faithful remnant of worshippers was left as whole portions of the Church in Europe, the United States, and Latin America strayed into psychology, the occult, and materialism. Bishops disagreed about divorce and contraceptives, and just such dissension was supposed to be contained in the Third Secret.

Pope Paul VI decided not to reveal the secret, and his successor, John Paul I, didn't have enough time, dying after only 33 days as Pontiff. That brought us to the current pope, the great John Paul II, and he too felt that the envelope containing Lucia's hand-written notes was best left in a sealed box. The reason, according to Joseph Cardinal Ratzinger, prefect of the Sacred Congregation for the Doctrine of the Faith, was because "it adds nothing to what a Christian must already know from revelation: a radical call to conversion, the absolute gravity of history, dangers threatening the faith and life of the Christian, and therefore the world."

But both Ratzinger and John Paul II hinted that the secret pertained to more than just internal religious affairs, more than a loss of faith—that it was relevant, in fact, to the "last times." Rumor was that the pope even indicated a specific passage of *Revelation:* Chapter 12.

If we are in that period of events, then we indeed are in the midst of an historical confrontation between good and evil. For Chapter 12 of *Revelation,* like the last part of the Book of *Daniel,* is the apocalyptical clash between Michael and Satan, who is cast out of Heaven and onto the earth with his host of evil angels, deceiving mankind and full of wrath, knowing they have only "a short time" (*Revelation* 12:12).

Was there not an outbreak of evil in the world? Did it not seem like devils had been thrown into our midst? Were we not in an era of tremendous and largely unseen demonic infestation? Was the intensity not increasing? And weren't we going through what Pope Leo had warned about in 1884?

The furies were everywhere. No denying it. No more pretending demons don't exist. There were even cases of bishops and priests practicing satanic pedophilia—sex with children. Instances had occurred in South Carolina and northern Italy, and as Vatican expert Malachi Martin points out, "The cultic acts of satanic pedophilia are considered by professionals to be the culmination of the fallen archangel's rites."

There were also rumors of secret satanic rites conducted by renegade priests in St. Peter's Basilica.

These were admittedly rare and extreme cases, but the dragon was openly showing himself and that indeed signified Chapter 12. The only thing missing was the storm— hail—which, positioned at the very end of Chapter 11, thus indicated the beginning of Chapter 12. We now need only a sign of severe hail: "Then the temple of God was opened in Heaven, and the ark of His covenant was seen in His temple. And there were lightnings, noises, thunderings, an earthquake, and great hail" (*Revelation* 11:19).

I still didn't see a sign of any hail, but the other indicators were in place. *Revelation* 12! Was that why Michael was accompanying Mary at apparitional sites, because the war was in full vigor and Satan was on the loose everywhere?

During a trip to Germany in November of 1980, at the square of a cathedral at Fulda, the Holy Father, according to a periodical called *Stimme des Glaubens,* was asked by a group of pilgrims why the secret hadn't been revealed. Like the supposed Third Secret published by *Neues Europa,* there's plenty of room to doubt that this exchange actually took place. Many believe it would have been out of character for John Paul II to respond the way he supposedly did. When asked about the secret, the pope was said to have replied:

"Given the gravity of its contents, so as not to encourage

the worldwide power of Communism to take certain steps, my predecessors in the chair of Peter preferred, out of diplomacy, to delay its publication. On the other hand, all Christians must be content with this: if it is a question of a message where it is said that the oceans will entirely flood certain parts of the earth, that from moment to moment millions will die, hearing this, people should not long for the rest of the secret.

"Many people desire to know only out of curiosity and a taste for the sensational," continued John Paul II, "but they forget that to know implies a responsibility for them. It is dangerous to want only to satisfy one's curiosity, if one is not at the same time prepared to do something, or if one is convinced that we can do nothing to prevent the misfortune predicted."

Next the pope supposedly took out a rosary. "Here is the remedy against evil. Pray, pray, and nothing more! Entrust all the rest to the Mother of God."

According to *Stimme Des Glaubens* the pope told the small gathering that the Church was prepared for personal trials, even martyrdom—an ironic statement coming as it did just a few months before an assassin shot him.

It is necessary, said John Paul, "to give ourselves completely to Christ, and for Christ!"

Through prayer, he supposedly said, it is "still possible to diminish this trial, but it is no longer possible to avert it, because only in this manner can the Church be effectively renewed."

The Church had often been renewed with blood, and it wouldn't be otherwise now, he pointed out.

"Be strong! Be prepared! We should trust ourselves to Christ and His mother, pray often, and say the Rosary. Then, although we have done little, we have done everything."

Whether or not we are in Chapter 12, a good argument could be made that an apocalyptical time had started. In a cable to the Kremlin, John Paul II vowed to set down the crown of Peter and return to his homeland, Poland, if the Communists invaded his native country to quash the growing freedom movement known as Solidarity.

John Paul was joined in the war of words by President Ronald Reagan, who felt the Soviet Union was an "evil empire."

Soon, Reagan enrolled with the Vatican in sending underground supplies—photocopiers, transmitters, telephones—to Lech Walesa and Solidarity.

If Poland could be freed, they figured, the rest of Eastern Europe, and perhaps even the Soviet Union itself, might follow.

That would spell defeat for the red dragon.

Right now all those nations were still held captive by Communism and Satan still had time left in his century, a terrifying period indeed. Russia and the U.S. had thousands of nuclear warheads pointed at each other, each carrying more megatonnage than was dropped over Hiroshima.

A single nuclear submarine could wipe out an entire region.

No wonder visionaries saw fire. No wonder they felt burning rain. Appearing in one political hotspot, Nicaragua, the Virgin told a seer named Bernardo Martinez that she'd asked the Lord to calm His anger, *"but if you don't change, you will hasten the arrival of a third world war."* This was in Cuapa, an approved site, and again she materialized after flashes of lightning. *"Pray, pray, my son, for all the world. Grave dangers threaten the world,"* she said, before elevating on a small cloud and out of sight.

There were other, equally somber manifestations. Throughout the world, statues of the *Rosa Mystica* were shedding tears and within two years the tears would become drops of blood. Meanwhile, above Three Fountains, Italy, visitors claimed the sun remained in one place for 75 minutes and that in the sky they saw a Host and the letters *"IHS"* and *"M."* In Escorial, Spain, a series of apparitions began to stigmatist Amparo Cuevas, apparitions that would speak again of huge chastisements. *"The angel of Divine Justice, my daughter, is marking the foreheads of the chosen,"* Mary allegedly said. *"And the angel of wickedness, of lies, also stamps foreheads and hands."*

Forces of demonism were pulling all stops. The following year both Pope John Paul II and President Reagan were shot within six weeks of each other, and just a month before the attempt on the pope there had been another extraordinary display of the northern lights. The date of the attempted assassination, in St. Peter's Square, was May 13, 1981, the 64th anniversary of the Virgin's first appearance at Fatima. Like Bruno Cornacchiola at Three Fountains, the assassin was a Communist-inspired fanatic, named Mehmet Ali Agca, with ties to the Bulgarian KGB. His shots should have struck John Paul in the head, inflicting mortal wounds, but just before they rang out the pope suddenly bent toward a young girl in the crowd because he saw that she was wearing a picture of the Virgin of Fatima. Although Agca shot twice more, wounding the pope in his abdomen, his life had been spared and once more the woman clothed with the sun had deflected the red dragon.

"Look how the evil forces were put in our way," said President Reagan, "and how Providence intervened."

Still, John Paul was seriously wounded, and as he lay in convalescence he began to meditate intensely on the meaning of Fatima. He corresponded with Lucia, reread the secret, this time with a better translation, and was said, in August of 1981, while looking over the Seven Hills of Rome from Policlinico Gemelli, to have witnessed the miracle of the sun just as Pius XII did.

"Mary's message of Fatima is still more relevant than it was 65 years ago. It is still more urgent," he commented one year later, during a visit to Fatima on May 13, 1982, to thank Mary for saving his life. "Precisely at the end of the second millennium there accumulates on the horizon of all mankind enormously threatening clouds, and darkness falls upon human souls," he added on December 8, 1983, at Piazza Di Spagna.

But certainly John Paul II was not all gloominess. Two days after visiting Fatima and renewing Pius XII's consecration, the pope was reported to have commented that "the situation may appear desperate, and hint at a new 'apocalypse,' but in reality this is not the case at all. For humanity of the year 2000 there surely exists a hopeful outcome, and many good reasons for hope."

That hope hinged on all good men reforming culture and going back to the Gospel, he said. In the Gospel was all we needed to know about the future, a view stressed by Cardinal Ratzinger. In an interview with a journalist named Vittorio Messori, Ratzinger explained that the Third Secret had not been publicly unveiled to avoid confusing religious prophecy with sensationalism. "The Holy Father deems that it would add nothing to what a Christian must know from Revelation and also *from the Marian apparitions* (author's emphasis) approved by the Church, which only reconfirmed the urgency of penance, conversion, forgiveness, fasting."

Gospel. Revelation. We need to look again at Chapter 12. We had most of the components already. No hail yet, but indications of three major players: the archangel Michael, the woman clothed with the sun, and the red dragon.

According to Chapter 12, the dragon persecutes the woman and she flies under this persecution to her place in the wilderness.

That "wilderness" had been many places. It had been the lonely mountain above LaSalette; it had been the Cova da Iria; it had been the farm called Betania; it had been the remote hamlet of Hrushiw in Ukraine.

Now there was a new wilderness. Again it was a remote peasant village. Again it was behind the Iron Curtain. But this time it wasn't in the Soviet Union. This time it was in Yugoslavia.

CHAPTER 29

A Place in the Wilderness

On June 24, 1981, a fierce thunderstorm swept the Croatian village of Medjugorje. Although the peasants were used to sudden storms, its loudness frightened even the most seasoned farmers. It was like the Day of Judgment, remarked one woman, Iva Vasilj, who scurried through town sprinkling holy water while hail crashed furiously around her.

The sky itself seemed to be opening. Rain. Sheets of rain. *Hail.* Lightning darned the steeped early-morning horizon, striking where the young people had their disco.

The following afternoon at about four o'clock, on this the feast of John the Baptist, two teenagers named Ivanka Ivankovic and Mirjana Dragicevic were on their way back from a sheep pasture when Ivanka happened to look to a large, rocky hill known as Crnica or "Mount Podbrdo." There she spotted a strange light and in it a shining womanly figure, hovering. "Mirjana, look!" she cried. "It's the *Gospa* (Our Lady)!"

At first Mirjana didn't bother to look. "Be quiet," she told Ivanka. "Do you think Our Lady is going to appear to *us?*"

She said this a couple more times before finally looking up herself. When Mirjana's eyes found the light she fell

213

to her knees. So did Ivanka. "We were scared," Mirjana
recalled.

The girls later returned with friends who also saw the
luminous saint, and appearing again the next day, then the
next, she began to speak to them, confirming that she was
the Blessed Virgin Mary. *"I have come because there are
many true believers here,"* she said. *"I wish to be with you
and to reconcile the whole world."*

From that week on, through the present, Mary has spoken to one or more of the six visionaries on virtually a daily
basis. There has never been anything like it and may never
be again; the apparitions have been going on now since
1981. I know that some devotees of Fatima and other sites
will take issue with what I'm about to say, and I'm well
aware that the Church has yet to pass judgment, but barring
revelation of a brilliant, almost inconceivable prank, Medjugorje will end up as the most important apparitional site
of this century and for that matter in all the history of
Mary's appearances.

I've never encountered anything quite like the sensations
of Medjugorje. Not at the tarmac at Fatima nor the grotto
at Lourdes nor the mountainside of LaSalette. Not at
Guadalupe or Pochaiv or Knock. Not at charismatic services in New York City or Mass at the Church of the Annunciation in Nazareth.

Not since Christ appeared in glory to His apostles has
there been a more direct interaction with the supernatural.

The feeling is that of standing at a point halfway between
Heaven and earth.

The feeling is also one of standing in the middle of all the
action. Since Fatima there had been at least 210 presumed
apparitions, and within just the next few years there would
be at minimum another fifty notable reports. But none had
the economy of language, the sweet grace, and the tranquil
power of Medjugorje. It was the hub from which the spokes
of other apparitions rotated, the very epicenter, along with
Fatima, of twentieth-century interventions, at the vanguard
of God's response to the devil, with roots all the way back
to the Miraculous Medal (Rue du Bac).

And there was an ominous scent in the air. *"I have come*

to call the world to conversion for the last time," Mary told the youngsters. *"After this period I will not appear any more on this earth."*

So began the final and most powerful stage of apparitions, the phase we find ourselves in now, the climactic period that has spawned dozens of similar apparitions on every habitable continent.

Yes, there were apparitions every decade; we've seen how they continued since Rue du Bac; so many that we confuse them.

But Medjugorje is something else. Medjugorje is the touchstone for an entirely new flurry of reports. Medjugorje is the annoucement that the era which began at Rue du Bac is about to end.

The Blessed Mother was calling mankind to prayer, penance, and fasting for a final time.

"The hours of the apparitions follow a progression," Fatima specialist Luigi Bianchi points out. "At Lourdes, they took place in the morning. At Fatima, at noon. At Medjugorje, in the evening."

It was like the end of a long day, an hour before midnight. It was our spiritual entrance into a new era and time to break the power of Satan. She had come, along with the most extraordinary supernatural signs she'd ever displayed, to renew the diminishing faith not just of Catholicism but of all religions.

Pray, she implored pilgrims, pray for as long as possible every day. Prayer is the manna that will sustain mankind, and the Rosary should be said by everyone no matter what religion or beliefs they hold.

She called for Judeo-Christian unity and said that while not all religions are equal, all *people* are equal before God. It is not God but mankind who created religious divisions. *"You are not true Christians,"* she said, *"if you do not respect other religions."*

Moslems, Jews, and Protestants were equally touched by Medjugorje. Bring harmony, Mary begged, peace and harmony. She made clear that she wasn't there to usurp the power of her Son. *"There is only one mediator between God and man, and it is Jesus Christ,"* she said, adding that

Jesus preferred His people to address themselves directly to Him.

But in the meantime she'd come as a confidant and protector. She also came as a spiritual adviser. *"Keep faith, fast, and pray. Advance against Satan by means of prayer. Satan wants to work still more now that you know he is at work. Dear children, put on the armor for battle and with the rosary in your hand defeat him!"*

Usually Mary appeared after three flashes of light and the visionaries, falling to their knees in ecstasy, saw her as a young woman with blue eyes, black wavy hair, a shimmering graylike dress and white veil (though really not colors of this world), and a crown of stars that hovered over her head as in Chapter 12 of the *Apocalypse.*

On special feast days she wore gold or turquoise.

She came with angels, standing on a small cloud, and sometimes she held the Christ Child.

Her salutation was simple and direct. *"Praised be Jesus,"* she always said upon arrival.

Reddish violet clouds wafted toward the hill of apparitions and the Croatian word *"MIR,"* which means "peace," was seen by hundreds scrawled miraculously in the sky. The children seemed to dash with supernatural speed up the rocky hill, like the kids at Garabandal, with not so much as a scratch from the brambles, and when Communist operatives tried to keep them from Mount Podbrdo, the officials themselves were awed by the strange light.

Mary appeared in early evening and later in the night, on Podbrdo hill or atop Mount Krizevac where Pius XI had a huge concrete cross built after a dream in 1933. Sometimes other villagers got a glimpse of her as a vague outline of light, in the bearing of the Miraculous Medal, visible to everyone in the hamlet who looked up at the mountain. But mostly she showed herself to the six visionaires as a three-dimensional entity, more real than reality itself.

"I wish to keep on giving you messages," she said, *"as it has never been done in history from the beginning of the world."*

Why this new message?

"Because those of Cova de Iria had not been listened to," replied Father Bianchi, "and remain not understood."

Prayer, penance, conversion. Medjugorje is a continuance of Fatima, with greatly expanded instructions. Mary was putting special emphasis on Mass, Confession, and the Bible, calling on people to read Scripture *"every day in your homes and let it be in a visible place so as always to encourage you to read it and to pray."*

When the visionaries grew too curious, she replied, *"Why ask so many questions? Everything is there in the Gospels."*

Especially it was in the Book of Revelation. Unless it was all a grand hoax, we were nearing the end of Chapter 12 and approaching Chapter 13. Mary, persecuted by the dragon, had flown to her place in the wilderness, and the war, engaged by her and the Archangel Michael with Satan, was reaching a critical juncture. The chastisements, warded off, were now looming larger than ever. *"You must warn the bishop very soon, and the pope,"* she said in 1983. The war's greatest battle was about to unfold. The visionaries were given secrets, secrets that pertained to the future of the Church and mankind in general. There were going to be warnings, a great sign or miracle, and the punishments, she told them, just as she had told the girls at Garabandal. We'll explore those in the next chapters.

Pray, pray, and pray more still. Offer the Lord sacrifice. *"Through fasting and prayer,"* she said, *"one can stop wars. One can suspend the laws of nature."*

In prayer could be found the answer to everything, she said, even a situation *"that has no exit."* She was calling *"on each one of you to consciously decide for God and against Satan. I am your mother and, therefore, I want to lead you all to complete holiness. I want each one of you to be happy here on earth and to be with me in Heaven."*

While the future of the world was a prime concern, Mary was really coming to show mankind the way to eternity. It was true, she said, that there is Heaven, Hell, and Purgatory.

"In Purgatory there are different levels. The lowest is close to Hell and the highest gradually draws near to Heaven. It is not on All Saints Day, but Christmas, that the greatest number of souls leave Purgatory (for Heaven). There are in Purgatory souls who pray ardently to God but for whom no relative or friend prays on earth. God makes them benefit from the prayers of other people. It happens that God permits them to manifest themselves in different ways, close to their relatives on earth, in order to remind men of the existence of Purgatory and to solicit their prayers to come close to God who is just but good. The majority of people go to Purgatory. Many go to Hell. A small number go directly to Heaven."

It's hard to tell how accurate the messages have been conveyed. They were communicated by youngsters who may have oversimplified what she said and forgotten pieces of her quotes. Words are also lost in translation. But overall there was great power in the messages, and there was no mistaking what they saw. The Virgin showed them the various spiritual levels in visions that were like watching slides or a movie. Heaven was a terrifically pleasant place with meadows and trees unlike anything on earth, the people all about thirty years of age, wearing pink, yellow, and gray garments like Jesus wore, radiating an inner light and immensely happy. They sang and prayed, acknowledging the Virgin as they passed or communicating with her in something that looked like a "tunnel." These people, in the unearthly light, were those who loved God and sought Him. It was so beautiful, said one visionary, that "your heart stands still when you look at it."

But only a small number went there directly. Most people went to Purgatory, a place of purification, obscured by an ash-gray mist, and though the visionaries saw no one there, they could hear people knocking as if to get out, crying and moaning in the fog.

While the others saw such sights like a moving picture, two of the visionaires, Vicka Ivankovic and Jakov Colo, claimed Our Lady had transported them bodily to the eternal destinations. "The Blessed Virgin appeared to us and she took us by the hand and we visited Heaven, Purgatory, and Hell," insisted Vicka. "It was not a dream, for we really disappeared for twenty minutes, as Jakov's mother confirmed."

In the center of Hell was a great sea of fire, "like an ocean of raging flames," Vicka recounted. "We could see people before they went into the fire, and then we could see them coming out of the fire. Before they went into the fire they looked like normal people. The more they are against God's will, the deeper they enter into the fire, and the deeper they go, the more they rage against Him. When they come out of the fire, they don't have human shape anymore; they are more like grotesque animals, but unlike anything on earth."

These were people who denied and hated God. They went into the fire naked and emerged with horrifically blackened skin.

Another of the visionaries, Marija Pavlovic, saw a beautiful girl enter the flames. When she came out she was a beast, "no longer human."

There was special need to pray for unbelievers who risked the sea of fire.

"People will tear their hair, brother will plead with brothers, they will curse their past lives without God. They will repent, but it will be too late."

That was why she was appearing so often around the world: conversion. She was even manifesting at other places within Yugoslavia itself—for example, just sixty miles away, in Izbicno. She wanted conversions while there was still time. She said she'd appear in every home if she had to.

But she also warned against false apparitions, explaining that no authentic ones would be continued after she stopped appearing in Medjugorje. Those who made such fraudulent claims were the "false prophets" of latter times. *"Many pretend to see Jesus and the Mother of God, and to understand their words, but they are, in fact, lying,"* she said. *"It is a very grave sin, and it is necessary to pray very much for them."*

Peace. The Virgin came as the Queen of Peace. Peace of heart. At night strange lights shot by the hillside and the moon offered an oddly brilliant glow.

Every aspect of the village was unforgettable, the old peasant women in *babushkas,* the mortar stables attached to the homes, the cocks that crowed each morning in a spiritual wonderland where the Holy Spirit offered a plan to intervene in our world and neutralize Satan.

The center of that mission was St. James, a plain breeze-block church with two distinctive towers surrounded by vineyards trampled by the pilgrims. Each evening thousands of visitors flocked around St. James as one or more visionaries entered for apparitions that started at precisely 6:40 p.m., in the middle of the Rosary.

Outside, the sun pulsed and spun as a daily occurrence. It whirled in hues of blue and purple, hues unlike any from a normal sunset—green, turquoise, without hurting the eyes, a disc or host moving to blot out the hot solar center, leaving not a single sunspot, save on occasion for the afterimage of pink heart-shaped lights that drifted into eternity.

The messages of reconciliation and peace would eventually find their way to many millions, including President Reagan and Mikhail Gorbachev. Since 1981 pilgrims from more than a hundred countries have visited Medjugorje, a quarter of them from America, and while one of the Medjugorje priests, Philip Pavich, feels figures are often "grossly overstated" and that they were "lucky if there have been ten million" pilgrims, other estimates, including one in *Life* Magazine, ran as high as 15 million.

Singer Lola Falana was cured of multiple sclerosis in Medjugorje, and visits were made by the presidents of Brazil and Italy, along with dozens of cardinals (some conservatively incognito), hundreds of bishops, and thousands of priests—about 30,000. I myself ran into the football coach Don Shula walking across a vineyard.

Mary was here. Of that I was personally convinced. At no other apparitional site except Fatima and Lourdes had she spoken with such thrift and eloquence. Rare indeed was the visitor who didn't come away deeply transformed.

But could it be "scientifically" documented? Were there instruments to detect an otherworldly presence? Did the Virgin emanate a measurable force field?

Most tests showed no abnormal ionizing radiation, but on one occasion experiments with a device called the electroscope recorded 100,000 millirads p.h. of energy in Medjugorje, where at the very most twenty would have been anticipated.

Examinations of the visionaries themselves turned up equally baffling evidence. Tests of their auditory and visual impulses indicated profound states of ecstasy, with little or no awareness of their surroundings while the Virgin was there. Using a device called the algometer, which measures the reaction to a warm stimulus, investigators found that the visionaries had an insensitivity to pain during the apparitions. An analysis of videos taken during the ecstasies showed great synchronisms, that is, movements and reactions that occurred simultaneously among all the seers. They knelt and raised their eyes in near-perfect harmony, and their voices disappeared together. One of the investigators, Henri Joyeux, a professor at the Faculty of Medicine in Montpelier, France, and a surgeon at Montpelier Cancer Institute, concluded that the ecstasy phenomenon was "scientifically inexplicable," with no signs of hallucination, neurosis, catalepsy, hysteria, or deceit.

But as Joyeux also pointed out, Medjugorje was far too huge for a laboratory. In the end it could be documented only in the human heart. It was a grand plan by the Holy Spirit, perhaps, as I said, a desperate final plan, and the Virgin made it clear from the outset that Medjugorje was an apocalyptical event. She was at a place in the wilderness. She was clothed with the sun. She was issuing new secrets and warnings. And as in *Revelation,* she was wearing the 12 stars.

Let's look at that aspect now, the war with Satan and Medjugorje's secret messages.

CHAPTER 30

The Woman Persecuted

Satan didn't have much time left. His century was nearing a close. He *raged* against Medjugorje, persecuting the woman and attacking every aspect of the apparitions. *"Great alarm is being felt at your coming here,"* Mary told the visionaries. *"Satan and the forces of darkness are alarmed; those who have turned their backs on God are alarmed. We have become a sign of the Church's reawakening to its mission."*

In a message on January 28, 1987, Our Lady said, *"Whatever be the place where I appear, and where my Son comes with me, Satan comes also."*

When I asked one of the visionaries, Ivan Dragicevic, if they'd had any problems with the devil, he said simply, "Satan is everywhere around here."

He was bold. He was bold and desperate. Medjugorje was converting people with a strength of the Holy Spirit I'd never seen before. It was the light of the world. In June of 1982, a year after the first apparitions, Mirjana locked herself in her room, knelt down, and was waiting for the Madonna when suddenly there was a flash of light and the devil appeared—blackened and horrible. "I felt weak and fainted," she said. "When I came to, he was still standing there, laughing. He told me I would be very beautiful and happy in love and life, and so on, but that I would have no need of the Madonna or my faith. 'She has brought you nothing but sufferings and hardships,' he said. He, on the other hand, could give me everything I wanted. Then something inside me shouted, 'No! No! No!' I began to shake and feel sick. Then he disappeared and the Madonna came and immediately my strength returned, as though she had given it back to me. I felt normal again.''

He came in various guises. He came camouflaged as the Virgin, or in the form of an extremely handsome, seductive man—though with eyes rolling grotesquely. When he wasn't physically visible his presence could be felt in the way of confusion. He tried to get everyone angry at each other, creating divisions and disorder. He had the power to distort impressions and memories, causing deep misunderstandings.

"Excuse me for this, but you must know that Satan exists," Mary told Mirjana. *"One day he presented himself before the throne of God and asked permission to try the Church for a period of time. God permitted him to try it during one century. This century is under the power of the devil, but when the secrets which I have confided to you have been fulfilled, his power will be destroyed. Already now, he is beginning to lose his power and he has become aggressive."*

The reason God granted him a period of special testing, the Blessed Virgin explained, was due to disbelief. We believe in God when things are going well but shun the Eternal Father when things go badly. And even when matters are going well, we give ourselves and not God the credit. "God, therefore, allowed the devil one century in which to exercise dominion over the world, and the devil chose the twentieth century," Mirjana said. "Today, as we can see around us, everyone is dissatisfied, many people cannot stand one another. Look at the number of divorces and abortions. All this, the Madonna said, is the work of the devil."

"You must protect yourself by fasting and prayer, especially community prayer. Carry blessed objects with you. Place them in your houses. Return to the use of holy water."

He was destroying marriages, the Madonna told Mirjana, stirring up divisions between priests, causing obsessions and murder, instilling people with a satanic pride that was noticeable now in all walks of life, at all levels of society. Pride was Satan's most distinctive characteristic and he'd infected us with his disease. He'd engineered a century of egoism and jealousy. One of the parish priests, Philip Pavich, who came later to Medjugorje, criticized "disinformation" coming out of Medjugorje (feeling that many messages were communicated inaccurately) and disagreed that Satan was any more powerful than in previous centuries (the "tremendous activity of Satan" didn't wax or wane from one century to another, felt this astute priest).

But what Mirjana had been told (or at least what she *reportedly* had been told) seemed like a ringing confirmation of Pope Leo XII's 19th-century vision. The 1980s were a decade of great confusion. The American divorce rate had almost tripled since 1945, with about half of those married since the mid-1970s likely to end in divorce. And there was a 70 percent increase in child homicides. In some major cities like New York nearly half the pregnancies ended with abortion.

Where schoolteachers once worried about students chewing gum or running in the halls, now they watched for assault, robbery, and drug abuse.

Listen to some of the figures! Each day, by the end of the 1980s, 3,000 children were running away from home, 2,200 illegitimate children were born, and nearly 1,100 teens were having abortions. Overall, two million American babies were being exterminated each year as killing the unborn became a means of birth control. In some cases the abortions occurred in the eighth or even ninth month of pregnancy, and the babies—limbs, torsos, heads—were disposed outside the clinics in trash cans.

On Wall Street, downtown from the abortion mills, greedy financiers wrecked whole corporations in quick-money merger schemes. Money had always been an idol, but never quite like this. Greed was glorified and "junk bonds" allowed Wall Street to claim money that didn't even really exist.

Capitalism was showing that it had a side as ugly in many ways as socialism.

Pride. Everyone was self-important. Materialism. The new icon was the "material girl," Madonna, who simulated sexual intercourse on a set designed to look like a church. She was embraced by the major media as an "artist." As Pavich said, every epoch had its evil. In the 13th century they had Genghis Khan. But no other era had weaponry that could demolish the planet, no other century had scientists tinkering with the very materials of life, no other century had millions watching a semi-nude "singer" in a church, and no other century had a Hitler, a Lenin, a Stalin, and a Mao as only the *beginning* of its immorality.

Many things had gone well for Satan. In many ways his century was turning out better than expected. No one was shocked anymore at dismemberment and frontal nudity at the movies. And it was chic or at least avant garde to associate with the New Age Movement.

But he still had not quite accomplished total dominion and, watching the cosmic hourglass, he knew he was approaching his final hour. He was going to give it all he had. He was mustering every available demon. *"The present hour is the hour of Satan,"* warned Mary. *"The hour has come when the demon is authorized to act with all his force and power."*

They were tough words, very daunting, but the Queen of Peace had not come to extinguish hope. She'd come to arm us for the final battles. Pray. Fast. Fast on bread and water twice a week, she said, on Wednesdays and Fridays. Fasting disengages the devil's hideous energy. *"My dear children, Satan is strong,"* she said in 1985. *"He wishes, with all his strength, to destroy my plans. Pray only, and do not stop doing it. I will also pray to my Son, so that all the plans that I have begun will be realized. Be patient and persevere in prayer. Do not permit Satan to take away your courage. He works very hard in the world. Be on your guard."*

Never before had Mary taken mankind into such an open conflict with the devil. His rage was tangible. The diabolical attacks were now manifesting as a conflict between the bishop, Pavao Zanic, and the Franciscans who ran the Medjugorje parish. There was a struggle for control of parishes in Hercegovina and Bishop Zanic was becoming increasingly hostile to the Franciscans. While at first favorably inclined toward Medjugorje, he now openly and truculently denounced the apparitions. In January of 1982 the livid bishop formed a commission to investigate Medjugorje, a commission designed from the outset to declaim and halt the visionaires. "The propaganda for Medjugorje is appalling," he wrote in early 1984. "We are preparing for war." He said the apparitions were "the greatest lie and swindle in the history of the Church."

It was a nasty internecine battle. Zanic's own superior, Archbisop Frane Franic, *supported* the apparitions, and so did the greatest scholar in the Marian movement, Abbe René Laurentin of France, who'd written the definitive works on Rue du Bac and Lourdes. When Zanic's commission came to an unsurprisingly negative conclusion, Cardinal Kuharic of Zagreb ordered Zanic to install a larger and more serious committee of investigation, which he did in earnest—but again stacking the commission with his own supporters. One bishop observed that disapproval of Medjugorje seemed to be a condition for selection on the commission. Meanwhile Zanic wrote to the parish ordering Father Tomislav Pervan to "cool and eventually extinguish" the apparitions. The bishop demanded that the visionaries make no more public appearances. They weren't to have any more apparitions in St. James, and they had to hand over all written material about the apparitions. Pious devotions and other practices inspired by the messages were to stop, and there was to be no more reference to the apparitions in sermons. Souvenirs and publications aimed at promoting Medjugorje were disallowed, and the statue of Our Lady fashioned according to the visionaries' description was to be removed from its position near the altar. Zanic also circulated an unsubstantiated and apparently false rumor that a Franciscan who had served at Medjugorje had gotten a former nun pregnant. He raged when another village girl, Jelena Vasilij, who received interior locutions, announced that Mary's birthday was not September 8, as the Church celebrates, but August 5. ("Anti-ecclesiastical rubbish," frothed Zanic.) His commission sent one of its members to test if Vicka was truly in ecstasy by plunging a large unsterilized needle into her left shoulder, causing her to bleed, and as one British journalist dryly noted, Bishop Zanic dealt Medjugorje a bigger blow than the Marxists had managed.

"If the hallmark of Satan is chaos and confusion," commented René Laurentin, "one is driven to discern his presence in this conflict."

I'm not telling the story in a strictly chronological way but you get the point. *"Dear children,"* Mary said on July 12, 1984. *"These days Satan wants to frustrate my plans. Pray that his plan not be realized. I will pray to my Son, Jesus, to give you the grace to experience the victory of Jesus in the temptations of Satan. Thank you for having responded to my call."*

She urged the children to pray for the bishop, who was carrying a *"heavy burden."* It was a self-imposed burden of humiliation. When Zanic went to Rome with the negative report from his second commission, the Vatican took away his authority in an unprecedented action and ordered creation of a more objective commission composed of bishops from throughout Yugoslavia. Zanic no longer had such an iron-handed control over approval of Medjugorje, and when some of the new members pointed out that there was little basis for his opposition, he "began to cry and to yell and the bishops gave up insisting," according to Archbishop Franic.

What the Yugoslavian bishops will eventually conclude is still a matter of conjecture but it's known that Pope John Paul II is favorably disposed, for he has commented that Medjugorje is "a great center of spirituality" and that if he weren't pope, he'd already have visited the village. "Pray for me there," he told bishops who were on the way to Medjugorje. "There are some bishops, as in Yugoslavia, who are against," the pope told other visitors, "but one must also see the crowds who respond, the numerous conversions. All that is within the framework of the Gospel; all these events, we must study them seriously."

Pilgrims flock to Medjugorje, Yugoslavia to experience conversion and listen to messages received by the young visionaries. Pictured are Vicka, Jakov, Ivanka, Maria, and Ivan during an apparition.

*Overwhelming crowds at St. James, Medjugorje
have led to the construction of an
outdoor altar behind the church.*

Earthquake destruction of unprecedented force
and abundant poverty ravage the earth.

231

The multitudes of sick and homeless provide ample opportunity to reflect God's love for us and fulfill His command to love one another.

Pilgrims visit the apparition site in Betania, Venezuela.

Maria Esperanza, Michael H. Brown, and Geo Esperanza

Apparition site at Oliveto Citra, Italy, and

Visionaries Umberto Gagliardi and Raffaello Ferrarra.

*Maria Kizyn (left), with a friend in front of
Blessed Trinity Church at Hrushiv, Ukraine.*

The miraculous well inside the church.

*The Chernobyl disaster heightened awareness
of the plight of our environment.*

*Josyp Terelya with
Pope John Paul II.*

Chornij Zenovia.

*Chornij Zenovia and other peasant women were
privileged to see the Blessed Mother
at Zarvanystya, Ukraine.*

The product of our modern age.

*The apparition site at El Cajas, Ecuador
and the visionary, Pachi.*

239

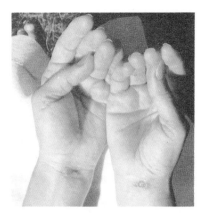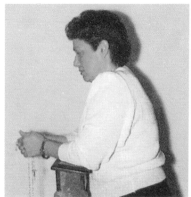

*Stigmatist, Gladys Quiroga De Motta
of San Nicolás, Argentina.*

*Jimmy, Mary, Steve, Wendy, Susan, Stefanie, Gianna
and Fr. Jack at St. Maria Goretti Parish.*

*Fr. René Laurentin and
the seer, Gianna Talone
of Scottsdale, AZ.*

240

Irish visionaries Christina Gallagher and Mary Casey.

Father McGinnity.

Josie Dayton near the apparitions grotto in Spinkl, Ireland.

A French nuclear test in 1969 produced an unexpected result—the image of Christ crucified in the rising mushroom cloud, and to His left, the image of Our Lady. Proof of a greater power than atomic warheads.

Statues of Our Crucified Lord bleed and images of Our Blessed Mother shed tears worldwide as societies turn away from Heaven's love.

243

This image of Our Resurrected Lord, Jesus Christ (as presented to Sister Faustina) pours His mercy and love over all His children and promises all who trust in Him that they will be eternally rewarded.

CHAPTER 31

The Secrets of Medjugorje

Like many, what I was interested in studying were those secrets. Each visionary was to be given ten of them, and by the mid-1980s, both Mirjana and Ivanka had received all ten.

No one knows if each visionary received the exact same secrets, but this we can determine: they all have secrets pertaining to the Church and the world, they all seem awed by what they were told, and those willing to talk do so in the context of warnings, a great sign, and chastisements. "There are some things that are good," said Ivanka. "And some things that are bad."

It is precisely the order we encountered at Garabandal. First there will be events that will shake up disbelievers, then the Miracle and Chastisement.

Or *chastisements*. Plural. There seemed to be a number of events. And indications were that some and perhaps the majority are anything but pleasant. Vicka cried upon learning her ninth secret on April 22, 1986, and when Mirjana had seen hers she begged the Virgin to lessen them.

Although Mirjana's regular apparitions stopped after she was given the last secret, so frightening are aspects of what she has been shown that the Virgin occasionally appears to Mirjana to help her cope. "She wants to prepare us for this, so I do not make a mistake," Mirjana said. "And she talked to me and said we need to pray more and more until the first secret. And do penance and sacrifices, especially now before the first secret. If you knew how it gets to me when I think about it! If Our Lady wasn't with me I would probably go crazy, knowing what is waiting for us. The young people don't know what's awaiting them. I cry and pray for them and ask Our Lady to enlighten them."

Mirjana added: "I think Our Lady came at just the right time because there are very few who honestly and sincerely believe in God, who are honoring God, fasting and praying. The world has never been like this. God has never been prayed to less than this time. Everything is more important than God. That's why she is crying. God is not needed for many people in the world. I'm sorry for the people because they don't know what they're headed for. If they could look into the secrets, how they are, they would change right away."

According to Mirjana, who is the most mature and educated of the visionaries, the first three secrets involve the warnings. She claims that besides a verbal description, the Virgin wrote them on a strange piece of material that's a cross between cloth and paper but really nothing of this world. Only she can "read" what's on the "paper" and she knows "the day and hour" of each warning. Ten days before the happening mentioned in the first secret she will reveal it to Fr. Petar Ljubicic, a priest she has chosen as her confidant, and he will then pray, fast for seven days, and decide whether and how to reveal it. While the satanic fighting in Yugoslavia, including the very vicinity of Medjugorje, is obviously the devil's attempt to squelch pilgrimages, Mirjana says this hideous civil conflict is not included in the secrets she was given.

In 1985, the day after she was shown a visual preview of the first secret, Mirjana gave Father Ljubicic several hints about the nature of the warnings. She said the first was "nothing good" and that it was more severe than some of the others. She was asked whether the warning would be spiritual or physical. "It has to be seen," she replied. "This has to shake us up so the world will start thinking."

A catastrophe?

"Not a catastrophe in a huge sense," she said, "but to

prove there is God."

The huge catastrophe, she said, would come later.

Would people try to explain away the first warning as a natural phenomenon?

"Some might say after the first and second that these have a natural explanation. But for many people," said Mirjana, "the first warning will be 'self-explanatory.'"

How long will it last?

A short time.

Were there any indications now in the world—pre-signs—of its coming?

No. It will stand on its own.

When Ljubicic asked who would see it, Mirjana replied, "All those who are going to be present where that secret is taking place."

Will it take place in Medjugorje?

Mirjana declined to answer.

Would people rush to wherever it occurs?

"Father," she replied, "no one wants to go and see the kind of event that will take place. For example, people would not want to go to Italy to see how a dam collapsed. There's no desire for that, and the same is true for that secret."

We know only that the first warning is not a phenomenon the entire world will witness, except perhaps via TV, but that for those nearby it will not only be visible but devastating. Between that secret and the second will be a period of grace during which people will be allowed the opportunity to convert. But Mirjana refused to say how much time there will be between the first, second, and third secrets. "The time between secrets varies," said the visionary. "One secret could be today, another tomorrow, as just an example."

Of all her experiences with Our Lady, said Mirjana, seeing the first secret "was the worst. Although I wasn't threatened because I've known all ten secrets for a long time, it shocked me really. Yesterday I saw it for the first time like a projection in a film."

While there's some confusion about the first three secrets, two are obviously awe-inspiring events and the third involves a supernatural sign that will prove God

exists and in Mirjana's words will be "permanent, inde-
structible, and beautiful." It will be seen on Podbrdo hill,
at the site of the first apparition, and it will be something
like fire but not really fire (which reminded me of what
Conchita said about the great Miracle at Garabandal). In
1981, hundreds of people saw flames erupting on Mount
Podbrdo but when they investigated nothing was scorched.
Afterward Mary told the children, *The fire, seen by the
faithful, was of a supernatural character. It is one of the
signs, a forerunner of the Great Sign."*

Warnings and a great sign: It was identical to what had
come out of Garabandal. A hill, just as the sign in Garabandal was supposed to take place on the mountain, and an
ethereal light, similar to the great Miracle announced in
the Spanish village, where it had been described as rays
of light or a pillar of smoke. "It's going to be obvious,"
said Mirjana, "that it was not made and placed there, that
someone didn't bring it from Medjugorje and place it
there."
Whether people would die during the warnings was
another matter of confusion, but judging by Mirjana's reactions, it certainly seemed so. I was left with an impression
of chaos and desolation. *Devastation.* Right now, according to Mirjana, we are in a "time of grace" during which
Heaven is trying to change our lives. But that time of grace
will run out shortly. The warnings, say the visionaries, will
come within their lifetimes. Since most of them were born
in the mid-1960s, they will be only 35 at the turn of the
century, which would leave plenty of time for any such
events to occur in the next millennium. The warnings will
serve as a purification, ending the era of Satan's extended
power.
    Let's hear that again: at the onset of the secrets, Lucifer's
reign will be broken.
    "When the sign appears, no one will any longer doubt
that God truly exists," Mirjana said. "But it will be too late
for many to convert. The encounter with Divine reality will
be catastrophic for those who have not already turned
toward God. But for those who have done so, it will be
a time of great joy."
    It sounded like Garabandal again, a moment when

people would see themselves as God does—a horrifying self evaluation, exposing all sin like a spiritual mirror. What did Mirjana think of the other mystics who throughout the century had prophesied storms, earthquakes, and fire? "My opinion is Our Lady chose them as she selected us," said the young Croatian woman.

While little was said about the fourth, fifth, and sixth secrets, leading to speculation that these were the ones having to do with the Church (or else secrets of a purely personal nature), the last four seemed to constitute the great Chastisement. When asked if mankind had entered the end times, or whether Mary had said anything about the Second Coming and the apocalypse, Mirjana told her inquirer, "That is part of the secrets. I would not like to talk about it."

Mirjana explained to Ljubicic that every time she or the others came close to revealing too much, a force of some kind would descend upon them and halt transmission of anything further. But there were still peripheral details to explore, some fascinating. As long ago as 1982, for example, there were reports that at least one of the chastisements—as opposed to the warnings—had been lessened. *"I have prayed,"* the Virgin said on November 6. *"The punishment has been softened. Repeated prayers and fasting reduce punishments from God."* In locutions to Jelena Vasilij, Mary seemed to downplay the negative possibilities. *"I have always said: Punishment will come about if the world is not converted. Call all mankind to conversion. Everything depends on your conversion."* One punishment that was lessened is contained in the seventh secret given to Mirjana—lessened, not erased. *"Repeated prayers and fasting reduce punishments from God, but it is not possible to avoid entirely the chastisement,"* Mary told Mirjana. In the opinion of Father Slavko Barbaric, another parish priest, "The Madonna did not come to announce catastrophes, but more to help us avoid them. We all know that a nuclear war is possible, even without apparitions. If a house burns, it doesn't burn because the mother cries 'fire.' On the contrary, the mother comes to save the house which is burning and in that there is hope."

In spite of everything, said Jelena, the world "will be saved." During an interview on the Eternal Word Television Network (EWTN) in 1992, the visionary Marija Pavlovic also emphasized that as far as she was concerned the main messages were to pray and hope—not any dire "warnings."

Yet the other visionaries often referred to the secrets as grave. "The eighth secret is worse than the seven before it," said Mirjana. "I begged for it to be made less severe. Every day I beseeched the Madonna to get it mitigated, and at last she said that if everyone prayed it might be averted. But then she told me the ninth secret and it was even worse. As for the tenth, it is terrible, and nothing can alter it. It will happen."

While the optimists pointed out that both Mirjana and Ivanka, now adults, had married and started families—something they presumably wouldn't do if the entire world was going to go up in smoke—others argued that the visionaries have no fear because they've already seen Heaven.

"After the time of grace will come the time of purification which will culminate with the third secret," said Mirjana. "After this sign, the world will certainly know that God exists. But it will be too late to convert. The encounter with the heavenly reality will be sad for those who have not profited by the warnings and have not converted. But there will be great joy for those who have opened themselves up to God in this time of calm."

There was also confusion about whether there might be a third world war. A message in 1982 was relayed to this effect—*"the Third World War will not take place"*—but there may again have been problems in translation or conveyance. Understandably, the visionaries didn't like answering questions at great length, especially if they drew near to the secrets, and Mary rarely mentioned specific countries by name. One she did cite was supposedly Poland, where she said *"the just"* would prevail and even added that the world had begun to convert, though there was a long way to go. It reminded me of Maria Esperanza, who also noted improvement on earth. The Poland prediction was in 1981. Mary also alluded to the Russians, whom she predicted would become *"the people who will glorify God the most. The West has caused civilization to progress, but without God, as if they were their own creators."* When I asked Ivan and Vicka if they had any comments on China and Russia, which at the time were experiencing the first rumblings of democracy, they declined to answer. "Worry about your own country," Ivan said, paraphrasing what the Virgin said. With prayer, said Mary, the works of Satan could be transformed *"in favor of the glory of God."*

In 1989, eight years after the first messages, the Blessed Mother was still persevering. *"One more time I beseech all of you to pray, to help by your prayers the unbelievers, those who do not have the grace to experience God in their hearts with a living faith. I do not want to threaten again! My wish is just to warn you all as a mother. I beg you for the people who do not know the secrets. . ."*

A third Medjugorje priest, Father Tomislav Vlasic, pointed out that one could never really know what's meant by "last times." It's a relative term, and we should recall that Christians in the first century thought Christ's return was imminent. "But," said Vlasic, "beyond this relative meaning, we must really be aware that we are now in the time of the great events when God wants to work a change for us, and thus the visionaries say that these apparitions are the last for humanity and that with these events the time of Satan is finished. It is true: a new page has turned, something will come."

There are many signs at Medjugorje, Vlasic pointed out, and I experienced that firsthand. When I visted the village in 1989 I was startled the first night to see the full moon split and form two orbs. Fearing I was encountering an illusion, the result of jetlag, I called to another pilgrim and asked what she saw. The woman witnessed the same thing without my telling her what I was seeing. In the orb to the left was what both of us swore was the profile of a veiled woman. We knew who that symbolized, but in the right I saw the profile of what looked like a bearded man.

Was it jetlag? Was I imagining? Hallucinating? Too much Croatian wine at dinner? The bearded man didn't seem like God or any saint with whom I was familiar, but the next day, visiting a church in nearby Tihaljina, I encountered two large statues in front of the altar, one of the veiled Virgin to the left, and at the other side, as in the other orb, a statue of a bearded man who I learned was the prophet Elijah.

I didn't know *Malachi* 4:5 then but I know that biblical passage now. *"Behold,"* it says, *"I will send you Elijah the prophet before the coming of the great and dreadful day of the Lord."*

The crowd atop Cross Mountain in Medjugorje.

CHAPTER 32

The Hours of Justice and Mercy

While Medjugorje was the center of attention, there were other apparitions occurring at the very same time with the very same messages.

Three thousand miles south, in the mountainous farm region of Rwanda, Africa, the Virgin appeared to six girls and a young man who were all roughly the same age as the Medjugorje visionaries. The apparitions were located in the southern area of Kibeho and began on November 28, 1981—just four months after Mary's first appearance in Yugoslavia.

It was deepest Africa. On one side were the wild savannas of Tanzania, where the last of the rhinos roamed, and at another border, Uganda, where the despot Idi Amin had savagely murdered countless of his countrymen. During 1981 and 1982 natives in the outbacks of Rwanda, and for that matter neighboring countries, murmured that something horrible, something far more frightening even than a savage like Amin, was about to occur. The hearsay was thick with bathos and mystery. The world, it was said, was about to end. Strange sights could be seen in Rwanda's skies, the sun spinning and pulsing or splitting into two separate suns. In Bantu and Watusi lore, signs in the sky were without question an indication

of major upheaval, even doom. The world was about to end
and Jesus Christ was returning. They knew this because His
mother was here. *"Bikira Mariya Yakonekeye i Kibeho"*—
the Virgin Mary was appearing in Kibeho.

"I could not determine the color of her skin, but she was
of incomparable beauty," explained the initial visionary,
Alphonsine Mumureke, who encountered Mary at a Catholic school called Sisters' College. "She was barefoot with
a white dress with no seams and a white veil on her head.
Her hands were joined together and her fingers turning
toward Heaven."

She called herself *"Mother of the Word"* and with
phrases distinctly similar to those spoken at Medjugorje
called for *"prayer from the heart."* It was a time of recall.
The Virgin urged Rwandans to forsake attachment to
worldly things and follow the narrow road to Heaven. She
told another visionary, Agnes Kamagju, that the people
must renounce fornication and *"make of their bodies an
instrument destined to the glory of God and not an object
of pleasure at the service of men."*

The road to Satan is easy and wide, Mary told a third
seer, Vestine Salina, whose parents were Muslim. And
everyone was taking that road because there were fewer
obstacles. The world wasn't just indifferent but had turned
against God. We must repent and ask pardon, said Mary,
a grace obtained by meditating on the suffering and passion
of Jesus and His mother. The result of not doing so was
shown to them in visions of Hell and Purgatory. At one
point, while taking a "trip" to "a different universe," Vestine was comatose for forty hours. She saw a place with
fire where the greatest torture wasn't the temperature but
the total absence of God. Then Vestine was shown a large
group of children playing and singing—happy and yet
suffering. That was Purgatory, a place of reconciliation.
Lastly Vestine saw a place of splendid light and perfect
happiness. Heaven. According to visionary Anathalie
Mukamazimpaka, Mary was telling mankind to "wake up,
stand up, wash yourselves and look to her tenderly. We
must dedicate ourselves to prayer, we must develop in us
the virtue of charity, availability, and humility. If Mary

comes to us it is because she loves us. She asks, do we love her? Are you washing yourselves?"

The true road, Mary told her, *"is the one of suffering."*

Those were some of the moral mesages. As in Medjugorje: prayer and sacrifice. But there were also apocalyptical undertones. It was said the visionaries at Kibeho were shown terrifying glimpses into the future: a tree in flames, a river of blood, and many abandoned, decapitated corpses. The world, said Our Lady of Kibeho, was on *"the edge of catastrophe."*

According to visionary Emmanuel Segatashya, a pagan who claimed to have received similar messages, Christ appeared to him dressed in a tunic on July 2, 1982, while Segatashya was on the way back from picking beans. "He taught me the Lord's Prayer," Segatashya told a film crew from Marian Communications. "And how to pray from the heart. He filled my heart with such joy. When I saw Jesus, He was surrounded by a bright light. He told me we don't reach Heaven by special gifts or compromises, but only through prayers coming from the heart. There's not much time to prepare for the Last Judgment."

The Virgin had come, stressed Alphonsine, to pave the way for her Son.

During an apparition on October 2, 1982, Alphonsine, with the exaggerated gestures common to the culture, fell to the ground seven times. She seemed very sad, almost hysterical—crying but continuing her prayers and song. "On the day you will come to call your children, have mercy on us!" she was heard imploring the Madonna.

Justice. Mercy and justice. As always, Mary was trying to stretch the period of mercy as far as she could before the time came for justice.

Her arrival in Kibeho, which lasted at least until 1989, was foretold by the Italian priest Stefano Gobbi, who, ironically, visited Africa on May 13, 1981, six months before the first apparitions in Rwanda and for that matter more than a month before the first appearances in Medjugorje.

"This is the time when all are bound to become aware of my special motherly presence," she had told Gobbi. *"I have come down from Heaven to manifest myself, through*

*you, along all the roadways of the world: along those
traversed by the poor and the desperate, along those grievous roads of sinners and the wanderers, along those of the
sick, the agonizing, and the dying.''*

In various other messages Mary again used precisely the
language she used at Medjugorje. She spoke of God's
"plan" and the importance of responding to His call. But
she lamented that many of her legitimate appearances, in
places like Kibeho, in *"faraway and dangerous places,''*
were ignored and given little credence.

Had the requests made at Fatima been fulfilled, she told
Gobbi, the Church would have achieved its greatest sanc-
tification.

Instead, there was loneliness and emptiness.

Satan had succeeded in waging war at the Church's very
summit, threatening, said Mary, *"the rock on which the
Church is founded.''*

Through the power of God she had let Satan fall under
the illusion that he'd conquered the Church, when suddenly she obtained from God a great new hope, Pope John
Paul II, *"who had been prepared and formed by me."* He
was to be a stumbling block for all God's enemies, *"the
rock against which the great division will take place."* The
Virgin was going to defeat Satan by drawing up her army
from the simplest of believers. These soldiers would attain
victory not with bravado but with their humility.

*"Not to the great, or the powerful, or the rich, or the
proud is it given to understand my voice and to penetrate
the mystery of my heart,''* she said on June 19, 1982. *"It
is granted to the little, to the poor, to the humble servants
of the Lord. With them, I have formed my cohort.''*

Her army was gelling and their prayers would pierce the
clouds and defang the demons. As for sacrifices, those not
only further weakened Satan but served as a formal invitation to Jesus. Father Gobbi too was predicting the return
of Christ, but it didn't seem like there was going to be
another humble scene at a manger. Instead he spoke of the
return of Christ's *reign.* Jesus was going to come in light
and splendor, re-establishing His Kingdom on earth.

*"The hour of justice and of mercy has begun and soon
you will see the wonders of the merciful love of the Divine*

Heart of Jesus and the triumph of my Immaculate Heart,"
Mary said in 1982, adding the next month, *"Humanity has
reached that time when it is to live through the bloody
hours of the great scourge, which will purify it through fire,
hunger, and devastation."*

The *"golden door"* of Christ's Divine Heart was *"about
to open,"* said Mary, and Jesus was about *"to pour forth
upon the world the torrents of His mercy. These are floods
of fire and grace, which will transform and renew the
whole world."*

While the *"fire of the love of the Holy Spirit"* was about
to come, Mary told the Italian locutionist Fr. Gobbi that
it was also still the hour of Satan.

The devil had managed *"by guile"* to draw to himself
"scientists, artists, philosophers, scholars, the powerful."
Atheism had spread, she said, *"to a degree that mankind
has never before known."*

Her adversary *"has taken possession of everything: never
before as in these present times has the world become so
completely his kingdom over which he exercises his power
as ruler* (8/24/77)."

And that was why she was now performing *"great
wonders:"* because she'd been *"appointed by the Most
Holy Trinity as leader of this terrible battle, which involves
Heaven and earth, heavenly and earthly spirits. It is a
great and continuous struggle, often invisible, and at this
time it has become general."*

She warned that while much of her plan would be carried forth by apparitions, the devil would succeed in
infiltrating and imitating them. He would seduce God's
people *"by false manifestations of the supernatural in
order to bring about deception and confusion on all sides.
He will succeed in working many prodigies which will
beguile the minds of even the good."*

Satan, she told Gobbi, *"will set snares for you in all sorts
of ways with pride, with lust, with doubts, with discouragement, with curiosity. You will be sifted like wheat and
many will be allured by his dangerous deceits."*

If there were times bishops may have been too quick to
condemn, there were also times when such condemnations
saved countless thousands from what Our Lady described
as deceit and discouragement. In America around this

time, Francis John Mungavero, bishop of Brooklyn, signed condemnation of the Bayside apparitions, finding after a "thorough investigation" that the visions of a woman named Veronica Lueken "completely lacked authenticity." They created just the type of "confusion" Mary warned Gobbi about, and were declared "contrary to the Faith of our Catholic Church."

Elsewhere and everywhere, Satan also seduced us with his great weapon of pride. Pride! Pride was never more rampant than in the 1980s, planting the seeds of selfishness and egoism. Everyone was proud! Everyone saw themselves as special and above the others! If AIDS was a physical disease, pride was the spiritual equivalent!

And like Lucifer, whose pride led him to challenge God, mankind too sought to sit on the heavenly throne. Everyone, the New Agers told us, had the potential of becoming a "god," and that type of occult sloganeering was pure danger. It was pride that more than anything led people down the wrong road, and according to Mary, mankind was preparing the chastisement *with its own hands.*

The sin of abortion—*"the great crime of killing children still in their mother's womb"*—especially cried out for God's vengeance.

There was need of *"a great miracle,"* she explained, because of the flood of filth propagated by means of social communication, *"especially the cinema, the press, and television."*

"With messages I have given and apparitions I have granted in many parts of the world, with my numerous weepings, even with blood, I want to make you understand that this is a grave hour, that the cup of Divine Justice is now full," she told Gobbi.

"I will make my presence felt in an extraordinary way because great indeed is this battle which we must fight against Satan, sin, and all the great armies of evil," she'd said on another occasion.

Long before the victory of Solidarity in Poland, which led to the downfall of Communism throughout Europe, during a cenacle in Vienna, Austria, on August 31, 1988, the Virgin, scooping all political journalists and foreign experts, told Father Gobbi and a group of priests from Hungary and Yugoslavia, *"With Austria and Germany, from here I bless the surrounding countries which are still under the yoke of a great slavery and today I announce that the moment of their liberation is close."*

In 1984, before a trip to Zompita, Udine, Gobbi heard Mary say, *"Like a mother, I am telling you the dangers through which you are going, the imminent threats, the extent of the evils that could happen to you, **only because those evils can yet be avoided by you, the dangers can be evaded, the plan of God's justice always can be changed by the force of His merciful love** (my emphasis). Also, when I predict chastisements to you, remember that everything, at any moment, may be changed by the force of your prayer and your reparative penance."*

"Even in this Second Coming, the Son will come to you through His mother," said Mary. *"He will come suddenly and the world will not be ready for His coming. He will come for a judgment for which man will find himself unprepared. He will come to establish His kingdom in the world, after having defeated and annihilated His enemies."*

The glorious reign, the reign of light, was in preparation.

But before that was possible an army had to be gathered and the earth, through chastisements like the famine about to strike Ethiopia, had to be cleansed.

CHAPTER 33

The Hour of the Apostles of Light

In his jail cell deep inside the Soviet Union, Catholic activist Josyp Terelya continued to record mystical experiences.

On July 17, 1983, he wrote his wife Olena that he had a vision in which he was at the shrine of Zarvanystya, in the center of a meadow, when suddenly an intense light illuminated the vegetation. A large white eagle came and settled on the field and told him he should not fear.

In the distance Terelya saw an old man dressed in white. The man introduced himself as the Archangel Michael and predicted that great miracles would occur in several years, miracles that would be witnessed by hundreds of thousands.

"The Lord is now gathering the good against the evil," said Michael. *"The world would long ago have been destroyed but the soul of the world would not allow this. As the soul preserves the life of the body, so do Christians preserve the life of the world. God needs fervent and constant sons. You shall go through the ways of the world and give witness, and in the end God will punish the apostates because only through this punishment will God be able to bring man back to sound reason. And when the faith and love shall be reborn, Satan will begin a new persecution of the Christians. Times of persecution will begin, of priests*

*and the faithful. The world will be divided into the mes-
sengers of God and messengers of anti-christ. After the
great revelations of the Virgin Mary, renewal of love of
Christ will begin."*

Michael and the eagle: Once again we're reminded of
Revelation, which describes the eagle as a creature from
the "throne room" of Heaven (4:7) whose wings are given
to the Virgin when she flies to the wilderness (12:14).
"The great eagle," Mary further explained to Father
Gobbi (5/6/89), *"is the Word of God, above all the Word
contained in the Gospel of my Son..."*

The eagle had landed, the Virgin was at her place in the
wilderness, and now came the next event in *Revelation,*
the serpent spewing water "like a flood after the woman,
that he might cause her to be carried away by the flood."
The devil was vomiting a deluge. He was going to sweep
her off the face of the earth. Or at least he was going to
drench her. The floodwaters were the flow of satanic filth
and negativism. They lapped over the shores of every
nation, a high and frightening tide on a planet that was
covered in darkness.
*"Because of these attacks of the dragon, in these years,
piety toward me has steadily diminished among many of
the faithful and, in some places, has even disappeared,"*
Mary pointed out to Gobbi in 1989.
Thus did Mary need messengers. Thus did she continue
to gather God's sandbaggers. Thus did she head for the
corners of the world, the unlikeliest corners, the downtrodden nations, looking for the simple and humble to carry
her light and illuminate the great and growing night.
In Magomano, Kenya, images of the Virgin were actually
seen in lamps and torches.

It was what she described to Father Gobbi as *"the hour
of the apostles of light."* And she wanted those apostles
to come from all walks of life and all religions. During
1982, in Damascus, Syria, Moslems, Catholics, and Greek
Orthodox watched in common wonderment as an icon of
Mary exuded oil starting on November 27. Within days the
Virgin began appearing to the woman who owned the icon,

Mirna Nazour, coming in a globe of light and leaving with three flashes.

The message was religious unity. Damascus had played a role in the schisms between East and West, when what is now the Orthodox Church split from Rome. It was in Damascus that a saint named John Damascene defended the veneration of religious images, which Emperor Leo III tried to ban in A.D. 726. Now an icon was shedding holy oil there! Unity. Clearly unity. Followers of Christ needed to unify against a common adversary. It was ridiculous how Protestants carped at Catholics and Catholics carped at Moslems and Moslems detested the Jews.

The Church is the kingdom of Heaven on earth," Mary said. *"He who divides it sins. He who is happy with these divisions also sins. . . Do not be afraid. I am with you. Through you I will educate my generation."*

There were those who argued against unity, spreading alarm that such solidarity would lead to a single world religion, which would then make it easygoing for the Anti-Christ to assume power, but Mary wasn't asking Orthodox, Moslems, and Protestants to become Catholics, only to recognize her special role and unify against Satan.

The messages were approved by the Greek Orthodox Church and didn't come solely from Mary. Jesus too appeared to Mirna, as a blinding, all-encompassing light. On August 14, 1987, He made clear again that His mother was not to be denigrated. *"She is my mother from whom I was born,"* He told the Syrian visionary. *"He who honors her honors me. He who denies her denies me."*

Clearly, especially in downtrodden Third World nations, Mary was the Holy Spirit's way of attending mankind with a motherly presence. But her role was under constant attack. The verbal floodgates were open. Certain Catholic priests removed statues of her from their churches, statues that often portrayed her as stepping on the head of the serpent, while non-denominational preachers, confused in their definitions, persisted in proclaiming Marian devotion to be idolatry.

"Just as in Jerusalem all the prophets were put to death, just as in this city the very Son of God, the Messiah

promised and awaited for so many centuries, was rejected, outraged, and condemned, so also today in the Church, the new Israel of God, the salvific action of your mother, the heavenly prophetess of these last times, is too often obstructed by silence and rejection," she told Father Gobbi on March 5, 1982, in Jerusalem.

A year later, in 1983, the Virgin showed herself on a wall at Beit Sahour, Bethlehem, a city dominated by Palestinians.

That same year she also manifested on a plain glass window in an Orthodox church in East Brunswick, New Jersey.

Yes, it was a message of ecumenism, and yes, as Father Gobbi said, she was especially prominent among the small and humble and impoverished. *"You have seen with what great fervor they recite the holy Rosary, and with what veneration they surround my images, how they place me in every room of their poor homes,"* Mary told Gobbi during a cenacle in Enugu, Nigeria. *"To these I will manifest myself even more, by apparitions and by means of my maternal presence, aiding them and soliciting Providence so that they may not lack food or clothing."*

In Argentina, where locutions and apparitions of Mary and Jesus were experienced by a 46-year-old woman named Gladys Herminia Quiroga de Motta, Christ pointed to the satanic flood and repeating the Syrian messages said, *"Before, the world was saved by means of Noah's Ark. Today the Ark is My mother. Through her, souls will be saved, because she will bring them toward Me. He who rejects My mother rejects me!"*

These apparitions were taking place about 145 miles north of Buenos Aires, on the outskirts of a city called San Nicolás, and in all there were about two thousand messages, messages seeking adoration of Jesus, prayer to the Holy Spirit, the reading of Scripture, peace of heart, and a turning away from envy.

Evil continued to spread, the Virgin said, and she would overcome it with the *"humble ones."* The Lord had a time for everything *"and this is the time for the call. It is up to you to answer."*

We are in *"very dramatic moments,"* Mary told Gladys,

and for the moment Satan was triumphant. But it was a victory that was superficial and *"will last briefly."*

Gladys had a vision in which she saw serpents with great eyes but eyes that couldn't see. They seemed stuck in a light green or blue fog, no longer able to slither. *"Daughter, the Prince of Evil pours out his venom today with all his might, because he sees his sorry reign is ending and little is left to him,"* announced the Virgin. *"His end is near."*

While it seemed like Satan was all-powerful (omnipotent), it was God who reigned in the Universe, she said, *"only He."* We were to humble ourselves before God, not the devil. Victory was assured. The victory of her Immaculate Heart. The victory of Jesus.

But Satan wasn't going to go without a fight, and he wasn't going to go before inflicting yet more damage and trying to lead mankind into catastrophes. The earth, said Mary in 1985, *"is in great danger,"* covered with God's warning. Atheism and indifference to the supernatural was especially acute in the larger cities, where Satan was able through the pride of "sophistication" to focus his energies and spread blindness like a spiritual plague.

God had not abandoned mankind. Man had abandoned God. In places like Greenwich Village it was considered offensive to display any form of Christian symbol unless it was a crucifix worn like junk jewelry. The pentagram was more acceptable than ashes on Ash Wednesday. I know from having spent years in Manhattan that there is an extreme resistance to the Holy Spirit and that some people mistake this resisting energy—the energy of confusion and anxiety—as New York's "electricity."

I remember walking into one New Age bookstore in the Village and quickly leaving after spotting the clerks at the back of the store—all decked in pyramids and snake rings—shipping books that appeared to be satanic bibles.

Abortionists openly advertise their services on subway posters, and so do practitioners of astrology.

The devil has run riot in New York City. In front of St. Patrick's Cathedral militant homosexuals wore imitation clerical garb and fake miters scrawled with the words,

"Enjoy Safe Sex," demanding that the cardinal, John O'Connor, condone the use of condoms.

They also carried placards showing a nude Christ, and they disrupted Mass on December 10, 1989. As *The New York Post* reported, "The radical homosexuals turned a celebration of the Holy Eucharist into a screaming babble of sacrilege by standing in the pews, shouting and waving their fists, tossing condoms into the air."

One protester grabbed a consecrated host and threw it to the ground. Afterward Cardinal O'Connor felt the need to reconsecrate the cathedral.

It was the spirit of Marques de Sade. It was the spirit of Aleister The Beast. It was the spirit of Marxism and every other anti-Christian outburst. Condoms in church! How happy Margaret Sanger would be!

It seemed like mankind was quickly dividing into two camps, those with allegiance to the Almighty and those with allegiance to sensuality and other dehumanizing sins. Humanity, said Mary, was just about totally *"contaminated."* In a vision the year before the demonstration at St. Patrick's, Gladys saw the earth divided into two parts. One part represented two-thirds of mankind and the other, one-third. Mary was with the minority. Gladys saw her holding the Infant and from her bosom were rays of light that radiated toward the two-thirds who represented sin and corruption. *"Gladys,"* she said, *"you are seeing the world half destroyed. These rays of light are sent from my heart that wants to save as many hearts as it can."*

Did this vision explain the many other visions that saw the majority of mankind "destroyed"? Was the destruction physical or spiritual? Did the fire so many saw falling from the sky represent hellfire—God's Justice?

Gladys saw enormous monsters that "appeared like dinosaurs and others like frightful human beings with huge heads and ears. When they were very near me, a blue wall appeared and came between the monsters and me."

The "wall" was the Virgin's cloak, and it suggested that with prayer, the devil was not omnipotent but *impotent*— more bark than bite, disarmed by those who invoked the Holy Spirit.

"The prince of evil knows that his sad kingdom is com-

ing to an end. In this way, he sheds his poison with all his strength. There is only a little time left."

It was a time for hope, for peace instead of anxiety. We were coming to the hour of the Holy Spirit. We were experiencing guidance just as the Jews of old had the guidance of the pillar of fire.

But those who sinned still found themselves in a precarious condition. They were *"hanging by a thread,"* in the words of a 1984 message to Gladys, and there was no time left for procrastination.

Again, there were rumblings of a Second Coming, or at least a major manifestation of Christ's power. Mary asked Gladys to have a medal struck with seven stars. The seven stars are a symbol in the first three chapters of *Revelation*—which discuss persecution of the Church but also hope for believers.

"Because you have kept My command to persevere, I also will keep you from the hour of trial which shall come upon the whole world, to test those who dwell on the earth," says the Lord in *Revelation* 3:10-11. *"Behold, I come quickly!"*

CHAPTER 34

The Hour of Exodus

And just as quickly, God was collecting His people. I have no idea what visionaries mean when they claim the Second Coming is "imminent," nor even whether to believe it.

But this I'm sure of: the Holy Spirit has been drawing the true believers from the land of heathens.

He was calling us to separate from those of cold hearts, blind ambition, and materialism.

He was nudging us away from "enlightened" and "rational" types who, like Marx, espouse a superficial morality.

He was beckoning us to the wilderness, for prayer and sacrifice.

We were like the ancient people of Israel when they were living among the oppressive Egyptians. God was leading us into the wilderness so we could escape from mankind's new amorality—as the people of Israel traveled through the wilderness on the way to the Red Sea.

We've been focusing on *Revelation* 12, but there are also indications that we're in times like those in the Book of Exodus. Take a look at that account and you'll see some of the same things that seers now perceive. In *Exodus* there was fire, thunder, hail. There were three days of darkness. There was a river of blood. There were swarms of locusts,

267

gnats, flies, and frogs, which have long symbolized demons. There were horrible plagues.

That was the fate of the oppressive Egyptians, the pagans who were so like the atheists, rationalists, occultists, earth-worshippers, humanists, Masons, and money-grabbers of our own era. While we saw evil in Qaddafi and the Ayatollah Khomeini, or in the shooting down of the Korean airliner, we failed to see it planting itself right here at home. While we saw the more obvious forms of evil—Jim Jones and Son of Sam—we missed it when it infiltrated television, movies, and magazines.

While our attention was diverted by Watergate, we missed larger evils that, ironically, were beginning to dominate the media.

There was no one around who was quite like Hitler and Stalin, but evil had graduated to a new level. It was more refined and insidious. And when that happened around 1200 B.C., God drew His people from the domain of the enemy, shielded them in the wilderness, and geared them for battle. Is that what the Holy Spirit is doing now, calling His people out from the land of the enemy, testing their courage, purifying them, marking them as His own, and asking them to prepare for a more direct refutation of the adversary?

The "great trial" so often mentioned by visionaries is in reality the temptations of our modern society. Those who haven't gotten lost in the forest, those who have found or are now finding their way back to God's camp in the wilderness, those who'd navigated around the miring swamplands of Marx, Nietzsche, Huxley, Sanger, Crowley, Freud, Hugh Hefner, and any number of other materialists—those who'd avoided or turned from greed and lust, hearing the bugle call of places like Medjugorje, or the simple call of His Word—now qualified as a kind of chosen people.

This was the cohort. This was the humble army with which Mary planned to disarm the enemy.

The signs and messages are like the signs and messages in *Exodus*. They often occur on mountaintops, as they occurred on mountains in the Old Testament, and just as there was smoke around Mount Sinai, so do pilgrims spot

unnatural gray vapors—along with columns of supernatural light—atop Mount Krizevac in Medjugorje.

That's not to say Krizevac is the new Mount Sinai. I'm
not trying to exaggerate the importance of Medjugorje or
any of the apparitions. But no doubt about it, specific biblical phenomena are repeating themselves. At Betania,
Venezuela, pilgrims see many manifestations of fog and
light—bubbles of purple around the sun, or rays of inexplicable light that illuminate a small crucifix.

Others have seen a rose-colored cloud near the waterfall,
with images of Our Lady.

Mary has also been spotted in the pose of the Miraculous
Medal, formed with rays of sun and streaming through the
canopy of trees.

One photograph taken by a pilgrim showed a mysterious
sparkling red column of light encircling the grotto *like a
pillar of fire.*

Was Betania a missing piece to the puzzle, a remarkable
puzzle that was forming along the lines of *Exodus?*

Was the "pillar of fire" like the pillar of fire seen in
Exodus 13:21?

Was Betania yet another place in the wilderness, on the
way to deliverance?

Thousands reported remarkable experiences there. This
was Maria Esperanza's territory, where she had spotted the
Virgin on March 25, 1976. Precisely eight years later, following a noon field Mass on March 25, 1984, the Virgin
appeared again, but this time in seven apparitions and this
time not just to Maria or a small group of pilgrims but to
108 people who had come to celebrate the anniversary.

"After this liturgical act took place in the old sugar mill,
the attendants moved to the porch of the farmhouse in
order to have lunch and rest," wrote Bishop Pio Bello
Ricardo in his pastoral letter. "Meanwhile some children
were playing in the leveled area by the cascade. Suddenly,
they saw Our Lady over the cascade. It was a very short
apparition. They immediately ran to tell the others who
were 150 meters away. They all hurried to the place of the
apparition and they were talking about what had happened
when the Virgin appeared again and all the people who
were present were able to see her. During that same after-

noon she appeared seven times, each time for five to ten
minutes, except for the last time, at dusk, when she
appeared for approximately half an hour.''

I spoke to several people who were there, and they
described the remarkable formation of a luminous fog that
took Our Lady's shape. Maria's family was present and her
husband Geo saw the white image inside the brush. ''It
looked like a marble statue,'' said Geo. ''White, with some
blue in the center which I recognized as the Holy Immaculate Virgin of Lourdes. Everyone agreed on this opinion.
The image stood immobile for about 15 minutes as we
prayed together.''

There was one apparition after the other, and the scent
of roses was overpowering.
So was the sensation of peace.
''During her fourth appearance I was able to see her in
much greater detail and much closer than before,'' recalled
another witness, General Jose Luis Tarre Murzi. ''My
daughter Marianela and I saw her garment and sash much
more defined. I asked my daughter not to distract me
because I wanted to see her disappear. A few seconds later,
she disappeared instantly just as if one were to turn off the
image from a movie projector. I was so overjoyed and filled
with such emotion at that moment, I started to cry.''

That was what impressed the bishop so much, that rank-
ing members of Caracas society (including a former
general!) were among the more than one hundred people
who signed affadavits of events on March 25. By the time
of the pastoral letter, another 390 people had signed decla-
rations, and the bishop estimated that a total of at least
eight hundred saw the Virgin at Betania by 1992, for she
was (and is) still appearing. There were tremendous
similarities to Medjugorje, noted Bishop Ricardo, as well
as to older apparitions. Mary appeared at Betania both as
Our Lady of the Miraculous Medal and Our Lady of
Lourdes. The apparitions of the 19th century, the apparitions which had initiated the modern age of Mary, were
coming full circle.
The Virgin with grace streaming from her hands, the

same Virgin as at Rue du Bac, was at Betania, Venezuela.

During a visit to Rome the following September, Bishop Ricardo was received by the Sacred Congregation for the Doctrine of the Faith and given a set of guidelines for evaluating the phenomena. After personally conducting the investigation he reported to Rome that the visions were authentic. Further, he declared Betania sacred land, a place for worship and sanctuary. Of Venezuela's 37 bishops and auxiliary bishops, only two disapproved of Ricardo's decisive and momentous declaration.

"I spoke to Cardinal Ratzinger twice about this, and he had no intentions of interfering," says Bishop Ricardo. "I also spoke to the pope about it. It was a general observation about prudence. The pope said it seemed like a sign of the times, the many apparitions around the world. He recommended a book about Medjugorje by Laurentin. He seemed to me to believe, but he was very prudent. My personal impression is that the pope believed the apparitions of Medjugorje were authentic. I explained to him the apparition of Betania and the main message of reconciliation. He said we must be prudent but that this seems like a sign of terrible times. The pope said the Spirit was using Our Lady as an instrument of evangelizing the world."

There were a host of other phenomena, some unique to Betania. At times the waterfall took on the silhouette of Mary, and at other moments a mysterious blue butterfly, unlike any others in size and color, fluttered from the Lourdes grotto and circled the crowd. Maria was told it was a sign of the Virgin's presence, as were the sudden, soothing breezes.

"My children, I call on you this day with the fullness of life to live with a clear conscience the responsibilities of the mission entrusted to you, with the virtues of faith, hope, and charity," she told Maria. *"I particularly recommend purity of intention, humility, and simplicity. The Lord's laws and doctrines are a part of you . . . the promise to keep the straight road of the innocents."*

Rise, Mary was saying. Rise and fight with the weapons of love and purity. Forsake obsession with material "success." The time had come to rebuild the morals of God,

or the future would be unpleasant. There was still time.
The situation was anything but hopeless. Pessimism was
the work not of the Holy Spirit but Satan.

Help those who are still afflicted with evil, she said, and
*"bring them forward to live in a healthy environment and
in peace of the spirit."* She wanted zeal for work of the
Church. *"A great moment is approaching, a great day of
light!"*

The main message was hope and prayer.

God existed and was healing His children.

He was drawing them out of enemy regions.

What about prophecies of world cataclysms?

The bishop observed that many visions were symbolic,
and not necessarily of actual future events. "A terrible
earthquake can be a symbolic version of terrible things surrounding the world," he noted.

And a symbol of God shaking up the world.

After visiting Bishop Ricardo I thought about his
serenity. He certainly didn't seem paranoid about any coming chastisements, and the Virgin certainly hadn't come to
create anxiety. She'd come to promote conversion, prayer,
and peace of heart, and already, as I said, Maria Esperanza
saw the world starting to improve, if only slightly, and if
only in certain perspectives.

The more it improved the greater the chance of lessening
punishments.

Really, Mary was a messenger of tremendous hope. For
too long, I thought, people have waited for great
cataclysms or even the end of the world like morbid thrill-
seekers. "Terminator," "Planet of the Apes," and "The
Day the Earth Stood Still." Maybe we'd seen too many
movies.

The real point was that God was calling His people;
those who were responding, whom Josyp Terelya referred
to as the "soul of the world," and their prayers were helping Mary hold back any real chastisements.

Pray, hope, and don't worry, Padre Pio always said.

But the Virgin also warned Esperanza that mankind was
abusing the gifts of grace and *"moving toward perdition.
If there is no change or improvement of life, you will*

succumb under fire: war and death. We want to halt the evil that suffocates you. We want to overcome the spirit of rebellion and the darkness of oppression by the enemy. This is why, again, in this century, my Divine Son arises. . ."

It was, said the Virgin of Betania, an *"hour of decision for humanity."* Economics, she said, had turned us cold and egotistical. We had to remove ourselves from the evil of society or succumb to plagues like those of ancient Egypt. She was coming to look for us amid *"the brouhaha of an atomic awakening that is about to explode."*

While noting that difficult times will "make us better people," Esperanza added that mankind would face a very "serious" moment—soon. She told me that before their conversion the Russians would have difficulties "among themselves," implying regional conflicts in the former Soviet Union. She had also said that there might be conflict with the "yellow races" and that 1992 to 1994 would be the onset of God's "justice in the world."

CHAPTER 35

Patches of Heaven

I wanted more evidence. I wanted more dates. If chastisements are coming, or at least some kind of warning, I wanted to know what I'm sure *you* want to know: how, where, and when?

Greater detail, I soon learned, could be found in that most Catholic of nations, Ireland. It was the hotspot for a new kind of Marian phenomenon, and we'll explore that before we get into more secrets.

Across the emerald island, statues of the Virgin seemed to be coming to life. The statues were at roadside shrines or "grottos." Strange fogs were descending on the miniature shrines and when the fog cleared these grottos would seem to temporarily "disappear," replaced by the spectacle of a shimmering heavenly meadow with the living three-dimensional figure of the Virgin standing there instead of a statue.

The damp Irish peat was replaced by little patches of Heaven!

So similar were these visions that it was like one gargantuan national occurrence. Grottos were coming to life from Armagh to Galway. The Virgin was even seen, at 11:50 a.m. on July 8, 1984, at the old apparitional site of Knock, dressed in a silvery gown, but with the brown cloak of a Carmelite nun.

While newspapers mocked the reports as a product of "the silly season," adults and children insisted they were seeing Mary and receiving messages about the world. It was the Virgin's most vigorous campaign yet. There were dozens of seers in all corners of Ireland, for by the mid-1980s, at least 25 grottos were the foci of supernatural reports.

The statues were smiling, frowning, or turning. They were disappearing and giving way to living apparitions with messages similar to Betania and Medjugorje. Anyone who wanted to hear forecasts of coming events was in the right place along Ireland's winding roads.

The epidemic seemed to have started in 1985 near a village south of Cork called Ballinspittle. There a 70-inch statue of the Lourdes Virgin, in a small cave up a steep vine-laden knoll, gained instant notoriety. "The first thing noticed was that the statue of Mary seemed to move," said a woman who lives in the nearest house. "Lots of people have seen images superimposed on the statue, and lots of people have been cured here. Our bishop has pooh-poohed the whole thing, but I've seen it move, and I've seen the face of the Sacred Heart imposed on it. Normal, intelligent people have seen the images. I've seen Padre Pio superimposed there too."

Reporters at the *Cork Examiner* treated such accounts with cynicism and amusement. It was a confirmation, in the words of one journalist, "that the Irish people had finally done what they had threatened to do for generations—lost their national marbles." But when the *Examiner* sent a dozen people to observe the Ballinspittle statue, seven came back saying they too had seen odd movements.

"There was a wave over the country and it couldn't be properly assessed by journalists because they weren't writing from faith," said one expert, Father Gerard McGinnity of Saint Patrick's College in Armagh.

"They were looking for explanations, but there *was* no rational explanation. Our Lady was asked if the moving statues were only in Ireland, and she said this was happen-

ing especially for Ireland—a kind of preparatory stage.
Why throughout Ireland? At the present time I could see
Ireland as the place where the residue of faith is strongest.
Our Blessed Mother is turning to this nation in the hope
that we'll spread this to the rest of the world—in hopes
she would find a foothold here."

It wasn't the kind of blurring or twitching one would
expect in an optical illusion. The statue movements were
pronounced, continuous, and at times nearly violent. Even
disbelievers saw the statue quaking, and a month after Ballinspittle, similar oddities were noticed in the hill country
between Cork and Killarney.

This time it wasn't just movements or superimpositions.
This time it was full-fledged, speaking apparitions.

The grotto was at a spot near Inchigeela known as Gortaneadin and had been erected in 1968 at the prodding of
a devout and seriously ill girl named Mary McCarthy, who
suffered a heart ailment and in fact died before the grotto
was actually built. Statues of Mary and St. Bernadette of
Lourdes, along with a cross, stood on a rise of rock next
to a small waterfall.

The phenomena began on August 5, 1985, when two
other village girls, Rosemary O'Sullivan and Marie
Vaughan, were bicycling around the roadside shrine and
saw the glowing figure of a tall and exquisitely beautiful
woman.

The Virgin was suddenly a moving, breathing person—
not a stone monument.

And though the girls were held awestruck by her gentle
smile, once what was happening sunk in, they hopped on
Rose's bicycle and sped home as fast as Rosemary could
pedal.

"It was just after Ballinspittle, and we thought they were
having a laugh on the locals," recalled Rosemary's mother
Elizabeth. "No way did we believe it at all. They said there
was a light, a fog, a high wind. There were even pillars
of light, which Rose called 'tubes.' The third evening when
they saw it again, Rose was hysterical because no one
believed her."

The apparitions occurred daily for the first few months
at the Gortaneadin grotto and later at another nearby grotto

known as Rossmore. Marie sprinkled holy water on the apparition and told it to leave if it was of evil. Instead the celestial female smiled brightly and said she was from Heaven. Like Medjugorje, the visionaries entered ecstasy simultaneously. Their eyes (fixed on the apparition) didn't react to flashes of light and their lips moved with no sound. Such observations were made by a doctor named M. J. Collins.

The Virgin identified herself as the "Queen of Peace" and requested families to pray the Rosary together. She also instructed the girls not to pray so fast, and she began appearing to others at the Gortaneadin grotto, where phenomena still occur. The message was prayer. *"Pray more for the conversion of sinners,"* Mary told one of the pilgrims, Mary Casey, the mother of nine children. *"This month I want you to remember bishops, priests, nuns, and all in the religious life in your prayers. Satan has begun to thwart my plans. I am always with you. Be not afraid of temptation. I want your prayers continuously."*

She urged the people to pray to the Holy Spirit because when the Holy Spirit descends, said Mary, *"you have everything."* In language nearly identical to the faraway appearances in Africa, Mary also admonished the people, especially the youth, not to use their bodies as *"instruments of pleasure,"* because their bodies *"belong to God and God alone."*

She warned that the devil would try to make them doubt, and indeed, he showed himself as a large black shadow and also as a hairy animal-like creature with red eyes and tusks. After a series of false apparitions, Mary said, *"This was a test to see if you knew the difference between love and hate. . . Ask my people to pray. Tell them to pray. This is the only way they will be saved."*

If Satan was lurking near Inchigeela, his presence was offset by the soothing arrival of angels. The O'Sullivan girl saw a "teenage" cherub holding a tall lighted candle with strange writing on it, and Marie witnessed a light coming toward the Virgin, a light that grew bigger and brighter until the figure of a young boy stood at the grotto.

This angel had blond hair and wore a knee-length white

robe and though he seemed to be male, he bore a remarkable resemblance to Marie herself.

When she asked who he was he replied that he was her guardian angel.

Again Mary requested prayers for souls in Purgatory and urged the people to fast on Fridays and pray from the heart. She also requested use of the Brown Scapular. Special attention was focused on *Matthew* 7:15-20, which speaks about testing the spirits according to their fruits, and 6:34, about the futility of anxiety. *"Beware of false prophets. My child, the devil will tempt you and is fighting for you but I shall be with you always. Go in peace."*

To build peace in the heart, said Mary, it was necessary to remain in a state of forgiveness.

As elsewhere, Mary came in accordance with the local culture. Mrs. Casey, who witnessed 81 apparitions, described the Virgin as "Irish-looking" with rosy cheeks that dimpled when she smiled. *"I have come for the sake of my Son. I cannot restrain His hand much longer... Prayer is the best weapon you have. The devil is strong with those who fear him and weak with those who despise him. Satan can do nothing to those who have surrendered themselves to God."*

Padre Pio was also seen at Inchigeela, and so was Saint Ann.

That was another nationwide phenomenon: people claimed to see the face of the Lourdes Virgin turn into the bearded countenance of Christ, especially as the Jesus of Mercy, or into holy figures like Pio, Saint Joseph, Saint Therese the Little Flower, Saint Anthony, Saint Maria Goretti, and even Pope Pius XII.

At Inchigeela pilgrims also claimed to see the visage of a young woman who fit the description of the deceased McCarthy girl. Mary McCarthy had taken a place alongside Bernadette and the Virgin!

Especially in southern Ireland, Heaven seemed to be descending and calling out to a kind of chosen people. At Mount Melleray in the Knockmeald Mountains, where there was a Lourdes grotto above a small river in a tall rockface, Mary manifested herself on August 16, 1985, to a teenager named Ursula O'Rourke.

"It was between half seven and half eight and just out of the blue we decided to go to the grotto and we said the Rosary," Ursula told me. "It wasn't as if I was staring at the statue. My little brother and I were playing. After the Rosary I was running around with him, and as we were leaving I looked back to the statue and it was *changing*. Her gown was blowing in the wind and the green shrubbery formed an unusual dark green that spun. Her head was turning in four directions. At first I thought it was my imagination. I looked at the state of Bernadette and felt it would do the same if I was imagining. I looked again at Our Lady and she was still there. I looked a third time and realized I was seeing what I was seeing."

A farmer named Michael O'Donnell, who lived just up the road, also saw the back of the grotto spinning.

"Then I saw images of Padre Pio, Our Lady, and Our Lord, where the statue was," said O'Donnell. "I could see them plain. We were praying the Rosary. The next thing I could see were steps with roses on either side and Our Lady walking down the steps. And as she was walking she was coming nearer and I kept going backward and then I collapsed. I was scared stiff and shocked—amazed. A lot of people who don't know me thought I was drunk, but I don't drink or smoke. She was 23 or 24 and with light skin. She had her hands up, like on the statue. The next thing, she went back into the statue."

At Melleray, as at most other sites, Satan tried to disrupt the heavenly serenity. On August 22, 1985, he showed himself to two local boys named Tom Cliffe and Barry Buckley, materializing to Our Lady's left with a pockmarked face and bulging eyes. He also had little stumps for horns, a sharp jaw, and brownish skin with red swellings. He laughed and jeered at the Virgin.

To their great relief the demon disappeared after a minute, but Mary warned that if the world did not improve, *"the devil will take over God's Church in ten years."* Mankind had ten years to improve, Mary said in another message—meaning the deadline was somewhere around 1995. She showed them the biblical scene of Noah's Ark.

"I love the Irish people. I am praying with the people to God, to forgive the Irish people. I want the Irish people

to spread my message to the world.''

It was as if Ireland, a nation of missionaries, where divorce and abortion were still against the law, was in Mary's plan as a beacon to the rest of Europe and perhaps the world. In New York City the face of a Marian statue at the far back of Saint Patrick's Cathedral (the most important Irish church outside of Ireland) was seen to switch and smile around the same time as Melleray and Ballinspittle.

Meanwhile, not two weeks after Melleray, on September 2, 1985, at Carns in County Sligo, which was more than three hundred miles to the north, four girls returning home up a dark country road were chattering about pop songs when they suddenly felt very afraid. "Look!" screamed one of them, Mary Hanley. There was a woman in a white veil and flowing gown. She was hovering over a field with Bernadette kneeling at her feet. The apparitional tableaux followed the girls until they got to the Hanley house, then disappeared into a cloud. The girls were so shocked they went home and prayed the rest of the night.

The following evening, September 3, neighbors gathered at the field and witnessed similar supernatural happenings. The Virgin's face was seen in the moon, and her silent lips seemed to mouth the words "faith" and "hope." It was only the beginning. From then on thousands visited the site, and among them was a woman from nearby County Mayo who began receiving apparitions and providing just what I was looking for: details about the coming "chastisements."

CHAPTER 36

Come the Thunder

Her name is Christina Gallagher. She has since become one of the most famous visionaries in the world. She is the wife of a plumber in Gortnadreha, and, in her early thirties back in 1985 when Carns was first happening, she had no aspirations of becoming a world-known mystic when she first went to the place of Mary's apparition to the four girls.

"I'd heard there were apparitions of the Virgin there, and I went, not expecting to see anything, but for a feeling of peace," she says. "But the first night I had an experience there. A star came and became redder and bigger until it got to the size of the moon and into the shape of a grotto, like the grotto of Lourdes, formed with smoke from the star. Others saw the Sacred Heart dripping blood."

There were many things seen in the sky above Carns, crosses and halos of light, and one clear bright night, images of a lamb and the Infant of Prague appeared in the clouds. The sun danced here too, and like at Medjugorje, stars changed color.

On a subsequent visit Christina saw the face of Jesus suffering on the cross, wearing the crown of thorns, his head turned toward the sky, the thorns very black and a glow around His head. The Savior's face was very drawn, long and sunken, especially below the cheekbones. His beard had been pulled out in splotches and He was clearly dying. "Dying for me," says Christina. "I was shaken up, a trembling sensation through my body. This was a Sunday night and I trembled until Monday night. It was the terror of my sins."

The face resembled a NASA reproduction based on the Shroud of Turin and Christina had an immediate affinity with Christ's suffering, subsequently experiencing the stigmata. As we spoke, seven pinpoints that looked like they'd been inflicted by small nails or thorns appeared on her head.

Years after her first visit to Carns, on January 21, 1988, Christina had her first apparition of the Virgin Mary. She wore a blue mantle and a white dress and had a slim nose, thin lips, and big blue eyes—"a stillness of peace beyond anything of this world. I thought my heart would come out of my body." The Virgin had a globe in her hands, a globe filled with swirling smoke, and she blessed Christina before fading.

In all, with her bodily eyes, Christina saw Mary thirty times, and while there were Irish visionaries who saw the Virgin more often, it was to Christina that secrets and warnings were given. She was also given a vision of the Anti-Christ.

And of course she found herself in the war with demons. At one point she encountered a diabolical creature for hours. "All I know is that I was awakened and there was a noise. It was the most horrible terror. I knew it was evil. It was part animal, part human. I could see the devil trying to get at me, but there was something stopping him. I wanted to get my prayer book. When I put my legs out of bed, it moved back, to the degree I moved forward. There were times all my energy drained out of me—times I didn't know if I would live or die. It was with me until five in the morning. It looked like part gorilla and part man. The eyes were pure fiery red. The face was like human with strange reactions. It was more human than gorilla, like a combination of man, gorilla, and kangaroo. It moved with a hop."

These were tests, figured Christina, tests that God permitted to gauge her faith and purify her. It was as if those who were privileged to see Christ or His mother had to go through comparatively similar experiences with the devil. The warfare was all the more obvious, felt Christina, because the devil "knows he will lose his power." Satan was allowed to show himself at the same visible level as Mary, and Christina encountered demons at least a dozen times.

"After I saw the Blessed Mother there were more apparitions of the devil," she says. "On one occasion I saw him in a shape like a dog, but with pink eyes and strange feet, with claws, and a face like an alligator. But it talked like a human. There were like three huge black bats falling all over, descending on his back, and one or two more descending on the floor. At one point he promised me anything in his kingdom, which he referred to as earth. Then he would get furious and say he would destroy me; he would froth and blow it toward where I was and it would burst into flames. I was left shattered to pieces. Then an older woman came and told me to be at peace. I didn't know who it was. She said I wore her symbol around my neck. Then I realized it was Saint Bridget."

She also saw angels, floating around the front room of her house, singing glory to God. She wondered if she was going insane but the experiences kept repeating. The angels were in clouds of lights with sweetly mingling voices. They had wings but the wings weren't really used to fly. The archangel Michael appeared as a huge apparition with a sword, drawing it to reassure her. "The power nearly made me pass out," says Christina. "Michael felt so much more powerful than the devil."

But Satan's century still lingered, petering out, yes, but with us still, and Christina saw "many horrific things" happening before the next millennium. Like Maria Esperanza, of whom she had never heard, Christina felt the chastisements would begin to unfold in 1992, perhaps invisibly at first, and would be completed by the year 2000, if not sooner.

"I don't know exactly what is there, but I have been given three dates that I can't say, and I do know the purification is coming and all we can do now is pray," she told me in the autumn of 1991. "At one point it seemed like it could be lessened but not now, because people have not responded to Mary's call and returned to God. I was given that there are three episodes. There will be a great crisis of suffering and there will be an occasion when everyone around the world will know that it is of God. Pray for them, because if they don't pray and they drift back into their old ways, when the purification comes I don't know what is going to happen to them. I actually feel that fire will fall and a great number will be wiped out."

This, said Christina, was what Christ was telling her. It was her latest message from Him. *"My little ones,"* He supposedly said. *"My people, my people: Why do you not respond to My cries? I gather my little ones to be my army of love. You, My people who serve the flesh and its desire before My Mercy, I will cut you down in the light of My Justice. Oh, you say to yourselves, 'This will not be.' I tell you it is close. The alarm has been set. It cannot be turned back. Your cries will be heard now, if you throw yourselves under My Mercy and turn away from sin and your evil ways."*

Christina claimed to have had a vision of Jesus huge in the sky. He drew His hands over the world and said simply, *"Woe."* And she saw balls of fire everywhere. "I would see people at the side of the road screaming. They were all looking toward the sky. I was told in the year 1992 many will cry out to God but He will not hear them."

That wasn't to say that 1992 was the year there would be a huge visible event, but it would be the start of a new spirit moving in the world. Throughout Ireland, at those many grottos where Mary had allegedly appeared, I noticed a consistent pattern: there were always pictures of the Merciful Jesus, red and white rays coming from His heart, and this theme of mercy was relevant to what Christina was now claiming: that the period of mercy was running out.

When I obtained the same picture from Franciscan Publishers in Pulaski, Wisconsin, I saw that the red and pale rays represent a shield on the soul before the wrath of God. *"Fortunate is he who lives in their brilliance, for the just hand of God will never reach him,''* Christ told Sister Faustina.

A similar theme was expressed in Scottsdale, Arizona, where Jesus, speaking in locution to a pharmaceutical administrator named Gianna Talone, was pleading for his *"little children"* to come back to God and live in sincerity and righteousness. He identified Himself as *"your Jesus of Mercy."*

It seemed just that. It seemed like all the apparitions and news from Heaven, all the signs, were a gift of supreme and unfathomable mercy, but that such a period would not last forever. "The time of His justice is about to begin, and there's chastisement to come," said Christina Gallagher. "You can lighten that if you want, but I cannot lighten the words given to me. Some people say that the message given to me is very gloomy. Well, if you take the seriousness of what Jesus and the Blessed Mother are saying through the messages, they're not gloomy because there's hope, mercy, and love. We're called to come to repentance, and if we don't come back this is what's going to happen. God is all love and mercy, and if you do not respond you have to put up with the consequences."

Most important was to protect the eternal soul, pointed out Christina, who like the visionaries at Fatima, Kibeho, and Medjugorje, was given glimpses into Purgatory and Hell. She saw Hell as a place with "flames burning into flames," fire as far as she could see, and bodies swimming in it. "They were black, and it was like the flames were so enormous you could see the force," she said. "Jesus spoke and said, *'This is the abyss of sin, the place for all those who do not love My Father.'* I could look down and down. Hundreds of bodies. They were nearly helpless."

For her glimpse of Purgatory, Christina was taken down a narrow road and then some steps and then a dark tunnel. At first she thought it was Hell because it was so dismal, with black gates and slushy mud. Very dark. Christina spotted two people she had known, a layman and a priest.

"I really desperately desired that they be released," said Christina. "Then Jesus disappeared and it was like I was thrown against a stone wall—trapped there, that I couldn't move—and there were evil spirits playing with fire. I could feel the fire hit me. It didn't burn but it caused agony. I said, 'Jesus, I desire to stay here if it releases those two souls.' Then a great ball of light engulfed me and it was all over. Later the Blessed Mother told me the souls were released.''

That was a deep stage of Purgatory, but not the deepest. The lowest level was called "the chamber of suffering." At the higher levels she saw Purgatory as an enormous area of gray ashes with no one visible. They were waiting for their release.

That was the real message, the real message in all the supernatural interventions, that the spirit world exists and that we should prepare for our destiny every waking moment. The real chastisements are at the spirit level.

"It's our soul that's at risk," Christina emphasizes. "The Lord wants to save our souls and mankind doesn't want to listen. Nobody needs to wait for a chastisement, because we don't know, we could be taken today or tomorrow."

People tend to focus on the part of the messages dealing with Divine punishment, complained Christina, while ignoring the call to conversion, fasting, and prayer. The important message was detachment from things of this world and preparation for the next. "In fasting we take the luxury out of eating, and by depriving the flesh, which is dust, we allow God, through the sacrifice of the cross, to work in our souls," she said. "Fasting teaches us to surrender, and not to look for worldly things, like more power, more money, and all the other things that attract us.''

Those who lived the messages had nothing to fear, she emphasized. It didn't matter "whether their lives are taken or they are left.''

The devil's time was short and his force was strong. The battle, she was told by Catherine of Siena, was "but only at an early stage." To be sure, there were improvements. Already there were signs that the epic era of Eighties greed, the chaotic corporate mergers and obsession with paper wealth, the reverence for daily Dow Jones figures and the Mercedes Benz, was on the wane, exposed for its superficiality, and yet there was a huge spiritual vacuum, especially in sexual affairs. The travesties of televangelists and politicans were symbols of a society in decay, and so was the trend to violence and degrading sensuality. Indeed, there was a growing radicalism, an amoral radicalism, sweeping the modernized world, and while signs were hopeful that Communism was about to end—that *perestroika* was ushering in great winds of change, in the wake of Russia's implicit consecration by John Paul II, who on March 25, 1984, on the day apparitions were seen in Betania, renewed the consecrations of the world to Mary—this was only a diminishing of formal Communism. The errors of *generic* communism—that is, atheism, extreme rationalism, and secular humanism—continued to spread, personified in the English-speaking world by organizations such as the ACLU (American Civil Liberties Union) and the philosophies spawned by an excessive reverence for science. Marxism wasn't dead, it was just wearing different feathers.

"The devil was allowed to appear to me so that I would see the truth," says Christina. "When someone comes along and tells me there's no devil and there's no Hell— and I've heard religious talk like this—it's like a knife going through my heart, because I know what I've suffered at the hands of the Evil One."

The things of the earth, Christina was told, were only to tempt us. In a three-and-a-half-hour apparition on July 1, 1988, Mary told her that *"many people have made money or lust their god, but when they die they will be in darkness."* She was warned especially about fornication, murder, abortion, and test-tube babies. On January 30, 1990, Christina said she heard Christ tell her that humanity better prepare itself, for the time had come for its cleansing. *"A great darkness will come upon the world,"* He told Christina. *"The heavens will shake. The only light will be through the Son of God and Man. The lightening bolts will flash like nothing the world has ever seen. My Hand will come over the world more swiftly than the wind."*

It wasn't meant to spark fear, but to call people back to their Redeemer. The battle between light and dark, said Jesus, was indeed great. Its intensity could not be overemphasized. *"The demons rage upon the earth. They are loos-*

ened from their pit. Tell all humanity of the Seven Seals of God. Tell all humanity: pray, confess. Seek only the Kingdom of God."

The Virgin was just as direct, according to Christina, and warned that *"the justice of God is unthinkable!"* The angels and saints were crying out for the purification of the world. The calamity had already started, said Mary. *"The influence of the Prince of Darkness is all around you. Arm yourselves with the Rosary. My Church will be shaken, even to its foundation. My children who want to be saved must repent. My chosen children, you are now like lambs among wolves. Stand firm, have no fear, for the Hand of the Mighty One is with you."*

The calamity was a world plunged into the depths of sin, a world, said Mary, that would now have to drink of its bitterness. *"The hour is close. Pray, pray, pray!"*

The Virgin told Christina to have her spiritual director read the Seven Seals, especially the Seventh Seal.

Talk of the Seals rang the alarm again. I thought back to the star seen at Carns that turned into a blood-red moon, and found it in the Seals of *Revelation,* which speak of a time when "the sun became black as sackcloth of hair, and the moon became like blood." That was in *Revelation* 6:12, under the Sixth Seal, which is entitled, "Cosmic Disturbances."

It is the part dealing with God's wrath, and in the very next chapter come the angels to whom it has been granted to harm the seas and earth after seals are placed on the heads of God's servants. This was very similar to what the visionary from Turzovka, Matous Lasuta, and the seer of Escorial, Ampara Cuevos, had been told. According to Matous, the Virgin said that *"all my children will receive and carry the sign of the cross on their foreheads. This sign only my chosen ones will see. These chosen ones will be instructed by my angels how to conduct themselves. My faithful will be without any kind of fear during the most difficult hours."*

Father Gobbi also spoke about the seal placed on the heads of those following God—and how Satan was placing his own mark on sinners. Those marked by God, Christ, and the Virgin Mary seemed to be those responding to the movement of the Holy Spirit, whether at Medjugorje and other apparitional sites, or by a renewed reverence for God and new attention to His tenets and Bible. Fundamentalists were speaking of the end times, and so were Orthodox Jews and charismatic Protestants. The spirit, it seemed, was marking His own in various ways—and continuing to form a cohort out of the land of Egypt.

If all these events are truly following the train of *Revelation,* and if the Apocalypse is to be taken literally, we are in the period when seals are being placed, when foreheads are being marked, when the cohort is being formed, when the "exodus" is being organized—or what Christina Gallagher and the visionaries in Arizona knew as the "period of Mercy."

But after the seals are in place, according to *Revelation* 7:9, comes the Great Tribulation. When the Seventh Seal is opened the angel takes the censer, fills it with fire, and throws it to the earth.

And then comes what we discussed in Chapter 19: the sounding of the trumpets, whereby trees catch fire, the seas turn to blood, a great star falls from the sky, poisoning the waters (a star called "Wormwood"), and the stars are darkened.

Christina believed the messages of Medjugorje. She said she was told the same thing. She was told the world would be given a warning, through a sign, and if the sign was not accepted, the chastisement would follow. "I can feel it within myself," she said. "I can feel it coming at a great speed."

Mary said she was uniting her own bleeding heart to that of her Son, in the hopes of withholding the great punishment *"that is quickly coming to my children of Ireland."* The *"great deluge"* (perhaps not an actual flood, for *Genesis* says the great Flood will not be repeated, but a flood of *some* kind) was *"at hand."*

Were these all metaphors? Was it not true, I asked Christina, that mystics had been predicting the "imminent" arrival of a great scourge for many decades? Was it not like the fanatics with bullhorns screaming, "Repent! Repent!" in Grand Central Station?

When I was in grade school there were annual scares that the world was going to end on such and such date at the noon hour.

Imminent, imminent, imminent. Quakes, darkness, tidal waves.

"It wasn't given to me, 'imminent,'" said Christina. "However, what was given to me is that the chastisement will come. It *must* come. So, it is coming. I'm not giving a time. From my understanding, it will be complete by the year 2000, if not before. When people hear that, they become afraid and say, 'The end of the world!' It's no such thing. It's the end of sin. God's Justice is going to demolish sin. You can take for instance AIDS, heart trouble, and people dropping dead when they're in good health. All these things, disasters and earthquakes, whatever's happening, is brought on by sin—not necessarily by the (sick) people themselves, but yet as a result of sin (in the world). Within it, as awful as it seems, God can use it by it being offered up (AIDS and other illness), by the offering of their suffering God sees His Mercy returned to Him. The personal suffering is to get greater and greater. That would be Phase One of it. Then there will be a time when everyone in the world, even if they've never heard of God, will become aware of God's presence."

Was mankind improving, as Maria Esperanza said?

There were improvements. There was cause for hope. But it was too little, and soon it might be too late.

"The Blessed Virgin says the errors have spread through the *entire* world," said Christina. "Now the biggest disaster is through abortion, which has drawn down the hand of God. This awful catastrophe that is happening through abortion is accepted by mankind as a normal fact of life. Any country accepting that into its society and crying out for abortion is a bit like crying out, 'Crucify Him! Crucify Him!'"

What, I asked her, about the dissolution of the Soviet Union? Were the United States and Russia not talking about disarmament? Were these not times of great hope?

"The time you see peace that's the time to be more wary, because it is not a genuine peace, it's a false peace," she responded. ''There's a lot of things to occur, and a lot of things hang from the balance of people's response. It can be a war. If another war starts between Russia and China, which I've been led to believe is possible, and if that happens through lack of response in prayer, well then you can be sure a horrific disaster will be the consequence.''

Visionary Jim Singer from Canada.

CHAPTER 37

Rumors of War

The mention of China and Russia was galvanizing. It was the message Terelya claimed to have received in his Soviet jail cell, the message seen at Amsterdam, what was also implied at Lipa, and I recalled that Maria Esperanza had mentioned the "yellow races standing up."

While it was reported the Virgin of Medjugorje had announced that there would be no Third World War, many disputed that such a message had ever been given and even if it had, there was room for regional conflicts.

Christina saw hatred spreading and wars that would "increase in intensity." When I saw her in late 1991 the world was calmer than at any other time in my life, with both the United States and Russia turning into allies, but she waved this away as the "false peace" and predicted there would be "another war that will develop and will spread quickly."

The issue was crucial. War is the first thing that comes to mind when a seer mentions worldwide destruction, especially destruction caused by "fire from the sky."

In the view of her spiritual director, the devout priest from Armagh named Gerard McGinnity, who agreed with Christina's assessment of a false tranquility, the world is following a "mirage of peace" when in actuality Satan "has never been more powerful than now. The Virgin says the world is in greater sin than ever in its history, and she seems to imply that the estrangement of mankind from God is reaching its epitome."

The calamities, in McGinnity's view, will be "the working out of this century of evil." Before all the demonism is purged, however, the divisions between people will become "more outright and obvious." What loomed at the very least was a spiritual civil war.

"As I interpret it, these difficult years, which seem so immediate, will cause those left on earth to fully witness the power of God," commented McGinnity. "The pride will give way to an acknowledgment of God and those who remain will enshrine the glory of Him. There will be a true peace. Never before has Our Lady explained true peace. Now she has done this, and it is clear that peace is not something diplomatically contrived, but the effort of surrender to the Creator—from the heart."

Father McGinnity was also a close adviser to two visionaries named Mark Treanor and Beulah Lynch who encountered apparitions at a Lourdes grotto inside Saint Peter and Saint Paul's Church in Bessbrook, which is about eight miles from Armagh, on the way to Belfast—an area of armored checkpoints because of all the terrorism in the North. For five years Beulah has been seeing Mary on a daily basis, and when I met them, both she and Mark were still experiencing what they claimed were full-bodied apparitions of Jesus as the Christ of Mercy.

Treanor said he'd seen the Lord in twenty apparitions. He described Jesus as highly masculine—not nearly as delicate as so many paintings portray Him—and very handsome. "His eyes are brown but even to say they're brown isn't right," Mark claimed. "They're not like anyone else's. They're on fire. I'm 5′9″ and He's taller than I am, dressed in white but at times with a brown or red robe over the white. The attire usually relates to what He is going to talk about. He's in a bright light. When Our Lady came the light arrived first and then she appeared. With Jesus, He and the light come together, which tells me Jesus *is* the light. To say it's white is unfair. It's brilliant, like opening a window shade in a dark room."

While Treanor wasn't at liberty to discuss much of what Christ allegedly said, both he and Lynch did speak of catastrophic events that were shown them by Mary during her many apparitions in 1987. One Saturday in November, said the 21-year-old visionary, "I was back in my seat after Holy Communion, praying in thanksgiving, when I saw what seemed like a film in front of my eyes, even though my eyes were closed. I saw a street. Very suddenly the street began to shake and vibrate very violently and then a split came in the center of the road. The road separated and into the opening fell the cars. The houses on each side began to crumble, the windows fell out, and the houses began to fall into the crack in the road. There seemed to be a lot of people falling into the road. Then immediately after this I saw what looked like a huge football stadium upside-down in the air, with thousands and thousands of people falling out of the stadium."

The day after, on November 8, Beulah, a middle-aged woman, also saw a split in the earth, and trees flat on the ground. Horses and sheep were running in terror. She also saw a great flood. "It was clear water trickling over rocks and heather and then rushing and I looked up and saw a huge sea," she said. "It'll start gently and then build up without stopping. A sea swelling—a surge.

"Then I saw very, very tormented waves. They seemed to be round. The sea became very, very rough and very thick and heavy, the color of mud. There seemed to be a lot of mud in it. Then I saw houses bobbing up and down in the water. They did not seem like tall houses, they seemed ground-level houses, with only the little windows like the cottages in Ireland years ago. I saw people in the water and some of them had their arms up as if they were trying to swim with these huge, huge waves, which seemed to be in curls and to be rolling. This scene was very fast. It seemed to take place and to roll very quickly. I saw pieces of trees and stuff sticking out of this, which was a bit frightening."

Was the tidal wave caused by the same earthquake? Was this one of the warnings mentioned at Medjugorje? Was it what Mirjana alluded to when she told Father Petar that no one would want to run and see the first secret any more

than people would "want to go to Italy to see a dam
collapsed?"

Was it a regional event or worldwide?

There were several visions of the disaster and Beulah
always saw the tidal wave *before* the split in the earth.

"The seas rose miles above my head," she said, and
"seemed to be in the vicinity of a village called Donegal."

But she also saw the destruction of "tall, tall buildings"
that brought to mind New York. She saw a long island surrounded by water. Beulah, who claims she has received
daily apparitions from the Virgin for five years now, along
with those of a Jesus in His mid-twenties, said she'd
experienced a vision on January 12, 1992, during recitation
of the Sorrowful Mysteries, and that during the vision
Christ showed her a globe with two angels at the top,
facing each other.

"My angels are touching the earth," Christ supposedly
explained. *"They haven't struck. Mark what I say: They
haven't struck."*

But they were ready to strike, said Beulah, and she saw
the waves again. "It seemed the earth had been picked up
and shaken." There was a terrible clap of thunder above
the earth and the sensation of an immense wind. "I was
shaken beyond my being," said Beulah, whose apparitions
are taken seriously by Father McGinnity but have as yet
met with no formal Church approval.

The same is true for Gallagher and Treanor: no official
approval, and none in the foreseeable future. But the lucid-
ity of what they claim was disarming. It was Treanor's intu-
ition that the events were going to happen "within a few
years," a "strange combination" of both natural and man-
made catastrophes. Like the visionaries at Medjugorje and
Garabandal, Mark was told the events would happen
within his lifetime. He saw clocks and watches with their
hands spinning, and a plaque with the words "Hong
Kong." When I asked about a vision he'd received of tanks,
guns, and Japanese soldiers covering the world, he clari-
fied that it was Japanese or *Chinese* at war.

Mark made clear that China bore close watching.
Already, he saw Satan at work in Yugoslavia, trying to
close off Medjugorje, which he said Our Lady called *"the*

light of the world.'' The devil concentrated his forces at apparitional settings, said Treanor, and he himself saw the demon with the face of a grotesque billygoat, while Beulah saw devils in the form of a black panther, an alligator, and even as "a lady full of light with two small horns."

What seemed to bother Beulah most were the impressions she received of the Anti-Christ. During an apparition from Mary she saw Pope John Paul II looking worn out, his eyes sunken; and it was as if he were being replaced by a dark-complected young man with a short black beard and golden vestments. Beulah saw a devil come out of the ground, a devil with the sharp features of Lenin. The devil went into the body of the young man.

When Christina Gallagher saw an image of the Anti-Christ, he was a man 45 to 50 years old, with very piercing eyes but nothing especially horrific about his physical visage. "I heard the echo, 'Anti-Christ, Anti-Christ,'" she says. "He's not Irish or English. He struck me as foreign. His skin was darker but he didn't have squinty eyes. There are many anti-christs and through them an army will unite and resurrect a leader."

When I asked Christina if that process was already underway, her reply was laconic: "Yes."

The evil, she said, was "multiplying." Satan was taking advantage of his "last chance," and the last chance, she said, was going to be an "awful battle and can do a lot of damage. There are many battles to come."

CHAPTER 38

A Moment of Consolation

She was going to win. You could feel that. There was no question that God was granting Mary the power over negativity. But for now the demons were at full rage. In Italy they chased a young boy away from an apparition and in Ecuador physically assaulted a young woman who was experiencing the Virgin high up in the Andes.

They attacked those who had forsaken a life of sin—trying to scare them out of God's cohort—and oppressed seers from Ireland to Korea.

It was a great agitation of the spirit. On a spiritual level mankind was already encountering its purification. We were given a clear choice between the way of God and the way of the world. It was a separation process, a spiritual cleansing, and a test of faith. Those who chose God, who fell into the ranks of Mary's cohort, experienced crushing attacks and found themselves separated from friends, business associates, and even relatives who'd chosen to scoff at the supernatural and concentrate on materialism. Those who chose the world seemed outwardly successful but were really in far more turmoil, lacking grace, happiness, and inner peace. They had no idea, most of them, that they were victims of a grand deception. Worse, they were infested with the spiritual equivalent of fleas and scorpions. It was an intangible, spiritual chastisement. Working with unrecognized force, the devil distracted everyone he could from looking toward eternity.

The Italian apparitions I mentioned started on the evening of May 24, 1985, when a dozen children in the fashionable little town of Oliveto Citra, population 3,950, high on a mountain south of Salerno, were playing near the gate to an old castle on the feast day of St. Macarius, the town's patron. "There were a lot of people in the square and no place to goof around, so we decided to go up to the square near the castle," says one original visionary, Dino Acquaviva. "We were there when we heard a baby crying. We thought it was someone trying to scare us. One of the boys took a rock and threw it and it came rolling back and we heard the baby crying louder—like it was bothered or mad. We went and looked toward the gate of the castle and we saw a ball of light that little by little got bigger and in the middle you could see a lady with a baby in her arms."

It was 10:30 p.m. in this impious, modern town, where the riviera-like cafes buzz into the night. The apparition lasted for nearly two hours. A waitress in the nearest cafe went to see what all the excitement was about and came back so shaken she went into shock and was taken to the hospital.

"The Blessed Virgin was there, like a real person, but in a light," continues Dino. "A real person, and young—16 or at the most 18. The only thing we could really remember was the eyes, which were blue. At her feet was a cloud, but it was like her face was erased. I fell on my knees three times. We ran back and forth three times. She was making gestures to come up. When she was there it was like the gate opened by itself. The gate had disappeared! We didn't know what to do. She was about a meter above the ground."

Mary was dressed in white with a sky-blue mantle and yet once more had the crown of 12 apocalyptical stars. *"Peace to you, children,"* she said in greeting. Actually the white light appeared to burst into colors when Mary appeared.

As the others stood watching and mesmerized, Dino hap-

pened to look in the other direction near the narrow road
coming up past the town's church and spotted a "skinny"
man with a beard holding a chain with a demon at the end
of it. "It was a small monster," says Dino. "It was all green
with black eyes and like he had bubbles on his body and
short legs and it was going back and forth." His twin
brother Carmine also saw it, saying there was no way to
explain it. "It didn't look like an animal or a human being.
The creature went back and forth, back and forth."

The appearance of a demonic entity at the very onset of
the apparition made me wonder if the entire incident was
demonic, an attempt to divert attention away from Medjugorje, with which it shared many features. I still wonder
about much of Oliveto Citra's phenomena. But it seemed
like the creature was coming to scare the children from the
apparition itself (succeeding, in fact, in making Dino run
away) and from later fruits, including conversions among
many others who saw her, it appeared that it might indeed
be Mary. The local priest, Monsignor Giuseppe Amato,
known as Don Peppino, was convinced it was the Blessed
Virgin and told me that since the start of apparitions,
which still continue, at least 12 or 13 people have seen
Mary as a three-dimensional apparition, some every week,
inspiring crowds of pilgrims who have experienced more
than two hundred healings. I myself saw the sun act
strangely, pulsing with great strength, and others have
seen purplish clouds, stars falling like a large comet to the
old castle, flapping doves, and other phenomena. Mary
identified herself as "Our Lady of Consolation" and "Our
Lady of Graces," and it seemed she came to inspire prayer
(*"pray, pray, pray,"* she repeated here too) and to give
encouragement in trying spiritual times.

"My children, come to me," she said. *"Open your hearts
and they will be filled with good things. Jesus is with you,
together with me, to save you from temptation. Satan
becomes always stronger; pray that he loses his power and
that you all grow closer to God. The evil one has taken
over many, but do not be afraid, my Son will free
them . . . Pray not to enter into temptation. Now I bless you
all in the name of the Father, the Son, and the Holy Spirit."*

Striking an optimistic note, Mary remarked on July 7,

1986, that *"the world is turning to me."* She asked for fasting twice a week for the conversion of the whole world
and thanked them *"for responding to my call."* Jesus
wanted to be merciful, but if mankind didn't pray and convert, He would allow His justice to operate. Her appearance
to young people in a town of materialists—where the
mayor was Communist—underscored Heaven's tremendous concern for our youth.

"It is the same message as Medjugorje," says Don Peppino. "There have been a few secrets given, three for the
world. The demon action corresponded with the action of
the Madonna. Generally everyone who has seen the
Madonna has seen the demon. At the beginning the demon
used to be more insistent. Now he is backing off. The time
of the devil is ending. He's like this because he knows his
time is ending. The message is to pray, make penance, go
back to God. This is what she said at Medjugorje. To this
day six or seven see her. The bishop at the beginning was
against this. Then something happened. A lot of pilgrims
started coming and there were a lot of conversions, under
the sign of Christ, and spiritual fruits. And together with
these events were cures of terminally ill. She says TV des-
troys and that we should try to shut it off. TV is an instrument of sin and destruction. She also appears at the church
during Mass, during Communion. She kneels in front of
the tabernacle and she points to Christ, as the guide of our
lives. The Virgin says all the time that the world is in danger but if we pray the punishment can be shortened or
eliminated. During the wars in the (Persian) gulf and in
Yugoslavia she appears sad and in a dress stained with
blood. I have the impression that something is imminent
this decade."

It was as if Oliveto Citra were seeing the culmination of
a warning directed specifically at that region, for in 1980,
five years before the first apparitions, its old section,
including the castle and church, was largely destroyed in
an earthquake. Two years later a local artist, Dina Apata,
had a dream about a pilgrim woman surrounded by a yellow or golden aura, walking on a rural path in the mountains. As at Medjugorje the apparition proclaimed that

Mary's real birthday was August 5, and on that day she arrived in special splendor—in shining gold.

On January 10, 1986, appearing to Mafalda Caputo, wife of a local accountant, Mary purportedly gave this interesting explanation: *"My dear children. God has sent me to earth to save you because the whole world is in danger. I'm here with you to bring peace to your hearts. He wants peace to reign in the hearts of all humanity and wants the conversion of all mankind. So, my dear children, pray, pray, pray. If you don't pray, you will receive nothing. The time left for you is very short. There will be earthquakes, famines, and punishments for all the inhabitants of earth. Dear children, when God comes among us, with some manifestation, He does not come as a joke. He isn't afraid of bullies, or of indifference, so take this message seriously. I will pray that God doesn't punish you...Humanity is full of great sins that offend God's love. The peace on earth is almost over. The world cannot be saved without peace. And peace can be rediscovered only if humanity returns to God."*

There was a good chance, said Mafalda, that people *would* return to God. "Our time is finishing," said this matronly and pious woman. "Humanity is going to change. The world is going to change."

We are not facing the end of the world.

But when I asked if there were going to be dire events, she replied, "Oh, disasters, si! But if we pray God will listen. God doesn't want to punish us out of revenge. He wants to shake us up. The Virgin says we have three weapons to save the world from wars and these are prayer, conversion, and penitence. The Madonna invites us especially to pray for the leaders of the nations because they don't pray. They prepare the world for the wars and they're going to use their weapons. The devil possesses these people and he is going to try to have them use these weapons. The Virgin told me many times we need to pray for the people of the Third World. I asked if there would be another war and she said yes. I asked if this war was going to be a world war. She said no. It's not going to be a war on earth. It's going to be a spiritual war: believers versus disbelievers. After this spiritual war there's going to be a period of peace.''

That was Mafalda's optimistic version, and I wondered if there was some miscommunication in the translation; at other times she left open the possibility of a third world war and said mankind was heading for a "precipice." Marco DeBellis, who saw Mary every day for five years and was given nine secrets, added, in an identical evaluation, that "the world is on the edge of the abyss." When I interviewed a middle-aged man and owner of the local Alfa Romeo repair shop, Umberto Gagliardi, who still sees Mary four or five times a month and has also witnessed apparitions of Jesus carrying the cross (on the left shoulder, says Umberto, not the right), he told me he was given four secrets, one of them sent to the pope. "Sometimes she says mankind is getting better but not like it should be," he explained. "Mankind takes more command from the demon than from Jesus. The Madonna said Jesus is going to come down soon. A lot of nations could disappear from the world. That's why the Madonna has been appearing. Mankind thinks only of natural things. There is no respect in families and no respect for anyone."

The situation remained in flux. I couldn't get a definite answer on the future at Oliveto Citra. But I liked the fact that it was not dismal. And it was emphasized that any possible chastisements would be not out of sheer heavenly anger but as a way of refreshing us. If major disasters do occur, said yet another visionary, Raffaello Ferrarra of Naples, they will "build a new era, a new future, a better one." Raffaello, who said he was chosen to convey messages because he didn't read or write ("and what I said would come from only her"), visited Medjugorje and saw Mary praying on Mount Krizevac. That was interesting in that Marija Pavlovic from Medjugorje had in her turn visited Oliveto Citra and supposedly had seen the Madonna up there at the gate—an incline of stone steps closed due to damage from the earthquake.

The gate. That was where the battle was. The demons came as a snake, a hunchbacked goat, or dressed as the Madonna but with a wolf's head.

"Satan tried to stop me from getting up to the gate one time," recalled Umberto, a mild-mannered man with thick black hair. "He had red eyes with feet like a horse. He had curly blond hair, like a good-looking man. The first night that the demon appeared, the Virgin motioned me not to come up. The same the second night. The third night I forced myself up, but the Madonna told me not to put my feet where the devil stepped. When I got to the gate I shook the gate. The demon was with his back to the gate, and I punched the gate to make him go away."

Others were pulled from bed, or saw a beautiful person who tried to seduce them. *"My daughter,"* said Mary to Jolanda Cimmino, *"wear the rosary around your neck. It will protect you from the devil. He tempts you and often he takes on my resemblance, deceiving you, as it has already happened on other occasions."*

Satan, she said, was *"making fools of you."*

She confirmed to Mafalda that the battle had started a century ago.

But the century was getting old, nearly done. At last he was beginning to lose his power.

CHAPTER 39

The Hour of Fire

The announcement that Satan's power was nearing an end came in the Soviet Union. In 1987, four years before the toppling of Communism, the Mother of God began to appear at the abandoned shrines and chapels throughout Ukraine. She came in great auras of light, fiery light, with Jesus and the angels.

The wave of events began in that old place of pilgrimage called Hrushiw, where the miraculous well had been damaged in 1840 and where Mary last appeared in 1914, when she sadly informed the 22 Ukrainian peasants that they faced eighty years of war, famine, and persecution. Now she was coming to reignite faith and announce the dawn of a new if uncertain era. On April 26, 1987, the first anniversary of the disaster at Chernobyl, an 11-year-old peasant girl, Maria Kizyn, returning from an outhouse, spotted the Virgin on a balcony at the front of the domed wood chapel of Blessed Trinity. Maria's house, surrounded by a heavy iron fence and attached to a small barn, was up a knoll perhaps two hundred yards from the closed chapel, and what she saw seemed like a statue standing on the balcony, visible from the waist up. The "statue," a woman dressed in black, gestured at Maria and moved about the balcony like a living person.

"I got scared and went to my parents and neighbors and

304

they came to the church," says Maria. "And my parents and neighbors saw the figure. It was as if she had something white in her hand. It appeared like a handkerchief. She didn't say anything. The face I cannot describe. A young woman. I saw her afterward a few times, but not as clear. She was there a short time. I'm not sure how long it was. My mother, father, and uncle were there. When my parents went closer to it, it disappeared. The church was closed and after a while my parents went to a church that was open and prayed."

Maria's mother Miroslova, a matronly farm woman with kerchief, maroon sweater, muddy blue boots, and sharp blue eyes, said they had knelt before the inexplicable woman, whispering in awe and disbelief. "That morning after Maria told us, we didn't know what to believe," says Miroslova. "We went to the church and didn't see anything from close, then we prayed, said an Our Father, and returned to the house. When we returned we looked back to the balcony and saw the figure. It had the appearance of walking on the balcony. I was so shocked I don't remember things. I thought it was some kind of warning. It was Sunday so we dressed and went to the other church in the village. Maria went with us to church and told what she saw to the other children and brought children to the chapel to show them what she saw and spread the word to parents and people coming here."

First in a trickle, from the village of Hrushiw, then in droves, as surrounding villages heard about the apparitions, hundreds of Ukrainian peasants began to congregate around Blessed Trinity Church, as if awakened from a deep dark slumber. It was the hour of the fire of the Holy Spirit. Just as her last apparition foretold the coming of Communism, these apparitions declared that it was coming to an end, that the eighty years forecast in 1914 were completed and a new society, a Christian society, was ready to form. It was still illegal to gather as the peasants were gathering, but risking heavy fines and arrest, the people continued to come from nearby cities like Drohobych and Lviv, then from farther reaches of the Ukraine and eventually from all corners of the Soviet Union, from as far away as Georgia and Siberia, until the hundreds had turned to thousands. According to Oksana Lazariv, assistant principal at the local school, there were days when 150,000 pilgrims passed through the small village.

"The roads were lined with autos for thirty kilometers," Lazariv told me. "All kinds of people, including the crippled, were coming across the fields. As a teacher I was interested to go there and listen to what people were saying. When I was there, I saw the Holy Mother. She was in black and I didn't see the hands but it was like a statue moving. Some people could see very clearly. For others she appeared and disappeared."

"Some people saw her, but not everybody was worthy," added Maria Andrijciw, a cook at the school.

"There was an unusual glow around the whole church," said Maria's mother. "Some people saw her in white, some in blue. Some said they saw stars moving and the sky opening. She appeared on the roof, on the windows, and also in the light around the church, which was like a wave. I was scared about how the authorities would act, once word spread and masses of people were coming here."

As Miroslova feared, the militia and KGB were sent to disperse the crowds and young Maria was whisked to the town of Bruchowichi, where she was secluded with her mother and older sister Hala. But the apparitions continued—witnessed even by the KGB—and roadblocks failed to deter the faithful. Many reported encounters with a mysterious old woman or nun who mingled with the throngs. Peering in the keyhole, others said they saw the church interior illuminated and a woman praying inside. When a resident of Buchach snuck in, looking for holy water to give her ailing child, a beautiful lady materialized and presented her with three pebbles. She told the woman to put these in a glass of water and the child would be healed. The child was cured soon after.

While it's difficult to confirm facts in Ukraine, there are estimates that as many as 400,000 people saw manifestations of the Blessed Virgin at Hrushiw, whether as a nebulous silhouette, a reflection in the windows, or an image—at times a living image—in the subtle, towering aura around Blessed Trinity. Occasionally Mary materialized near the cupola in a luminous globe of light surrounded by tongues of flame, or wearing fiery robes. She was said to be 18 to 21, smiling through tears and looking lovingly down upon the masses, who sang hymns and recited the Rosary. Within the field of luminosity, people saw auras of light around the grass, leaves, and their own fingertips.

According to Ivan Hel', who was deputy chairman of the Lviv Regional Council of People's Deputies when I met with him in 1991, the police tried to drown out the supernatural glow with searchlights. "But they could not achieve this," said Hel'. "The appearance didn't stay there all the time. It appeared and disappeared. At first I was skeptical. I'm an educated man, a university graduate, and I felt in this century there were not many such miracles. I stood there and didn't see anything. I asked, 'Where is the Holy Mother?' But after a while I saw an image of the Holy Mother within the glow. It was not a clear image but rather like the Holy Mother holding the baby Jesus in her arms. It was not like a live woman but more like an illuminated postcard. We prayed and sang until morning."

Hel' had spent 18 years in concentration camps, which played havoc with his emotions, but now there was an indescribable sensation of peace. "I had been tortured and beaten but I had this wonderful feeling," he said. "When I got there, there were about 5,000 people. I believe there were 150,000 during the course of certain days, during the course of holidays. (The major events) lasted until October. The Ukrainian people, you must understand, suffered very much—none have suffered more!—and Russia wanted to destroy our nation. In 25 years, they destroyed 25 million. I don't know why our nation suffered this amount. When God loves someone He'll give him a hard time—testing. The suffering was not in vain and the appearance of the Holy Mother is proof of this."

I learned of similar marvels across the western Ukraine, in the horribly repressed hinterlands where churches were being renovated and huge crosses installed at mass graves. Mary's image was seen in windows, in the clouds, in reflections of water. Sixty kilometers from Drohobych, in Hoshiw, where the 3,000-pound bell had been melted into Nazi bullets, I was told that in 1987, around the time of

Hrushiw, two men taking a shortcut through a forest spotted a young woman in radiant white and followed her until she reached the monastery's church, where she rose as if climbing invisible steps and disappeared at the top of the dawn-tinted domes. At the monastery of Pochaiv, where Mary appeared during the 12th century in a pillar of fire, she had been spotted again in 1987 or 1988 as an older woman wrapped in flames near the door of the monastery's secondary church. According to Vasyl Savich Darmogay, an Orthodox priest, people were also reporting mysterious candlelight or fires next to the building. Near Ternopil she was seen above a steeple, enshrouded in clouds, and in Pidkamin, between Pochaiv and Lviv, I spoke to half a dozen people, both adults and children, who witnessed a living picture or tableaux like the famous tableaux at Knock. For three days in July of 1987, hundreds came to catch sight of the Virgin on an exterior wall of the stone church at Pidkamin, St. Paraskovey's. Her hand was on the shoulder of the boy Jesus, who stood next to His mother and appeared to be eight or nine, dressed in dark clothes, a yellow glow surrounding the silent, living Virgin. Here too luminosity was seen in the church, as if Heaven was reconsecrating the building. "All the Christian people were happy," noted Dybyna Pavlo. "All the Communists were angry."

Near Buchach, where manifestations of Mary had occurred at the end of both world wars, she was seen with the infant Christ in a light above Trinity Orthodox Church. There had been strange pink and blue clouds above Trinity, and other phenomena, such as smaller images, manifested throughout town. "Some people said they saw the Mother of God with the small Christ," said Olga Lozynsko. "Others saw St. Paul and St. Michael." About seven kilometers south of Buchach I gaped in wonderment at the miraculous "etching" of a bearded man with a halo that looked like an apostle and appeared on a window pane on May 21, 1987, immediately after Hrushiw's most intense period. The image was not really etched, nor was it painted or penciled. It was just *there*. I wondered if Buchach was favored with so many signs because it had suffered so many KGB atrocities. In the basement of Pokrowa Catholic

Church, where images of Mary had been seen in the 1950s, I saw human skulls unearthed by workmen renovating the church, men who told me that among the remains were the bones of small children and two decapitated priests, the skulls now in cardboard boxes next to old dusty statues of the Virgin and Saint Anthony.

Something was happening here. Something that was both hopeful and foreboding. The strongest sensations came at the famous old shrine at Zarvanystya, where Communists had stolen the miraculous icon and then Mary's image had appeared in a pool of water. When I arrived in the village, which is 181 kilometers from Lviv, past the turkeys roosting in trees and the horse buggies, I learned that Mary began reappearing at Zarvanystya in the mid-1980s, around the time, I noted, that Pope John Paul II conducted what many feel was finally an adequate consecration of Russia. It was also around the time of Gorbachev's rise to power.

"One day on my way to cut wheat, I stopped to see why there was a crowd around the well," said Chornij Zenovia, a saintly woman who had spent years at a concentration camp in Siberia. "The people said they were seeing the Holy Mother. I knelt and started praying very hard and suddenly instead of the well I saw a big glow, like a mountain, and in it I saw a lady holding a baby in her arms. The light was like silver. The Lady was in blue clothes with a white sash, and a barefooted baby was in her arms. On her head Mary had a white shawl. I saw this for about half an hour. The glow was seen very often for two or three weeks in 1987, I think the autumn. The Holy Mother warned us to return to church and love one another. Personally I took it as a sign that Communists would soon disappear from the face of the earth."

Although the KGB moved in with force, unleashing attack dogs and clubbing pilgrims to the point where a number required hospital treatment, the apparitions continued at least through 1988, as I learned in speaking with Mykola Krushelnyckyj, a factory worker who was walking up a dirt road one evening in December of that year, when he spotted something in the sky over the vicinity of the well.

"I was going to the next village, approaching the river, and I saw above the forest a huge glow," he said. "In the middle was a round picture that looked like the Virgin Mary, from the waist up, holding Jesus in her arms, with silver clothes. On her head was a golden crown. I returned because I was scared. I had a feeling when she was holding the baby in her arms she was moving her head, bowing or looking toward the baby. I didn't hear any sound. The light around her was like the moon. There was a cross hanging from her neck and a heart. She was rather sad. She was looking toward the sky and making this head movement."

The glowing mass, which was at least twice the height of a tall tree, moved north over the woods and meadows, fading beyond and behind a mountain like an ephemeral cloud.

It was another portent, and within three years Communism collapsed in the Soviet Union and Ukrainians declared their independence from Russia, a move that led to the unraveling of the evil empire and new, unprecedented freedom. On October 13, 1991, forty million Soviet citizens were able to watch a live broadcast of ceremonies at Fatima, where 900,000 pilgrims from around the world were pledging themselves to the conversion of the materialistic West and Russia. Wherever I traveled I saw workmen laboring feverishly to reinforce church walls, repaint frescoes, and rebuild roofs that had collapsed during the eighty years of forced neglect.

"This Church has suffered the most for unity of the universal Church," observed Sonya Hlutkowsky, spokeswoman for the Ukrainian Greek-Catholic Church Archeparchy of Lviv. "People are now traveling to Siberia and digging for the bones of loved ones and even if the bones no longer exist they bring back earth. We don't even know how many entire communities were shot when they tried to hold underground services."

The leader of all Ukrainian Catholics, Myroslav Cardinal Lubachivsky, had returned only recently from exile and was unsure what to make of Hrushiw. "The people here say it is not true," he commented, "and I was not in Hurshiw, so I do not know." He had not heard of the events at places such as Pidkamin and Zarvanystya, and the archeparchy was swamped with other business, struggling to tend to a barrage of applications for the priesthood, address the needs of the five million Catholics who had suffocated in Marx's hellish vapors for nearly an entire century, and keep up with all the churches that are reopening.

"The cardinal is not negative," explained Sonya Hlutkowsky. "He's cautious. And he's concerned about Ukraine. Ukraine is a country of rumors, and rumors become facts. We don't have a structure to investigate it. If you ask us in our hearts, we believe God has a special plan or mission for Ukraine and it manifests through the Mother of God. I firmly believe these things occurred regularly in this country. It was only this kind of heavenly support that kept them going."

I appreciated the cardinal's reserve, but the archeparchy was not well informed about Hrushiw, believing that the phenomena had occurred over just a three-week period in 1987 and then ceased. In fact, a month before I arrived, in October of 1991, a priest from Chicago, Father Walter Klimchuk, himself witnessed an apparition at Blessed Trinity, and Maria Kizyn still glimpses Mary on occasion. "After we had taken a few pictures and drank from the miraculous well, I led our group in the recitation of the Rosary," said Father Klimchuk. "It was during this time that I glanced up beyond the well and saw a young woman—standing there above the well. At first I thought that I was hallucinating. I kept opening and closing my eyes, thinking that the image was not real. But then there were tears flowing from the eyes of Our Lady and I realized that I was given to see the Mother of God."

Maria, now 16, with fawnlike eyes and tousled brown hair, felt, as others did, that the tears were a warning. "I think the purpose was to appear so that people will change because hard times—catastrophes—are nearing," she said. "I didn't hear the voice, but this is my understanding. I don't know when they will occur, but I believe one catastrophe was avoided. I am speaking about the whole world."

It was said that the message from Hrushiw was *"Pray, pray, for tomorrow may be too late."* Above the loft in

Blessed Trinity I noticed the painting of a chalice above a crowd of people who were in red smoke and hellish agony. I thought of how dymanic the situation is in the former Soviet republics, which are now forming their own armies and could easily become involved in simmering ethnic tensions or territorial disputes. Ukraine, which has thirty percent of the former U.S.S.R.'s military officers, and its own navy, was already at political odds with its arch foe Russia. As Hel' observed "The Holy Mother wants us to return to belief and fight for the Church. The times are very unknown—unknown times are coming."

Although neither Hel' nor Maria heard Mary speak, one who did, the activist Josyp Terelya, who arrived at Hrushiw on May 9, 1987, after release from prison, conveyed this message: *"Oh daughter of mine, Ukraine, I have come to you, for you have suffered the most and through all your sufferings you have maintained your faith in the Sacred Heart. I have come to you so that you will go and convert Russia. Pray for Russia. Pray for the lost Russian nation. For if Russia does not accept Christ the King, the Third World War cannot be averted."*

Terelya claimed that the Virgin delivered him lengthy visions and lectures, just as she had on two occasions when he was imprisoned at Vladimir. A fuller account of his visions is contained in the book *Witness.* He said the Blessed Mother warned of fields aflame, even the air and water burning, smoke and fire everywhere, rivers of blood—and the Anti-Christ rising from the ocean.

"How many warnings must mankind be given before it repents?" she asked. *"The world continues on the road of self-will and hedonism."*

As a result, the seal of the devil, she told him, had been placed on the foreheads of many. But now, in the U.S.S.R. also, Mary was rallying her own troops just as the archangel Michael had predicted when he appeared to Josyp in the 1983 jailhouse vision. *"The world would long ago have been destroyed but the soul of the world would not allow this,"* Michael had told him. *"As the soul preserves the life of the body, so do Christians preserve the life of the world. God needs fervent and constant sons. You shall go through the ways of the world and give witness, and in the end God will punish the apostates because only through this punishment will God be able to bring mankind back to sound reason. And when the faith and love shall be reborn, Satan will begin a new persecution of the Christians. Times of persecution will begin, of priests and the faithful. The world will be divided into the messengers of God and messengers of anti-christ. After the great revelations of the Virgin Mary, renewal of love of Christ will begin."*

While the Kingdom of Heaven is at hand, Terelya was told, there might be great holocausts before it arrived, if mankind doesn't repent and convert. The Third Secret, the Virgin told him, *"is all around you."* He saw the Anti-Christ with a golden cincture around his neck—an ecclesiastical undertone like the visions of Beulah Lynch—and in the beast's mouth were flags that belong to Czechoslovakia, East Germany, Romania, Hungary, and the Soviet Union.

From the ends of the globe Terelya saw a man begin to grow, rising to the heavens. In his hands he carried an immense red flag with the insignia of the Anti-Christ. This insignia included portraits of Marx and Lenin. It had been given to this man, explained the vision, to take peace from the earth. One day, Mary told other visionaries, including Vassula Ryden of Switzerland, Russia would be the country in which God would be most glorified. Healed and resurrected by God's strength, Russia's stature of holiness would attract all her neighbors. But was the Anti-Christ coming first?

"Lucifer is losing strength," Mary told Terelya. *"To maintain himself on the throne of darkness he began portraying himself as repentant, but this is not true. Lucifer is cunning and clever. He is preparing a great deception for all of God's creation, and especially for the people of God. For a short time a godless kingdom shall maintain itself from one end of the earth to the other."*

CHAPTER 40

The Hour of the Knowledge of the Anti-Christ

Terelya was a controversial figure, given to strong politics and stronger opinions, but when he stuck to the messages he was uncannily accurate, predicting the independence of Ukraine four years before that unlikely event occurred, as well as the Soviet coup in August of 1991. No visionary, in fact, had yet hit with greater specificity. I was most interested in what he saw of the Anti-Christ, because similar indications, that a satanic spirit was manifesting in the flesh, were coming from the Andes highlands of Ecuador.

These indications arrived from August 28, 1988 to March 3, 1990, during 112 recorded apparitions to Patricia Talbott Borrero, better known as Pachi, a teenager from an aristocratic family in Cuenca. Pachi was no religious fanatic. Her aspiration was to be a model. She was already traveling to shows in New York and Mexico City displaying the folkloric dress of Ecuador and promoting tourism for the government. And she thought stories about places like Medjugorje were "crazy." Until she saw Mary for herself that August night in her bedroom. Falling into a deep ecstasy, her head back like the visionaires of Garabandal, Pachi soon encountered Mary at dozens of locations, especially in churches around Cuenca and 12,000 feet up the

cloud-enshrouded Andes in a bowl-like ravine on a mountain known as El Cajas. She was directed to El Cajas by
the mysterious sound of bells, and Mary appeared there
with golden skin and 12 stars—calling herself "Guardian
of the Faith." Crowds of up to 120,000 ascended the
heights, like a scene out of *Exodus.* During the ecstasies
lights like golden raindrops fell from the sun, the *paja*
grass turned golden, and the clouds formed holy images.
A huge silhouette of Mary was seen in the sky, backlit by
the moon, and when a statue was placed on a rock at the
site, it often moved and turned crimson.

Pray slowly, said the Madonna of El Cajas, because
prayers said in a hurry do not reach Heaven. Be humble
and constant in prayer. Pray to your guardian angel every
day and to the archangels Michael and Gabriel—Michael
to keep from temptation, Gabriel for truth. *"Tell parents
not to offer too much freedom to their children, because
this freedom is the reason my little ones become victims
of the tricks of Satan,"* said Mary. She warned about the
obsession with fashion, which was a trick of the devil's,
and urged family prayer. Prayers and penance were imped-
ing a third world war, she informed them. She wouldn't
appear to Pachi long (nowhere nearly as long as in Medjugorje) but would always be nearby. *"At the end of all the
apparitions in the world, I will leave a great sign in this
place and in all those where I have been."*

But first there was a battle to fight. According to Gaston
Ramirez Salcedo, a local architect, entrepreneur, and politician, thousands saw a silhouette of Mary descend from
the ramparts at El Cajas on February 3, 1990 at 4 a.m., followed closely by a gray fiendish figure that looked like a
mummy. "It was like a fight," said Salcedo, who had
served as postmaster general of Ecuador and was a city
councilman. "It was like something in the movies, an
apocalyptical fight. The image of the Virgin disappeared
and there was like a laser light show—flashes of light a
hundred meters long, thousands of them, like a war. Blue,
red, yellow. The rays of light were coming from the ground
and it lasted for two or three minutes."
Forces of contention also centered on Pachi, who told me

she was physically assaulted by invisible demonic hands and that only because of the Virgin did she get back her strength. "The devil used to hit me, and make me feel I was nothing, useless, and he would laugh at me," said Pachi. "I saw him as a normal man. I was studying at my grandmother's and was close to the door when I saw a tall man, very handsome, with dark dress and arms crossed, looking at the floor. I was completely chilled. He raised his eyes and they were metallic. I got very scared but I looked at the other side and there was the Virgin. I asked, 'Why was I left alone?' She said, *'You will have to pass by these tests so you can speak to people and warn them not to get close to the devil.'* "

Most disturbing was an experience Pachi had on March 4, 1990, the day after her last apparition. She was at her mother's home, which was full of visitors because holy pictures in Pachi's bedroom, where the Virgin first appeared, were shedding oily tears. A short, plump, bare-foot "nun," dressed in white with a mole on her cheek, came to the door saying she had received a message for Pachi and had to speak with her privately. "I felt uneasy about this but she was a religious woman and I said okay," recalls Pachi. "We went to my mother's room and the nun slammed the door. She said, 'Look at my feet. Look at my hands.' Her eyes were tremendously bad. Again, she said, 'Look at my hands, look at my feet.' Again I saw nothing. I started to pray to St. Michael and the nun stopped talking and her eyes squinted. Her voice changed to a deep voice, and again she said, 'Look at my hands.' On her hands and feet was the stigmata. I was very scared. And in her right hand, which I thought was stigmata, appeared the number of the beast in blood—666. At that moment she tried to jump on me and she put her thumbs in my eyes and asked, 'What do you see? What do you see? What do you see?' Pressing hard. I don't know how I got away. I know God was helping me. I said, 'Go away. Go away!' And she started to say the pope was the Anti-Christ and the Church was good for nothing. I said, 'In the name of God go away' and at that moment I thought it was a person possessed of Satan."

The "nun" left the room but seeing a priest on her way out greeted him in a nearly mocking fashion, bowing and saying, "Hello, *father.*"

No doubt the intensity of the attacks was due to the fact that Pachi had been given especially intense secrets. They were granted to her in October of 1988 during a trip to Guadalupe, Mexico, where she had an apparition of Mary on Tepeyac Hill, site of the 16th century apparitions to the Indian Juan Diego. "There were five girls when we went to Tepeyac," recalled fellow model Bernardita Jerves, "and we all knelt at the altar rail, all in contact with each other and we could feel the same energy. I felt I had to pray. When Pachi finished her apparition she looked very sad in her expression—not quite desperate, but very worried. Teary. She said it was terrible, that the world needs a purification and that a chastisement would come to humanity."

Later, in a dream, Bernardita herself saw a horrific scenario that Pachi told her was part of the great Chastisement. Through Pachi the Blessed Mother explained, *"Bernardita, you know a part of the sacred chastisement. This is the sign. You, my beloved daughter, know already one of the ten sacred secrets. It is the dream, when in reality your spirit came out from your body and you saw all that can happen in that day. Do not talk about it until I ask you. My little soul, I grant you that one month before this circumstance happens you can notify all my children."*

Mary made clear that conversion would soften the Heart of Jesus *"and the intensity can be diminished or be lost forever; if not, the great trial will come."* There always exists a happy tomorrow to a sad yesterday, Mary said in consolation. The sufferings of select people were currently being used for redemption of the world. But *"natural disasters created by man"* are coming. There were allusions to the ozone layer, schisms in the Church, and seismic disturbances.

These indications were available because Pachi was allowed to share certain details of the grand secret. While one part was to remain just that, a secret known only to

Pachi, and one part was only for the pope, presented to him when Pachi and her mother visited Rome on April 4, 1990, a third part was circulated within a small circle of friends. It concerned the Soviet Union, which Pachi, an unsophisticated girl, always knew to distinguish from "Russia." She foresaw the break up of the U.S.S.R. and even mentioned Estonia and Lithuania, the two republics that were among the first to secede from the Soviet Union, which Pachi correctly predicted would "destroy itself."

Pachi believed a third world war was coming, a nuclear war, and her mother told me that during the apparition in Mexico her daughter had seen "a great field all burned and children from all the races burned and full of sores and with no hair." The "burning field" was nearly identical in language to one of Terelya's visions. She saw a war coming "from the south." She also saw the possibility of a Communist revolution in Italy and destruction of the Vatican. The pope would go to France, then Poland, she said. She saw a Marxist revolution in France, lasting only a month, but Communism would return elsewhere and Germany would get nervous and invade Czechoslovakia, causing Russia to counterattack, which in turn would lead China, backing the former Asian republics of the U.S.S.R., to take advantage of the confusion and attack Russia in a surprising and terrible manner. This victory would shock the United States, which at first would not want to get involved but eventually would be forced to ally itself with Russia, sending a small number of troops. Estonia, Hungary, and Poland would avoid mass destruction, but Czechoslovakia (where apparitions, I'd learned, had also erupted in Presov) would be completely destroyed. There would also be an uprising in Caucasia. Russia would rid itself of Communism once and for all but Gorbachev would be assassinated and unless mercy was shown, nuclear exchanges would destroy much of mankind.

A comet might come as a sign before the war. The three days of darkness would be caused either by the comet, the nuclear dust, or earth being bumped off its axis.

I was very impressed with Pachi, who exuded enormous, quiet power and charm, and yet, again, the rumors of what her secret consisted of (the part available to close friends) were nearly as convoluted as Ida's visions in Amsterdam, and it was so similar to prophecies by the Polish mystic Wladyslaw Biernacki as to make me wonder if it borrowed from Biernacki's controversial prognostications, which were available in Ecuador and likewise pitted Germany against Czechoslovakia and had war beginning in Italy, with horrible consequences for the Vatican and the pope—who Biernacki too saw fleeing to France. Although I was assured that Pachi had never seen Biernacki's prophecies, I was again on guard against human and demonic counterfeits. There were all kinds of apparitions around Latin America—in Totorillas, Guayaquil, Santo Domingo, Es Meraldas, Pereira-Risaralda (Colombia), El Huatusco (Mexico)—and at least one of them, at Penablanca, Chile, seemed diabolical, with miraculous photos of the squiggly neon-like lights seen at San Damiano and Bayside and blood running from the forehead of the visionary during his "ecstasies" or appearing on the Host in his mouth. On a wall in Pachi's bedroom was a mark like a cross said to have been placed there in oil by unseen hands, and it seemed oddly irregular for a heavenly manifestation. While there was a possibility Gorbachev would once more resume power, making himself a more likely target of assassination, and that Communism would again rear its ugly head, the scenario sounded a bit too multi-faceted. Were they all to happen together, or was it a smorgasbord of possibilities?

When I asked Pachi if the chastisements might include, as certain visionaries in Ireland and the Soviet Union implied, a conflict between China and Russia, she, her husband, and Bernardita seemed startled at the question, affirming that this was part of the secret circulated among those close to the visionary. I knew she and her husband wanted a child and when I asked if it wasn't odd to want to bring a child into a doomed world, she said, "No, because I know God will protect the child. When God permits a child into the world, it is because there is still hope for the goodness of man.

"Still there is not enough prayer," said the attractive seer, whose eyes were more piercing and powerful than any I had ever encountered. "There is not a real conversion

of the people. We take a step forward and two back. The
Holy Virgin keeps crying all over the world. Men feel
happy with advances of science and the Holy Virgin says
when they see these buildings and monuments it's when
man feels proud. She says don't feel happy with things of
the world because these will be destroyed.

"She hasn't come to make us fear but to urge us to convert. She doesn't want people to become fanatics. She
wants us to gain Heaven. We have to be ready but prepared
with peace. The United States at the moment is a country
where Satan acts very strongly. It's incredible to see drugs,
AIDS. All the things that come out of that country are the
work of men. This country is going to suffer a lot. Many
cities are going to disappear. New York City will disappear. There is a coldness toward God. New York is a city
made for man and there is no nature. It is the idolatry of
man.

"(Mary) does speak of the Anti-Christ," continued the
young Ecuadoran. "He's already in the world. He's acting
all over the world through various fields—not directly, but
through such things as science. People don't know him.
He is *going* to act directly and we're *going* to know him.
He's very, very intelligent, and will look like a humble
good man and he's going to be very attractive, even beautiful, and have a very attractive personality, and he will get
to people through television and all the ways of the world.
But especially to youth in music and drugs. It is the work
of Satan. He is very young yet. He's going to act directly
in a terrible way after the punishment. I wouldn't want to
live for the days when he acts stronger. A way to recognize
him at the beginning will be that he will speak of humility,
but people will recognize that he is not such. He will bring
people to egoism."

This is not out of line with *Revelation*, which speaks
of the Anti-Christ in Chapter 13 after the Great Tribulation
just as Pachi says he comes after a "punishment." We
must remember, however, that such visions and prophecies are not always expressed in chronological order, and
that "punishment" could mean one of the warnings, with
the Anti-Christ arriving between the warnings or during
stages of a chastisement. Neither is it out of line with the

theories of Dr. Walvoord, the Baptist theologian who interpreted the Old and New Testaments as predicting the
"Mediterranean dictator" who will rise with tremendous
charisma, taking control of the area around the Mediterranean. As you may recall, Walvoord argues that Russia's
loss of power and formation of a "new world order" will
clear the way for him. Pachi spoke of war "from the
south."

The dictator, said Walvoord, will seize control of a new,
ten-nation European confederacy, and will seduce the
world by masquerading as a brilliant, indeed ingenious,
savior and prince of peace. He will be especially adept at
using the media. After hypnotizing much of the world with
his political skills he will move more openly into the field
of religion, convincing many that he is not just a great governmental leader but also possessed of such spiritual force
that he should be looked upon as godlike, a virtual deity.
Using satanic power—the energy given him by the dragon,
Satan—he will show great wonders and ruthlessly crush
believers of the true Christ. The reign of this evil leader
will bring down God's wrath—the Great Tribulation.

"All that I tell you is in Sacred Scripture," Mary told
Pachi. *"A false prophet exists who will entangle (my little
souls) saying that he is God, but he is from the blood of
the demon. He will betray the Father. And the one who has
the heart and wisdom will realize that he carries the number of the beast, 666, on his right hand. Satan is set loose
to touch my little ones, but I am that woman whom the
Father announced, who will crush the head of the serpent
that is Satan."*

If we look at *2 Thessalonians* 2:8 11, we see the apostle
Paul forewarning that "the lawless one" will come in the
midst of a tremendous delusion, which will be broken by
the return, in some form, of Christ, destroying the lawless
one "with the brightness of His coming."

CHAPTER 41

The Hour of the Light
of the Trinity

"Dear children. The time has come that you can no longer survive without my direct intervention. The one you call Satan is the Shining Darkness who has poisoned all your souls and has deprived you of the dignity with which I gifted each one of my children. I created each one of you good. To each of you I gifted a whole and pure soul. Among you, children, there are no more souls which are whole. I am the Truth and there is only one truth. The Shining Darkness has taken away My gift from you, your dignity."

Lying in bed on May 28, 1989, Zdenko "Jim" Singer, 37, plant manager for General Printing, a huge Canadian ink manufacturer, was discussing plans with his wife Natalie for celebrating their 19th wedding anniversary when he suddenly seemed to doze off. Natalie, who works in the rectory of St. Raphael's Roman Catholic Church in Burlington, Ontario, noticed that within two or three minutes her husband's hands were raised and he seemed to be speaking to someone with great animation and joy. There was "a sort of warm, pleasant energy all around us which I find impossible to describe."

According to Zdenko, a native of Zagreb, Croatia, he saw in front of him "many colors which rapidly began to blend and transform into a brilliant shine. A form of a man started becoming visible from the center of this radiance, and as the brilliance intensified, this form became more obviously defined. At the same time I felt an intensely powerful presence of this being. It was immediately obvious to me in Whose present I was. I felt extremely comfortable, totally at peace and indescribably warm. During this event, and all subsequent apparitions, I was not aware of my surroundings. All I was aware of was the Lord's presence and all that He was showing.''

For the next 99 days, claims Singer, he experienced apparitions of the "Father, Son of Man, and Spirit," along with appearances of the Virgin. Most of them occurred in a wakeful state with his eyes open. The colors blended into a brilliant ball of white light—not really a "ball," since the glow encompassed his entire field of vision—and in it he saw the silhouette of a man he took to be "Lord the Father." He never beheld this Person's face, only the silhouette. On one occasion Jesus appeared in the brilliant light to the right of the Father, stepping close to Singer as a full-bodied apparition that Singer could virtually touch, a terrifically impressive personage with very dark brown hair and a short beard, appearing to be about thirty. Singer claims the closest representation to what he saw is the Jesus of Divine Mercy with red and pale rays coming from His Heart, the vision seen by Sr. Faustina. The Light itself was the Holy Spirit.

We could call this the hour of the light of the Trinity, and we could also call it the final hour. Throughout the world, and specifically North America, the Virgin's appearances, having stood as God's maternal presence for so many decades, seemed to be increasingly giving way to direct experiences with her Son. The baby she held in her arms at Fatima, and showed as a boy at Pidkamin, was now showing Himself as a young man, often as a man, as Singer perceived, of about thirty, which was about when Jesus in the flesh first revealed His public ministry 2,000 years ago.

On a spiritual and apparitional level, Mary was shown bringing Him back into the world, and with Him, around Him, and through Him was the Trintiy, of which He is an

integral part. The supernatural was descending upon the
materialistic West. There were claimed apparitions in Arizona, Georgia, Ohio, Minnesota, Canada, California, Texas,
Colorado, Wisconsin, and other parts of the hemisphere,
and the strongest messages were messages of hope. In the
sun was seen a door, this time not the gate of Hell but the
door of Heaven. Yes, these were unusual times, said visionaries like Singer, and perhaps apocalyptical times, but they
were also times of great hope. We are not nearing the end
of the world, they seemed to agree, but the end of an era,
the era of Satan, and ahead is the era of goodness and
peace. The era of godless materialism, the era of "man-as-
god," was about to end. As if to confirm the cycle's conclusion, Catherine Laboure, the visionary in 1830 at Rue du
Bac, was appearing in at least one American apparition.

It was now more than a hundred years since Pope Leo's
vision in 1884, but no one knew exactly when or in what
actual form Satan's official time began running and no one
knew when his time was up. Father Gobbi believed the ten-
year period beginning in 1988 is the decisive period and
said the Virgin described the current times as the final
phase of the "second Advent," as well as the period of the
tribulation and those threatening events currently hidden
in the Medjugorje and other secrets. This period of ten
years, Mary supposedly said, would be when *"there will
come to completion that fullness of time which was pointed
out to you by me, beginning with LaSalette all the way to
my most recent and present apparitions."*
Father Gobbi said Mary had explained that the number
of the beast, 666, is an indicator not just of the beast's
name, but of *time*. The year 666 was a period of history
during which Islam was destroying Christian communities;
and 666 doubled is the year 1332, a period during which
the Word of God, or "Parola," came under attack by a new
school of philosophers who began to give exclusive value
to science and then to reason. That gradual tendency
evolved into the French Revolution and then Marxism and
godless intellectuals, which in America took the form of
secular humanism, extreme rationalism, and the idolatry
of money. The number 666 tripled is the year 1998, by
which time Gobbi believed an idol would be planted in the

place of Christ. If we remember, the stages seemed to be: warnings, an end to Satan's domination, a great sign, rise of an anti-christ, or *the* Anti-Christ, which will be Satan's last gasp, and chastisements to purify the world.

Singer's time-table was not very different from that of Gobbi's, nor for that matter those of Christina Gallagher and Pachi. During his apparitions of the Light, he was told that something was coming in seven years, and since the particular apparition occurred on January 13, 1991, that meant 1997. It seemed to concern the final hour of Satan's extended power. *"Three days remain for you, by your free will, to consecrate your hearts to Me, to enjoy My rewards and victory over the malefactor,"* said the enigmatic message. *"Three days remain for you to allow the malefactor seven years of his particular aggression and oppression among you. Through the ages you have been warned what the malefactor is preparing for you during these final times. Only by your conversion and sincere love will you be protected."*

The year 1997 stood perfectly sandwiched between Gobbi's 1998 for the rise of an idol and the year 1996, which bore significance to what I'd heard in Ecuador, where, it was said, Pachi was told the beginning of the events in her secret would be just before a month of two full moons. There will be two full moons in September of 1993, July of 1996, and January of 1999. The year 1996 is closest to Singer's year, and fits with the Garabandal speculation that the great Miracle might come on the feast day of Saint Stanislaus, which will arrive on a Thursday in 1996.

If this wasn't just idle and eccentric speculation, or worse, a monumental deception, then it seemed like unusual events, events linked to the "end times," might commence just after the mid-point of our current decade and run on for several years, culminating, if Christina Gallagher was correct, by the end of the century.

If, perchance, the earlier events of the century fulfilled the first five seals of Revelation, and did not pertain to similar future events—if "conflict on earth" had been fulfilled already by the world wars, scarcity of earth by famines from Ukraine to the Horn of Africa, widespread death on earth by the associated holocausts, and "cry of the martyrs" by the Communist and Nazi persecutions of the Church—then we next face "cosmic disturbances" as part of the Great Tribulation.

We have seen how the prophesied events, subject to change according to mankind's response, seemed often to involve fire from the sky, darkness, flooding, storms, earthquakes, and general mayhem. These images could well be mere symbols (the fire of the Holy Spirit, the flood of God's Justice, the quaking of Heaven's righteous anger), but if they are to be taken literally, one can imagine many spectacular scenarios, the most unnerving to me being the unexpected approach of an asteroid or comet. At Garabandal, Conchita said the "warning" would be a horrible event more terrifying than actually destructive, and she seemed to see a cosmic event, "like two stars...that crash and make a lot of noise, and a lot of light...but they don't fall. It's not going to hurt us but we're going to see it and, in that moment, we're going to see our consciences."

A close call with a comet (which Pachi mentioned as the possible part of a warning before war) might fit Conchita's description of "two stars," since a comet, paired with the sun, would look like two stars, and it also reminded me of Gallagher's perception that whatever was coming was coming at "great speed." I remembered another visionary warning that "the fire has been lit." A comet was also foreseen by St. Hildegard and the occultist Nostradamus, who, in a quatrain called "The Comet, The Arab Mastiff, the Exile of the Pope," foresaw a "great star" that "shall be seen as if two suns in the sky should appear." The fire of Heaven, said LaSalette, *"will fall and consume three cities. All the Universe will be struck with terror and many will let themselves be led astray because they have not worshiped the true Christ who lives among them."* Was its approach symbolized by the sun that "fell" during the great miracle of Fatima? Or were we in for solar disturbances far greater than those which caused the aurora borealis?

If earth encountered a close call with an asteroid or comet, it would certainly qualify as a terrifying event, and if such an object were large enough and hit earth, or caused earth to pass through its gaseous tail, it might induce the sort of effects mentioned in various predictions of both warnings and chastisement: its red dust turning water to "blood" (if the comet in *Exodus* is any indication), its ash scalding the skin and eyes, its impact (if an asteroid or pieces of a huge solid-core comet hit) moving mountains, its dust or gases inducing meteorological effects, its meteorological effects causing both flooding and drought, its flooding leading to disease and famine, its hydrogen mixing with earthly gases and causing regional fire, then torrential rain clouds, its electrical charges leading to an unprecedented display of lightning, its tail dust causing cold and darkness, and its impact causing earthquakes, sun-stifling clouds of dust, and tidal waves.

If we look deeper into *Revelation,* specifically the events of the Seven Trumpets, we are given additional indications of a multifaceted cosmic event. Fire is thrown to the earth before the First Trumpet, and then vegetation is destroyed (burned up), the sea is struck with "something like a great mountain with fire thrown into the sea" (*Revelation* 8:8), and a third of mankind is destroyed by what seems like Armageddon.

In other words: natural disaster and war together plaguing mankind until the Kingdom of God is proclaimed. In the Sixth Seal, the sun becomes dark as "sackcloth," which the dust from impact (or an eclipse as an object passed) might cause, the moon becomes "like blood" (perhaps from a fiery tail), and "stars of Heaven" fall like leaves from a tree—an allusion perhaps to debris in the form of a meteorite shower from a passing object. In *Revelation* 16, the Bowl Judgments seem to repeat and add yet more detail to the Tribulation, including mention of the earth "utterly shaken."

In 1990 a sizeable asteroid missed earth by only six hours. According to *The New York Times* of April 7, 1992, if we set up an adequate monitoring system, scientists "might find 1,050 to 4,200 Earth-crossing asteroids that are at least 0.62 miles in diameter, a size judged large enough to begin to cause global upheaval by deranging climate and agriculture. Even quite small rocks are of possible concern since their enormous speeds endow them with kinetic energy that is converted at impact into quantities of heat comparable to that released by multiple nuclear explosions. Slamming into the earth at roughly 16 miles a second, a large asteroid could explode with the force of a million H-bombs, lofting enough pulverized rock and dust to block most sunlight. Cold and darkness could last for months, crippling agriculture and probably a good part of modern civilization, leading to the deaths of a billion or more people from starvation."

I realize that I'm involved here with speculation bordering on fantasy. The "star," as in *Revelation,* would more likely be a nuclear warhead, which would also cause many of the same effects: certainly fire from the sky, darkness, and "wormwood" in the waters as radiation spread across the planet and caused the sort of horrible boils Pachi saw on the skin of people of all races. Many prominent scholars in Russia and elsewhere in the U.S.S.R. were nervous about the Chernobyl event for more than technical reasons. They began to read *Revelation* and especially 8:11, which says, "Then the third angel sounded: And a great star fell from Heaven, burning like a torch, and it fell on a third of the rivers and on the springs of water; and the name of the star is Wormwood; and a third of the waters became wormwood; and many men died from the water, because it was made bitter."

Wormwood is a bitter wild herb used as a tonic in rural areas of the Soviet Union. And the Ukrainian word for wormwood is *"chernobyl."*

Singer didn't see any asteroids or comets. He didn't see a world war. He *did* glimpse a "strange" war that while not quite at world-war status would involve an odd combination of Eurasian countries arrayed in strange alliances. As for disease: *"The Shining Darkness has sown among you various vicious diseases. AIDS mows down lives. By your conversion back to me, you shall prevent two much more vicious sexually transmitted diseases which the malefactor is preparing as his future 'gift' to you."*

There would be tragedies, the Lord told Singer, *"tragedies being prepared by the Shining Darkness to draw away your attention from the Divine Intervention into your lives."* The voice predicted a particularly nasty war in

Yugoslavia, which soon came about and expanded to such an extent that Medjugorje was shut off to the world and itself threatened by Serbians who, as a last vestige of Communism, raised the devil's red star. My last attempt at reaching Medjugorje met with failure as phone lines were jammed in the spring of 1992 and fighting broke out in the fields next to Medjugorje, with MIG jets dropping cluster bombs and breaking the sound barrier in the skies above.

Fortunately, miraculously, (as of this printing) Medjugorje itself was spared damage, but as we all know, the viciousness in Bosnia-Hercegovina, where Medjugorje is located, became as bad as anything in Europe since World War II and threatened to spread to Macedonia, Albania, Turkey, and even Greece. "Ethnic cleansing," destruction of three hundred Catholic churches, concentration camps, the rape of Muslim women. Bullet holes scarred treasured crucifixes in Mostar and Dubrovnik. No wonder Mary had so often warned that peace was in crisis, and no wonder she had appeared in at least a dozen other locations in former Yugoslavia, including apparitions to a young girl in Split.

Yugoslavia seemed to stand as a microcosm of what could happen in the former Soviet Union and adjacent countries. Like Yugoslavia, many former Soviet republics—Moldova, Ukraine, Armenia—are involved in border disputes, religious animosities, and ancient blood feuds. There are 125 ethnic conflicts just within the former Soviet empire.

In Africa civil conflict descended upon Rwanda (site of the Kibeho apparitions) and famine took hold of Somalia.

If the same time-table held for other areas of the world as it did for Yugoslavia—where the hellish scenario unfolded ten years after the first Medjugorje apparitions—did that mean that Ireland, Western Europe, and the former U.S.S.R. would encounter *their* Hell between 1995 and 1997 (ten years after the first phenomena at Ballinspittle and Hrushiw)?

Would America come after that, just as it was now encountering its own outbreak of apparitions from Arizona to a shrine not far from Denver? Was the mayhem in Bosnia and Croatia a pre-sign for the Western Hemisphere?

"Satan is attacking My children of Croatia precisely because I have chosen them to be the model of My Love to all My children of the world," explained the Lord during the unique apparitions in Canada. *"While they are convinced that they are enjoying liberty and freedom, Satan's rage will not spare My children of the Western world either. Never have My children delighted in sin as now. In Noah's age I cleansed the world of sins that were of a lesser degree than these in which My children now take delight. In China the Shining Darkness will appear as the victor, since too few of you have enough faith in Divine Intervention. I tell you that the time when you will be the witnesses of My Intervention into your earthly lives is soon coming. But I admonish you to examine your love and faithfulness to me. The Shining Darkness will multiply his powers. The Shining Darkness is preparing for you great bloodshed in the Eastern world, especially the U.S.S.R. In the Western world, My children shall meet with great injustices, violence, oppression, and ever deeper and greater loss of dignity with which I gifted you. Convert and your prayers will be granted."*

Referring to abortion, the Lord said, *"Among these (aborted) children is a large number of them who were the gift to you for your good. The Shining Darkness knows this and he still rules your hard hearts. These very ones, these innocent ones, were intended to deliver you from the despairs from which you now suffer. These innocent souls were intended to rule and advance this world which I gifted you, in the manner that I teach you, in My love."* Only when *"every drop of the malefactor's poison"* is purged would there be true peace, and that could only come through strong and constant faith. *"The power of faith expels the malefactor from your lives,"* said the Lord. *"Through your sincere love of me you are rewarded with the power and wisdom to protect yourself from the malefactor and all his evil."* With conversion and prayer *"you shall destroy the empire of the Shining Darkness."* The Lord urged special protection and discipline of youth; a far more reverent attitude toward marriage; and the eradication of *"evil misuse of press, radio, and television for these are now powerful instruments of the Shining Dark-*

ness with which he blinds you and delivers the most amount of evil to you. With love that I give you, courageously put into question every institution which violates the family.

"*These are the times of my special graces for you, and the Shining Darkness is deeply aware of that,*" said a voice that Singer could feel as much as hear, a deeply penetrating voice totally unlike any human voice, felt physically as well as in the mind and emotions, speaking Croatian. "*This malefactor dares to enter into battle with Me. He even dares to make use of My Heavenly Truth. Convert, each one of you. The love, warmth, total peace and tranquility with which I will reward you is endless. For your conversion I give you the gift of Medjugorje. In the gift of Medjugorje you possess all the messages which the Immaculate Mother brings you. They are the only method for you to eliminate the Shining Darkness from your lives. His poisoned gifts lead you to eternal damnation.*

"*In My love and these times of My special graces I will send you many signs and heavenly apparitions. Even now, there are My children among you who are chosen to be witnesses of My signs. Many of them will become the witnesses of Divine apparitions. Let all these children be the reminder of My love for you.*

"*The Shining Darkness knows that the time of his evil is approaching the end. My children, be vigilant, for the Shining Darkness will multiply his evil powers, especially where he recognizes the Divine Heavenly Presence. Each of you, convert totally and, through My gifts, you shall be the victors over the malefactor.*

"*Because of your conversion,*" the Lord continued, "*the Shining Darkness shall lose this battle. But, the victims among you shall be many. In these special times you will soon be witnesses of My graces. Many among you who were disgraced, banished, exiled, and persecuted will soon take their place among those that are first. Convert and through My love you shall be the victors. Tragedies which the Shining Darkness is preparing as his 'gift' to you My children will be thwarted by your faith.*"

In North America, especially as the Lord began to show Himself, accompanied often by apparitions of the heavenly mother, a new and final theme was emerging: that we do indeed approach dangerous times, far more important times than what our newspapers and television would have us know—spiritual times—and that there is still time left to lessen or prevent any truly gargantuan catastrophes.

In affluent Scottsdale, Arizona, Our Lord and Mary appeared to a group of attractive young adults (some would say "yuppies") who saw the shortcomings of a materialistic world they once aspired to. They say that our times are more significant than we currently realize, that sin and materialism have blinded the nation, and that as a result there will be chastisements unless there is an abrupt change of course. America, they were told, is Satan's turf.

"The secrets I've gotten are mainly from Our Lord, and one is from Our Lady," says one of the visionaries, Gianna Talone, a 35-year-old woman who works as a pharmaceutical administrator. "It's important not to focus on the negativism, the panic, or the fear. Too much emphasis is put on fear and panic. I would caution about making a statement as to time and I'd put emphasis on action now and not postponing it because who knows, it could happen tomorrow. God has His own timetable. He is loving and tender. God will draw the army together. I think the emphasis has to be on change and prayer now. Right now. In urgency. Our Lady always speaks of urgency of prayer and conversion now—forgiveness, mercy, love, honesty, respect, dignity, compassion. It's a time where we will be weeded out and with our free will we have free choice. The Lord says there's no middle of the rope. There's only two ends."

Gianna points out that in Ninevah the positive reaction of those forewarned withheld promised punishments, which seemed to make a mockery of the predictions but in actuality showed the Love and Mercy of God. On June 5, 1989, she was given this inspiring message by Jesus: *"My people, do not wait for the chastisement for the beauty of My Father to be restored! If you will allow Me now to dwell in you, the beauty of My Father will be recreated. Do you not realize the power you have through love, faith,*

*and prayer? Through faith in Me and the One Who sent
Me, trust, love, and prayer, all beauty and peace can be
re-established, preventing chastisement! All goodness can
be restored if you open your hearts and believe and practice what I teach you. The chastisement shall be a result
of misbelief, lack of love, lack of faith, lack of respect and
from the lack of your mercy! I tell you, if you change your
hearts and live what I tell you, goodness, purity, and
beauty can be restored by destroying evil now. You have
the power to destroy evil if you all focus on Me and allow
Me to live in you. You can prevent the chastisement from
My Father!"*

In the sky above Scottsdale, another young mystic named
Susan Evans, saw a huge eagle.

Indications are that Scottsdale will become a major center of pilgrimage.

To an anonymous Midwestern visionary known as
Mariamante, Mary said, *"You will know by the sign in the
heavens which is me that the time is at hand for the instan-
taneous conversion of the multitude. This I will accomplish
through a tremendous outpouring of grace upon the earth
given at the hands of God to me for this purpose. This will
be the triumph of my Immaculate Heart of which I spoke
at Fatima. You must do all that I tell you now. It is very
important that you follow my instructions, as this will be
an aid to many in softening their hearts in order to be
receptive to such grace."*

Mariamante said Christ also appeared to her and
explained that after the Trinity, Mary should be most
loved. He emphasized that He certainly was not jealous of
her. Where she is, so is He. *"My mother's plan to accomplish the triumph of her Immaculate Heart has been underway now for some time and continues to gain momentum
as more souls consecrated to her are called forth to begin
their particular mission for which they are picked."*

The sun was spinning in America. The sun was dancing
in Conyers, Georgia, and Sabana Grande, Puerto Rico, like
it danced in Medjugorje and Betania. The same epidemic
of apparitions that had hit Ireland in 1985 and Ukraine in
1987 was hitting America. In Pasadena, California, Mary

was seen as Our Lady of Lourdes behind an apartment. In Duluth, Minnesota, Bishop Roger L. Schwietz had initiated an investigation of alleged apparitions and communications from Our Blessed Mother that warned of yet more demonic entities pouring from Hell. In Phoenix, Arizona, seer Estela Ruiz was told by Mary that mankind had created a new idol, a new golden calf, and *"that golden idol has now been made into the image of man."*

If it wasn't a case of spiritual plagiarism, psychological copycatting, a satanic trick to incite hopelessness and fear, or a plot to discredit future claims of the supernatural, the American visions seemed like a final attempt to form a new flock, and to replace war-closed Medjugorje with centers right here in the United States. Although criticized in certain quarters, I saw the messages from Scottsdale as especially clean and profound. *"I tell you, the chastisement will come from your not doing the wish of My Father!"* Jesus told Gianna. *"It will be because you have placed restrictions on the goodness of My Father, Who is all good and the Creator of all beauty."*

Up in Ontario, Singer was hearing the same thing. *"By your return into My embrace, I gift to you the power to thwart all of those malefactor's intentions against which I warn you. Satan knows that he does not have much time left. Resist him tirelessly, evict Satan from your lives, never allow him any place among you. Because of My love for you, never allow him peace in your midst, for soon, out of My love for My children, I will wash the face of this world."*

It could be a gradual process, and it might not even be realized as a purification or chastisement except in retrospect, as many of God's actions are not appreciated until later, nor are His warnings. The war may be on a spiritual level, but it will be war nonetheless, pitting believers against disbelievers, the spiritual equivalent of a civil conflict, with accompanying hardships. Singer sees the chastisements as coming in the form of increased violence in our society and increased personal suffering as sin is more directly and immediately punished by God. It doesn't mean God will wave a magic wand and cause one huge spectacular event. The very increase of evil is a form of chastisement, one that no one is able to elude. We face the moral (and perhaps with it the economic) collapse of America. The incredible darkness seen by visionaries is in many ways our spiritual darkness, a darkness brought upon us by the shadow of the media, which has convinced us that there is no such *thing* as sin, and that the devil is naught but a cartoonish character with a pitchfork. The darkness has blinded us to Satan, and as seers of the "three days of darkness" envisioned, spiritual entities known as demons have thus been given free flight in our atmosphere, affecting us without our knowing it.

Our greatest chastisement is the evil increasing around us. Jesus sought to make us realize that sin will bring a painful future, and he too gave indications of what will come. He said on the Mount of Olives (Chapter 24 of *Matthew*) that the signs of the times, the signs of the end of the age and the coming sorrows, will include nation rising against nation, famines, pestilences, and earthquakes *"in various places."* There will also be false prophets, cold-heartedness, and lawlessness. Immediately after the tribulation of those days, *"the sun will be darkened, and the moon will not give its light; the stars will fall from Heaven, and the powers of the heavens will be shaken."*

Then the sign of Christ will appear in Heaven, and mankind will experience the Second Coming. As the days of Noah were, warned Jesus, *"so also will the coming of the Son of Man be."*

Watch, He told us, *"for you do not know what hour your Lord is coming."*

Back in the 1930s, He told Sister Faustina that *"all those souls who will glorify My Mercy and spread its worship, encouraging others to trust in My Mercy, will not experience terror at the hour of death. My Mercy will shield them in that final battle..."*

The way to alleviation of spiritual ills is the way of the Gospels. There is no road to purification but the difficult route of self-control and piety. A great test has befallen mankind—not in the form, for now, of a world war, not yet with global earthquakes or any of the spectacular scenarios envisioned by seers, who seemed to glimpse the extreme possibilities—but on the plane of morality. The devil has blinded us to the very presence of sin, has even made many forms of sin look like a *good,* and now activities once recognized as abominations in the sight of God are accepted, rationalized, and even legally protected, with those who oppose such sinfulness subject to ostracization.

There is one route away from the devil's snare. It's the way of Christ, and that means humility, love, purity, long-suffering, sacrifice, and peace. There's no room for anger. There is absolutely no room for greed and jealousy. There's no room for adultery, sodomy, and fornication, which violate the gift of sexuality and offer it to Satan.

As Mary once said—once allegedly said—to a visionary named Barrio Rincon in Sabana Grande, Puerto Rico, in 1953, *"The times will come when the spiritual and moral deterioration of the shepherds of my Son's flock will be a matter of public knowledge...Spiritual growth will become very difficult for the children of God and further times will come when such growth will seem almost impossible. Beware, my children, because indifference and confusion will prevail along the way, and throughout the world."*

Our destiny and that of mankind are still ours to determine, not by political or military decisions but by the way we conduct our lives. That was the message of Fatima, and we should pay special attention to Fatima because that apparition predicted the end of World War I, the onset of World War II, and the rise of Russia at a time, in 1917, when it seemed ridiculous that Russia could one day cause problems throughout the world. As author Howard Q. Dee once commented, Our Lady came then and comes now to tell us that the time for her victory has arrived but not before we pass through a time of great distress and trials caused by sin, and conditioned on our conversion. She comes to provide refuge in deeply troubled times, in times when radical activists are allowed to desecrate our churches, assault pro-life marchers outside abortion clinics, set the agenda for media coverage, spread sexual propaganda through our schools, and dominate the entertainment industry. She came to give us refuge in her Immaculate Heart.

I believe the bad days, the bad days for those of the flock who have watched the surge of evil, are soon to end, hopefully within our lifetimes. I agree with a message given to Estela Ruiz on April 6, 1991: *"During these days when you see so much evil around you, you need to know that there is also much good—that times are coming when you will see the good overcome evil. Many of my children have turned to God. Many have listened to my call, have turned to God's Mercy and have become true children of God."*

But as steps are made forward, there are also steps backward, and we remain perilously close to the edge of an unknown abyss. Our society totters. We know not yet for sure which way it will go. Mary has requested fasting *"so that with your help everything I wanted to realize through the secrets which I began in Fatima may be fulfilled."* On March 25, 1992, at Medjugorje, Mary, disheartened by a recent turn of events, warned that we need to change our lives even more and keep to her messages because we have taken *"a path of misery, a path of ruin."* In a nearly angry tone, she admonished that the requests for prayers and fasting had been taken superficially, and that as a result she could do little for us. She sounded nearly as if her plan to create in us an oasis of peace was again failing, and thus the arm of God was once more heavy, the cup again overflowing. *"Satan is playing with you and with your souls and I cannot help you because you are far from my heart."* The previous autumn she told Christina Gallagher that *"part of my plan for the world has been destroyed."*

Her Immaculate Heart would triumph in the end, but at what cost? I had my own ideas on what the future held, and I believed, by 1992, that Mary had held back the Justice of God but that there was a stipulation, which was that people would be subject in the near future to a major new test. I have no idea what this new test will be, but it may be the rise of a new evil the likes of which mankind has never before encountered. This evil is not currently known to man. It will arrive almost imperceptibly, with few noticing the depth of its evil, for it will appear to have beneficial and convenient aspects. This is the great deception we have been warned that Satan is preparing, a last chance before his century is over. It will be an evil comparable to abortion—that is to say, that even if evils as great and widespread as abortion were to be eliminated, this would be enough to present mankind with an enormous challenge. How mankind responds to this new evil will determine the extent, length, and severity of purification and chastisements.

We have been given the remedy time and again, remedies repeated at most apparitions. We start with prayer, greatly increasing our supplications to God, we put proper importance on the most powerful prayer, the Mass, and we remember regular recitation of the potent Rosary. If we are Protestants or Jews we increase our traditional means of communicating with the Eternal One. We fast and do penance. We acknowledge and forsake our sins. We love everyone no matter his or her color or creed. And we remember the special devotions: the first Saturday of the month for Catholics, at which time Confession should be conducted, a Rosary said, a Mass attended. We should especially keep in mind the chaplets of Divine Mercy, repeating as often as possible the following words: *"Eternal Father, I offer You the Body and Blood, Soul and Divinity, of Your dearly beloved Son, Our Lord Jesus Christ, in atonement for our sins and those of the whole world."*

We should also memorize and repeat over and over: *"For the sake of His sorrowful Passion, have mercy on us and on the whole world."*
This will nourish and extend the period of mercy. This will appease at least some of God's wrath. We've seen how the prayers of hidden souls like Sister Faustina held back chastisements in the past, and if it's true that we're faced with larger catastrophes—and perhaps the return of Communism—then the time is now to multiply our prayers and put off chastisement again.

The warnings and punishments, if they come, will differ according to region, and like the great evil, in my opinion, will not always or usually be immediately noticeable for what they are. In this period will also be a warning that involves not so much fire from the sky as *fear* of fire from the sky, and strange loud rumblings. This, according to mankind's response, will then be followed by another chastisement and the inevitable, glorious onset of the change of era.

Our era is ending. One way or another, the world is going to change, and it will experience such major change—a sociological sea change—within the lifetimes of the Medjugorje visionaries, between now and 2040. We cannot go on much longer as a godless race, more prone to evil than to Heaven. It wouldn't surprise me if, through economic or other effects, much of our technology is broken down and our modern attitude takes on more the nature of a peasant's. It was to peasants who Mary so often appeared. Before or during this breakdown of our false society will come a new world order, which, if he does now exist, would give fertile soil to the Anti-Christ. If the Anti-Christ comes in our era, I believe he will have tremendous influence—not necessarily actual raw political power. Hardly anyone will notice him until he is accomplished. That is to say, he might not rule and control in a way that's obvious to the world at the peak of his influence, which means I disagree with some of what Dr. Walvoord said. The Anti-Christ will be a figure like Marx, except his ideas will be more powerful and immediate.

The artifice of our society is false and must be refashioned. It's a world at odds with nature and itself. Our science is corrupt, serving atheism, not God. Our science has provided us with much good but also much bad: nuclear weapons, ozone-depleting chemicals, human indignity in treating us as evolutionary animals, and the prospect of catastrophic changes in climate (the type warned about at LaSalette) from technological gases and a global warming. The world will not *end* but *change.* Our confidence in science will dramatically decrease as we see the evil behind many of its pretenses. I don't believe, by the end of the millennium, that we will know the coldness and hatred we know now. It may increase up till then, but eventually will come events, spiritual or physical, which will begin to break that hatred and egoism down. If we don't break it down, God, in His time, will do it for us, and the variety of possible ways has been expressed in the many apocalyptical visions. We do not need to look for any more signs so much as we need to look for faith. Christ will return, and no one knows that hour. It will be a great and terrible day that we need to prepare for, not become fearful of.

In the end, the most important mission, our main concern, should be the state of each and every one of our souls. The greatest chastisement is Hell. It's no coincidence that visionaries are so often shown its fire, its burbling mud, its demons, and its greatest agony: the total absence of God. Every one of us faces our final hour every waking moment, not knowing when it will come. And not knowing when it will come, we should treat each hour as our final hour.

We have seen the horrors of demonic entities and Hell; we have glimpsed the sufferings of Purgatory. But the same visionaries who've seen eternal torture have also seen eternal reward: the indescribably beautiful and happy expressions on people clothed in light garments like what Jesus wore, in landscapes of supernatural peace and color— terrifically encompassing peace and total love—joyously joined in singing praises in Heaven to a finally visible God.

If another nuclear reactor explodes in the Soviet Union, or if war comes, or if a cosmic disturbance threatens the planet—if the earth is knocked out of its orbit, for that matter—these are small matters in comparison to our eternal destination; and well-prepared, we have nothing to fear. *"In the end,"* said Our Lady of Fatima, *"my Immaculate Heart will triumph."*

And in the end, the main mission of the apparitions has been to show a materialistic world that God does exist, to indicate to us a maternal concern, and to make sure we understand the extent of devices available to God to put us back in order. The rise of Hitler, the advent of Communism, and the world wars should have served as warnings enough and foretastes of what else may come. We are in a lull, a period of mercy and self-evaluation. And that's what we must do: assess our spiritual state. For in the end, at the moment of death, we will all see the Light that visionaries have seen, and we will all have decided for ourselves an eternal destination.

Notes

Chapter One: The figure of 94 percent believers comes from the *Almanac of the American People.* It's a 1987 figure, but it doesn't vary wildly year to year. According to Alison Gallup of the Gallup organization, pollsters there found the same percentage— 94 percent in 1990—who believed in "God or a universal spirit." I'm always on guard against use of the term "universal spirit" but it certainly shows an inclination towards the supernatural that is not reflected in American schools or the mass media, which are virtually devoid of supernatural terminology. The Bible I use is the King James version, simply because I enjoy its elegant prose. I also employ the New American Bible, St. Joseph Edition. That David du Plessis visited Medjugorje and responded favorably comes from editor David Manuel in the foreword of a book entitled *Letters from Medjugorje.* For Martin Luther see *Mary in Protestant and Catholic Theology,* by Thomas A. O'Meara.

Chapter Two: The account of Rue-du-Bac comes largely from a book distributed at the apparitional site in Paris, *The Saint of Silence and the Message of Our Lady,* written anonymously. This apparition was approved in 1836, six years after the occurrence. I also draw from the book *A Woman Clothed With the Sun* (edited by John J. Delaney, Doubleday/Image). Information on the con- troversy over the secrets of LaSalette comes from *Encountering*

341

Mary, Sandra L. Zimdars-Swartz (Princeton University Press). The secrets given to Mélanie (or allegedly given to her) are in *Apparition of the Blessed Virgin on the Mountain of LaSalette the 19th of September, 1846,* published by the Shepherdess of LaSalette. It's available by writing Miraculous Lady of the Roses, 1186 Burlington Drive, Hickory Corners, MI 49060. Some historical apparitions are contained in *Cause of Our Joy,* by Sister Mary Francis LeBlanc, St. Paul Editions (Daughters of St. Paul) in Boston, 1970. Also, I visited LaSalette in 1989 and Rue du Bac in 1991.

Chapter Three: The story of the Foxes is taken from many sources, especially *The Spirit Rappers,* by Herbert G. Jackson, Jr., Doubleday, 1972. I visited Lourdes in 1989 and use a number of sources for backup, including *A Woman Clothed With the Sun* and *Encountering Mary.*

Chapters Four and Five: The legend of Pope Leo XIII comes from sources such as *'Neath St. Michael's Shield,* published by the Daughters of St. Paul, and also *Prophecies! The Chastisement and Purification,* by Rev. Albert J. Hebert, S.M. (P.O. Box 309, Paulina, LA 70763), p. 152. For more information on Masons and Illuminati, see *The New World Order* (Word Publishers) by Pat Robertson; also, *The Deadly Deception* by Jim Shaw and Tom McKenney (Huntington House) and John Bird's booklet, *Queen of Ukraine,* available through the 101 Foundation, P.O. Box 151, Asbury, NJ 08802-0151. The 101 Foundation has a long list of pamphlets on apparitions. For Freud I use *Freud* by Ronald W. Clark (Random House). The source for much of Marx is Richard Wurmbrand's fascinating and excellent book *Marx and Satan* (Crossway Books). The Pope's encyclical was *Humanum Genus,* April 20, 1884, and is available through TAN Books and Publishers, Inc. in Rockford, IL. For Knock I use such pamphlets as "The Glory of Knock," by Father Michael Walsh, and "Knock," by Father Berchmans Walsh, obtained from the site of apparitions. Sanger's book *Woman and the New Race* was published by Brentano's in 1920. Write PEACE of Minnesota, 611 S. Snelling Avenue, St. Paul, MN 55116 for more literature on Sanger. I draw information from their brochure "Exposed: Planned Parenthood," by Debra Braun. Among other Sanger books worthy of study is *Pivot of Civilization,* also Brentano's. The material on *Woman Rebel* comes from *Birth Control In America,* by David

Kennedy, Yale University Press, 1970. One can find other quotes in *Margaret Sanger* by Madeline Gray (the most revealing biography, published by Richard Marek Publishers) and *Pioneer of the Future: Margaret Sanger* by Emily Taft Douglas (Holt, Rinehart, and Winston).

Chapter Six: The accounts of Fatima were obtained from numerous sources, including *Fatima in Lucia's Own Words,* edited by Rev. Louis Kondor (Postulation Center, Fatima, Portugal), which I obtained during a 1989 visit to the site; *Our Lady of Fatima,* by William Thomas Walsh; *Cause of Our Joy* and *A Woman Clothed with the Sun,* which I've previously cited; and *Encountering Mary,* also previously mentioned. Also, I chatted with Francisco's and Jacinta's brother during the visit there. See also a book entitled *1917,* which also has information on Rasputin. Some say it wasn't a holm oak but an azinheira evergreen. As for Hrushiw, some of this comes from the accounts of the Catholic activist Josyp Terelya. A note on Lenin in that Finnish cabin: actually he'd returned to Russia by now after 11 years in exile.

Chapter Seven: Some of the information on Lenin comes from *The Young Lenin* by Leon Trotsky and *Lenin: The Compulsive Revolutionary.* Also, Payne's book *The Life and Death of Lenin.* Deriabin and Bagley are respectively former KGB and CIA agents who collaborated on their book for Hippocrene Books in New York. The quote is from page 214. As for Hitler and demonism, Ravenscroft's book *The Spear of Destiny,* G. P. Putnam's, 1973, is the seminal work. Joseph Carr's book *The Twisted Cross* is another seminal source and is published by Huntington House in Shreveport, LA. I also draw from a set of encyclopedias called *Man, Myth, and Magic.* And the regular encyclopedias such as *Britannica* as well. I also use John Toland's *Adolf Hitler* (Doubleday) and numerous other sources. Toland, like many mainstream biographers, seems almost to go out of his way to avoid discussing Hitler's occultic influences. Ravenscroft depends much upon another scholar of the spear, Dr. Walter Johannes Stein, who allegedly knew Hitler. In Stein's view a "mighty spirit now inhabited (Hitler's) soul creating within and around him a kind of evil transfiguration of its own nature and power." Author Bram Stoker, who wrote *Dracula,* was also a member of the Golden Dawn, and so was the president of the Royal Academy. The Swiss newspaper *Schweizerisches Katholisches Sonntagsblat* is supposed to have an account of Lenin's possibly diabolical death. In the standard biographies are less graphic accounts. Note on Wotan: also spelled Wodan or Woton. A painting of Wotan the year of Hitler's birth resembled the later Hitler so much that some thought it was a hidden Hitler portrait.

Chapter Eight: I take the descriptions of Banneux and Beauring from *A Woman Clothed With the Sun,* previously cited. Some of the information on the Ukrainian famine comes from the files of Congress (Report to Congress: U.S. Commission on Ukrainian Famine—1988). I also interviewed Ukrainian scholars from such places as Harvard. See also *The Black Deeds of the Kremlin—A White Book.* See again *Fatima in Lucia's Own Words* for experiences in the 1920s.

Chapter Nine: The information on Hitler and the spear of Longinus comes chiefly from Ravenscroft's *The Spear of Destiny,* published by G. P. Putnam's in 1973. Again I also refer to *The Twisted Cross* and Toland's *Adolph Hitler* for information on Hitler's occult proclivities. See also Shirer's *The Rise and Fall of the Third Reich.* See *Witch Hunting in Southwestern Germany, 1562-1684,* by H. C. Erik Midelfort (Stanford University Press), for the background of German occultism.

Chapter Ten: For more on Soviet repression, see *Witness,* by Josyp Terelya, the Riehle Foundation, P.O. Box 7, Milford, Ohio, 45150. Cardinal Slipyj's comments were taken from *The Church of Martyrs,* a pamphlet issued by a Ukrainian group in Belgium. The background on popes often comes from a concise biographical history entitled *The Popes,* edited by Eric John (Hawthorn Books). Again I employ *Encountering Mary, Fatima in Lucia's Words,* and *Our Lady of Fatima* for the information on consecration and the secret, along with various other sources. The Three Fountains apparition is taken from a book called *The Virgin of the Revelation,* issued at the Grotta Tre Fontane in Rome. It was written by Don Giuseppe Tomaselli. For Mao see *The Red Barbarians* by Roy Macgregor-Hastie, and *Mao* by Dick Wilson.

Chapter 11: For the accounts of the Third Secret and consecration I use two books by Frére Michel de la Sainte Trinité: *The Whole Truth About Fatima,* and *The Third Secret,* published by Immaculate Heart Publications in Buffalo.

Chapter 12: I draw from a list of apparitions provided by the 101 Foundation, P.O. Box 151, Asbury, NJ 08802-0151. This foundation has done an excellent job of publishing certain obscure material. The messages from Amsterdam are contained in the book *The Messages of the Lady of All Nations,* edited by Josef Künzli and available through 101. Hopefully the plea for a united world did not mean a single world government or "New World Order," which would certainly upset many fundamental Protestants and conservative Catholics. It would certainly make me wonder. During my visit to Montichiari I witnessed, as I did elsewhere, strange fluctuations, pulsations, and gyrations of the sun, directly over the basilica. The bishop's denunciation was posted in several languages inside. As for Amsterdam: Right off, there were questionable messages given to the Dutch seeress, messages that at the least were incomplete or poorly translated. During the fourth apparition in 1945, for example, the Virgin Mary supposedly commented that the trend to socialism *"is good."* While we can imagine Heaven looking kindly upon certain aspects of socialism—which in theory should be less materialistic and more equitable to the poor than capitalism—we have already seen that in practice it's the ultimate in materialistic philosophy, geared only to the physical world and oppressive to the masses. Moreover its modern founder was the malignant Karl Marx. There was also something about the Dutch apparitions and messages that missed the touch of other Marian appearances. They seemed unusually abrupt, lacking the majestic aura characteristic of a Lourdes or Fatima. In some visions the Lady is seen clenching her fist—a decidedly uncharacteristic gesticulation from the usually meek and if anything sorrowful Mother. But I reserve judgment on that apparition and believe it may be worthy of another investigation. The denunciation of Montichiari was issued by Bruno Foresti, vescovo di Brescia, on October 15, 1984. It reads in part: "The Bishop of Brescia, in accordance with which is written in Lumen Gentium N. 27 '. . . The Bishops have the sacred right and duty before the Lord to give laws to their subjects, to judge and regulate everything concerning worship and apostolate,' continuing what has already been stated by his predecessor and comforted by the authoritative mind of the Sacred Congregation for the Doctrine of the Faith states that: 1.) The so-called apparitions of the Blessed Virgin called *'Rosa Mystica'* at Montichiari do not give good reasons for credibility. 2.) Therefore the cult relating to the Virgin Mary *'Rosa Mystica'* is not approved and is to be neither practiced nor favored. 3.) Whoever promotes it, by distributing printed material or organizing pilgrimages, does not help, but disturbs the faith of believers, inducing them to act contrary to the teachings of the Church.

Chapter 13: The Lipa account comes from the Keithley Report, a tape available through the Center for Peace, Asia, Facilities Centre, Shaw Boulevard, Mandaluyong, Metro Manila, Philippines. (Phone 79-56-22). It's Frére Michel's book *The Third Secret* that I again draw from as far as the Fatima message and Lucia's remembrances. For further background on the "end times," see *Armageddon, Oil and the Middle East Crisis* by John F. Walvoord.

Chapter 14: See the Frére Michel books for accounts of the pope's experiences. For Balestrino I use *Guida alle Apparizioni Mariane in Italia* by Patrizia Bortolotti-Piero Mantero (SugarCo Edizioni Inc. in Milan). The accounts of Seredne comes from Ukrainian literature unavailable in the West. For the Turzovka account see Edition 8 of *Vers Demain*, the summer issue of 1970, by Louis Even.

Chapter 15: For the Hungarian account, see "Miracles of Mary," a series of pamphlets distributed by the Augustine Publishing Company, Chulmeigh, Devon, EX18 7HL. I use the pamphlet for the Zarvanystya and other accounts as well. It's available in the USA through the 101 Foundation in Asbury, NJ. See also Frére Michel's *Fatima Revealed and Discarded.* Michel's volumes on Fatima again serve as a source. Accounts of Hrushiw come from literature I collected in the Soviet Union, including "Hrushiw Chronicle" edited by Myron Utrysko and a pamphlet written by a professor of religion in Sambor, Ilarion Hmytryk.

Chapters 16 and 17: The accounts of Garabandal come from a visit there and subsequent phone interviews with the visionaries, as well as from *The Apparitions of Garabandal,* by F. Sanchez-Ventura Y Pascual (San Miguel Publishing Company, Detroit, available now through St. Michael's Garabandal Center for Our Lady of Carmel, 889 Palo Verde Avenue, Pasadena, California, 91104); *Our Lady Comes to Garabandal,* by Joseph A. Pelletier; *God Speaks at Garabandal,* another book by Pelletier; and *Star on the Mountain*, by Pelletier and M. Laffineur. I also draw from

The Tipperary Star, May 5, 1990. Liam Tuohy, a former priest from Ireland, wrote for that paper.

Chapter 18: The accounts about Padre Pio come from visits to San Giovanni Rotundo in 1989 and 1991, as well as from books such as *Padre Pio: The True Story,* by C. Bernard Ruffin, an excellent compilation of amazing facts (Our Sunday Visitor Publishing Inc.). Ruffin is a Lutheran minister. See also the Pelletier books about Garabandal. I visited San Damiano and relied upon pamphlets distributed at the site and in America, especially "Miraculous Lady of the Roses" and "San Damiano: Mary's Invitation To All Her Children." Also, see *Encountering Mary.* There are certain conflicts in detail that cannot be readily resolved but are usually minor ones.

Chapter 19: The text of the alleged Third Secret I obtained from a flyer distributed by groups promoting Fatima. Much of the information on the Third Secret comes from Frére Michel's *Third Secret,* available through Immaculate Heart Publications in Buffalo, New York—highly recommended, even if I don't share many of Michel's criticisms and views. See also Michel's "Fatima and the Last Times," a pamphlet issued by the Augustine Publishing Company, and Zimdars-Swartz's *Encountering Mary.*

Chapter 20: Terelya's accounts come from personal inteviews conducted in Toronto as well as the book *Witness:* Apparitions and Persecution in the USSR, available, again, through the Riehle Foundation (see address in notes for Chapter 10). The 50,000-church figure comes from *Red Empire,* by Gwyneth Hughes and Simon Welfare. For the anecdotes about the secret police, including the metropolitan (who supposedly took the name Nikodim) and the radioactive tracers, see *The KGB,* previously cited, by Deriabin and Bagley (Hippocrene Books). For Stalin I used *Stalin: The History of a Dictator,* by Harford Montgomery Hyde. The quote from Slipyj comes from a previously mentioned pamphlet, "The Church of Martyrs." Other information comes from the pamphlet, "Soviet Persecution of Religion in Ukraine," published by the World Congress of Free Ukrainians in Toronto (1976). Some of the information on Pochaiv comes from a pamphlet I obtained during a visit to Ukraine while other information can be found in John Bird's pamphlet, "The Miraculous Icon of Pochaiv'' (Veritas in Dublin, 1989). For the UFOs see *UFOs From Behind the Iron Curtain* by Ion Hobana and Julien Weverbergh. For Marx I once again resorted to Wurmbrand's *Marx and Satan.*

Chapter 21: The government quote comes from the *Journal of the Southern California Society for Psychical Research,* Volume 11, 1981. Other information on Zeitun comes from a sourcebook published by the Community of Saint Mary ("Our Lady of Light"), from a pamphlet by Pearl Zaki called 'Our Lord's Mother Visits Egypt'' (published by St. Mary Coptic Orthodox Church in East Brunswick, NJ), and from the pamphlet, *When Millions Saw Mary,* by Francis Johnston, issued by Augustine Publishing in Devon, England.

Chapter 22: The quotes from Sheen and Montfort were taken from the September-October, 1991 issue of *Soul* Magazine. Walvoord's book is *Armageddon, Oil, and the Middle East Crisis* (Zondervan).

Chapter 23: The best source for Akita is *Akita: The Tears and Message of Mary,* by Teiji Yasuda, English version by John Haffert, 101 Foundation, Asbury, NJ 08802-0151. See also *The Meaning of Akita* and the video tape "Hill of Redemption" (produced by John Bird, Westernhanger Productions). The *Rosa Mystica* information comes from the book mentioned, *Mary The Mystical Rose,* by A. M. Weigl (published by Rev. Raymond J. Jasinski of St. John of God Church in Chicago).

Chapter 24: The Gobbi messages are in *To The Priests, Our Lady's Beloved Sons,* available through the Marian Movement of Priests, P.O. Box 8, St. Francis, ME 04774-0008. Gobbi has also experienced a few apparitions, according to his American translator.

Chapter 25: Many such prophecies can be found in books by Father Albert Hebert, which can be obtained by writing him at P.O. Box 309, Paulina, LA 70763. Among them are *Prophecies!* and *Signs, Wonders, and Response.* See also *The Three Days' Darkness.*

Chapter 26: Stephen Ho Ngoc Ahn's experiences are from the pamphlet "Message of Our Lady of Fatima at Binh Loi," published by the Blue Army in Washington, NJ. It was reprinted from a British version distributed by The Little Way Association.

Chapter 27: I visited Betania and also draw from *La Virgen Maria Se Aparece En Venezuela,* Pbro. Otty Ossa Aristizabal (Ediciones Paulinas 1990) and *Apariciones de la Virgen Maria en Betania,* same publisher. My visit to South America was arranged by Lois Malik of Peace Center Tours in Elmhurst, IL (708-941-8057).

Chapter 28: The quote from John XXIII is from 712-713 of *The Documents of Vatican II,* edited by Walter M. Abbott, S.J. The pope's remarks in Germany, I should note here, are as controversial as the *Neues Europa* secret—unconfirmed by the Vatican. The Martin quote is from his book *The Keys of This Blood,* page 632. The Reagan quote is from *Time,* page 30, February 24, 1992.

Chapter 29: Most accounts have Mirjana leaving that first time without looking. This version, in which Mirjana *does* look and see Our Lady, I take from a taped interview six months after the first apparitions. The account of the hailstorm comes from Mary Craig's *Spark from Heaven.* This is a valuable book and includes some of the scientific testing. So does René Laurentin's *The Apparitions at Medjugorje Prolonged* (Riehle Foundation). Another Laurentin book, *Is the Virgin Mary Appearing at Medjugorje?* was the first I read on the topic and helped pique my interest. I visited Medjugorje in 1989 and 1990. See also *Words From Heaven* by two anonymous writers for Saint James Publishing, and Joseph A. Pelletier's *The Queen of Peace Visits Medjugorje.* The quotes from Vicka on Hell come from Laurentin's *Nine Years of Apparitions* and Jan Connell's *Queen of the Cosmos.* I also heard an account of this while interviewing Vicka with an American group. Many quotes come from *Words From Heaven,* and it's tough to vouch for the accuracy. The report on Reagan and Gorbachev comes from *Seven Years of Apparitions* by Laurentin. The message to Reagan, it was reported, was forwarded by Alfred H. Kingon, a representative to the European Community, before the president's 1987 summit with the Soviet leader. It was a simple greeting, expressing love and peace, but it conveyed Medjugorje's unique charisma. Reagan was touched. "Now I am going to this meeting with Gorbachev with a new spirit," he was said to have responded.

Chapters 30 and 31: Mirjana's quotes come from privately taped interviews conducted in July and September of 1985 by Father Petar Ljubicic. Also, from *The Queen of Peace Visits Medjugorje, Words From Heaven,* and *Spark From Heaven.* The latter book seems to be highly accurate and is the source for a number of facts and quotations on the Zanic controversy, as are the writings of Laurentin. These books helped greatly also in discussion of the secrets. I also relied upon Laurentin's *Messages and Teachings of Mary at Medjugorje,* co-authored with René Lejeune and published by the Riehle Foundation; another Laurentin book called *Ten Years of Apparitions* and his chronicle of sightings around the world, *The Apparitions of the Blessed Virgin Mary Today; Medjugorje Journal* by Lucy Rooney and Robert Faricy; *Mary Queen of Peace Stay With Us* by Guy Girard, Armand Girard, and Janko Bubalo; and *Medjugorje Up Close* by Rooney and Faricy. See also *Queen of the Cosmos,* from which a few quotations were extracted. I also used *Latest News from Medjugorje* by Laurentin (Riehle Foundation), *A Man Named Jozo,* compiled by Bill and Fran Reck of the Riehle Foundation, and Laurentin's *Ten Years of Apparitions,* yet another publication from the Riehle Foundation in Milford, OH.

Chapter 32: My main sources for Kibeho were *The Apparitions of Our Lady of Kibeho,* produced by the Marian (Guadalupe) Press in Galway, Ireland, an information paper called "A Last Farewell" by Raymond Halter, and another paper (actually a small book) by Father Gabriel Maindron with preparation by René Laurentin, entitled the same as the Irish production and available through the 101 Foundation. I also extracted quotes from the video, "Kibeho, Apparitions of the Blessed Virgin," produced by Marian Video of Lima, Pennsylvania. The Gobbi book of messages was cited previously (see Notes for Chapter 23). Condemnation of the Bayside apparitions was announced on December 4, 1986 and this declaration can be obtained from the chancery in Brooklyn.

Chapter 33: The information on Terelya comes from personal interviews and *Witness.* The information on Damascus comes from *The Miracle of Damascus.* The Argentinian apparitions come from two Riehle Foundation books, *An Appeal From Mary in Argentina,* by René Laurentin, and *Messages of Our Lady at San Nicolas* (513-575-4844).

Chapter 34: Esperanza had once asked the Virgin if it was true she was appearing in Yugoslavia and Mary answered, *"Yes, but my littles ones will suffer."* Maria got the impression of an invasion. The Virgin explained that it was *"like a test of love"* and that the war would not go on forever but would require outside intervention before tensions wind down.

Chapters 35, 36 & 37: The sighting at Knock was by Josie Dayton of Spink. Josie, a visionary, experienced one apparition during which she saw a nude Christ on the cross and Mary putting her veil over His waist—the flowing cloth we see in many renditions of the Crucifixion. On Halloween of 1985 a small group of "fundamentalists" upset about "idolatry" took a hammer to the Ballinspittle statue, but it was soon replaced and the fundamentalists were publicly ridiculed—apparently confusing reverence for Mary with worship of the sun, moon, and golden calves; to know idolatry, one had to know Egyptian history, not the history of Catholicism; it was a misuse of the term idolatry. In addition to my personal interviews, I draw quotes or other information from a pamphlet called "Inchigeela...A Call to Prayer," available through the Inchigeela Queen of Peace group (and in America the 101 Foundation); the *Cork Examiner,* an information sheet compiled by the Melleray Grotto Committee; a booklet by William Deevey entitled *Our Blessed Lady Is Speaking To You. Are You Listening? Her Messages From Melleray Grotto;* a leaflet produced by Our Lady of Carns Shrine; a pamphlet entitled "Jesus and Mary Speak in Ireland"; and a magazine called *Ireland's Eye,* which ran splendid articles about Christine Gallagher in its August, September, October, November, and December, 1991 issues.

Chapter 38: I visited Oliveto Citra and interviewed the visionaries. See also *Mary Among Us,* by Robert Faricy and Luciana Pecoraio, from which I draw quotes; and *I francescani nella storia di Oliveto Citra,* by P. Teofilo M. Giordano.

Chapter 39: Most information was from a trip to Ukraine in the autumn of 1991, just before Ukraine declared independence.

Chapter 40: I visited Ecuador through the help of Lois Malik of Peace Center Tours in Elmhurst, IL. I also draw from Sister Isabel Bettwy's *I am the Guardian of the Faith.* See also *Guardiana de la Fe,* published by Liberia Espiritual in Quito; *El Amor De Dios Triunfa,* by Julio Teran Dutari, D.J.; and *La Virgen Llora En El Mundo* by Francisco Sanchez Ventura for information on apparitions in Porto San Stefano.

Chapter 41: I spent time with Zdenko "Jim" Singer, whose Americanized surname was given him when he arrived in Canada, and Gianna Talone's messages are in the book, *I Am Your Jesus of Mercy,* published by the Riehle Foundation. I also interviewed her. Mariamante's messages are in *The Apostolate of Holy Motherhood.* I thank Paul Van Dooser for conducting interviews for me with Nancy Fowler of Conyers, GA. See *Catholic Prophecy* by Yves Dupont (TAN Books and Publishers, Inc., P.O. Box 424, Rockford, IL 61105) for more on older prophecies and the comet theories. The Faustina material comes from *Divine Mercy In My Soul,* the diary of Sister M. Faustina Kowalska, available through the Marian Press in Stockbridge, MA 01263. I also recommend *Apocalypse,* by Rev. Albert Joseph Mary Shamon, available through the Riehle Foundation. The Marian Library at Dayton University in Ohio assisted with some of the photographs.

Chronology

Major Apparition Sites of the 19th and 20th Centuries

1830	Rue-du-Bac, France	Catherine Laboure
1846	La Salette, France	Melanie Calvat and Maximin Giraud
1858	Lourdes, France	Bernadette Soubirous
1879	Knock, Ireland	Fifteen people
1904	Poland	Fr. Maximilian Kolbe
1917	Fatima, Portugal	Lucia, Francisco, & Jacinta
1918	San Giovanni, Italy	Padre Pio
1920	Verdun, Quebec, Canada	Emma Blanche Curotte
1925	Tuy, Spain	Sister Lucia
1932	Beauraing, Belgium	5 Voisin & Degeimbre children
1933	Banneaux, Belgium	Mariette Beco
1937	Poland	Sister Faustina
1945	Amsterdam, Holland	Ida
1947	Montichiari, Italy	Pierina Gilli
1947	Tre Fontane, Rome	Bruno Cornacchiola
1948	Lipa, Philippines	Novice Teresita
1952	India	Fr. Louis M. Shouriah, S.J.
1954	Seredne, Ukraine	Anna
1954	Ohio, USA	Sister Mildred Neuzil
1961	Garabandal, Spain	Four girls

1964 San Damiano, Italy	Mama Rosa Quattrini
1968 Italy	Mama Carmela Carabelli
1968 Zeitun, Egypt	Thousands
1970 Vladimir Prison, Russia	Josyp Terelya
1972 Milan, Italy	Fr. Stefano Gobbi
1973 Akita, Japan	Sister Agnes Sasagawa
1974 Binh Loi, Vietnam	Stephen Ho Ngoc Ahn
1976 Betania, Venezuela	Maria Esperanza & others
1980 El Escorial, Spain	Amparo Cuevas
1980 Cuapa, Nicaragua	Edward Bernardo Martinez
1981 Medjugorje, Yugoslavia	Six young people
1981 Kibeho, Rwanda, Africa	Six girls and one boy
1982 Damascus, Syria	Mirna Nazour
1983 San Nicolás, Argentina	Gladys Quiroga de Motta
1985 Ballinspittle, Ireland	Two O'Mahony women
1985 Carns Grotto, Ireland	Four girls
1985 Oliveto Citra, Italy	Children & many people
1985 Melleray Grotto, Ireland	Several people
1985 Naju, Korea	Julia Kim
1985 Switzerland	Vassula Ryden
1987 Terra Blanca, Mexico	Three children
1987 Bessbrook, N. Ireland	Beulah Lynch & Mark Trenor
1987 Ukraine	Josyp Terelya, Maria Kizyn & thousands
1987 Inchigeela, Ireland	Sally Ann & Judy Considine
1987 Ecuador	Patricia (Pachi) Talbott
1988 Cortnadreha, Ireland	Christine Gallagher
1988 Phoenix, AZ, USA	Estela Ruiz
1988 Scottsdale, AZ, USA	Nine young people
1989 Canada	Zdenko "Jim" Singer
1990 Denver, Colorado	Theresa Lopez
1990 Conyers, GA, USA	Nancy Fowler

Photo Credits